T0319798

Private Initiatives in Infrastructure

Private Initiatives in Infrastructure

Priorities, Incentives and Performance

Edited by

Sanford V. Berg

Public Utility Research Center
University of Florida, USA

Michael G. Pollitt

Judge Institute of Management Studies
University of Cambridge, UK

Masatsugu Tsuji

Osaka School of International Public Policy
Osaka University, Japan

Edward Elgar

Cheltenham, UK • Northampton, MA, USA

Published by
Edward Elgar Publishing Limited
Glensanda House
Montpellier Parade
Cheltenham
Glos GL50 1UA
UK

Edward Elgar Publishing, Inc.
136 West Street
Suite 202
Northampton
Massachusetts 01060
USA

A catalogue record for this book is available from the British Library

Library of Congress Cataloging in Publication Data
Private initiatives in infrastructure : priorities, incentives, and performance / edited by Sanford V. Berg, Michael G. Pollitt, Masatsugu Tsuji.
    p. cm.
    Includes index.
    1. Infrastructure (Economics)—Case studies. 2. Public–private sector cooperation—Case studies. I. Berg, Sanford V. II. Pollitt, Michael G. III. Tsuji, Masatsugu.

HC79.C3 P7 2002
388—dc21

                                                              2002017914

ISBN 1 84376 000 2
Printed and bound in Great Britain by Biddles Ltd, *www.biddles.co.uk*

Contents

List of figures

List of tables

List of contributors

Sanford V. Berg
Distinguished Service Professor, Director, Public Utility Research Center, University of Florida, Gainesville, USA

Maria Luisa Corton
Research Associate, Public Utility Research Center, University of Florida, Gainesville, USA

Jacqueline Hamilton
Research Associate, Public Utility Research Center, University of Florida, Gainesville, USA

Toru Hattori
Research Economist, Central Research Institute of Electric Power Industry, Tokyo, Japan

Mitsuhiro Kagami
Director General, Research Planning Department, Institute of Developing Economies, Japan External Trade Organization, Tokyo, Japan

Sunil Mani
Research Fellow and Dean, Institute for New Technologies, United Nations University, The Netherlands

Salvador A. Martinez
Research Associate, Public Utility Research Center, University of Florida, Gainesville, USA

Tanga McDaniel
Research Officer, Department of Applied Economics, University of Cambridge, UK

Michael G. Pollitt
University Lecturer in Business Economics, Judge Institute of Management, University of Cambridge, UK

John Tschirhart
Professor of Economics and Co-director, Public Utility Research and Training Institute, University of Wyoming, Laramie, USA

Masatsugu Tsuji
Dean and Professor of Economics, OSIPP, Osaka University, Japan

Introduction

Sanford V. Berg, Michael G. Pollitt, and Masatsugu Tsuji

The private sector may participate in financing, building, operating and managing projects involving the provision of infrastructure services, but governments have traditionally played a key role. In some cases, national or local governments have handled all phases of service delivery. In a 1998 workshop sponsored by the Institute of Developing Economies (Japan External Trade Organization, Tokyo), the three editors led research teams that tackled the strengths and limitations of privatization, regulation and liberalization in various sectors, drawing lessons from Japan, the United Kingdom, the United States and other countries (Kagami and Tsuji 2000). In early 2000, a follow-up workshop brought together researchers to explore private initiatives in infrastructure. The present volume builds on and extends studies from the second IDE/JETRO workshop. We wish to express our appreciation to the Institute of Developing Economies/JETRO for funding this research. Mitsuhiro Kagami deserves our special thanks for the leadership he has shown in this multinational collaboration.

Public–private collaboration is not unusual in mixed economies. As nations have turned from command-and-control mechanisms for raising and deploying capital, policymakers are revisiting the design of institutional frameworks that promote legitimacy, credibility and efficiency in important sectors. Legitimacy is relevant since customers must be convinced that they are paying appropriate prices for services received, and if there are government subsidies, taxpayers must view these as contributing to social objectives. Those who receive and value these services need to accept the public and private arrangements that attract and allocate resources to infrastructure activities, and the institutional design must be credible to attract funds for what are often capital-intensive investments. If the financial markets view the contractual environment as unpredictable and subservient to political whims, capital will not be available on attractive terms to those developing projects. Finally, unless incentives are in place for cost containment, the infrastructure services will not be affordable or reliable. Economic efficiency is essential for the system to be sustainable. Citizens and investors have access to information on the performance of comparable sectors around the world. If the various stakeholders view the system as inefficient relative to what has been achieved elsewhere, political leaders will be pressured to address sources of waste.

The purpose of this volume is not to offer a single recipe for creating successful infrastructure programs. No such recipe exists. Different models can co-exist, and different cultural, political and legal settings have led to a variety of institutional frameworks. These frameworks create incentives and may either promote strong sector performance or result in wasted resources and the withdrawal of capital from infrastructure. By focusing on concrete situations in specific countries, the editors and authors of this volume attempt to draw lessons for analysts and policymakers. The hundreds of billions of dollars that will be invested in infrastructure sectors in the coming decades represent a challenge and an opportunity for the global economy. Citizen tax revolts have forced governments to turn to private capital markets for infrastructure funding. Without careful design of governance structures and performance incentives, either investment will not be forthcoming or money will be invested inappropriately. However, successful projects have a demonstration effect. Innovative strategies that work will be copied and refined in other sectors and other countries.

The chapters in this volume capture some interactions among key features of reform in certain infrastructure industries, notably electricity, telecommunications, transportation and water. Social infrastructure includes such projects as hospitals, prisons, and government information technology (IT) initiatives. One theme is that policymakers must identify key policy objectives and prioritize them. A fundamental lesson of economics is that there is no such thing as a free lunch. A fundamental lesson from political science is that the next election becomes an important time-horizon for public policy. Taken together, these lessons suggest that policymakers may promote programs that benefit today's constituencies at the expense of future groups. In the case of infrastructure industries such as telecommunications, energy and water, the sunk costs associated with investments mean that opportunistic behavior by government and private parties can result in sub-optimal levels of investment and poor management of programs. Infrastructure performance can suffer because of the long-term nature of associated capital investments. Historically, state, local and national governments have often become involved with the financing, pricing and provision of network infrastructure in ways that can run counter to economic efficiency and even counter to widely accepted views of fairness.

No single factor determines the success of reform, but analysts such as Doug North (1990) argue that institutions establish incentives that promote the creation or destruction of value. Here value is taken to be the net benefit from market activity: the sum of consumer and producer surplus.[1] In the event of externalities such as pollution, impacts on other parties must be taken into account. The important point is that the rules of the game create or limit opportunities for economic agents to use information and resources to meet market demands and create value.

While many policymakers bring ideological biases to debates about strategies toward infrastructure sectors, they fortunately tend to be pragmatic. Globalization has meant that international experience serves as a form of political benchmarking for policies toward infrastructure. Some policymakers are confident that market-oriented solutions will yield the most acceptable outcomes, including innovations, improvements in service quality, service expansion and low prices. Others fear that other social objectives may not be met without appropriate governmental oversight. Over time, best practice for government agency oversight is identified and diffused across regions and nations.

Such oversight can take on a wide range of forms, from (1) data collection on sector performance to (2) light-handed regulation that focuses on constraining the exercise of market power to (3) comprehensive regulation where public–private partnerships become a code for micro-management and detailed intervention. When is each of these appropriate? The answer cannot be based just on theory. Political scientists and economists remind us that neither perfect governments nor perfect markets exist. Both are flawed and fraught with imperfections. Thus, the optimal mix of public and private activity depends on the institutional context of the particular country.

- Given the current level of development, what are the performance objectives for the sector?
- How well has the sector performed in terms of these objectives to date?
- What explanations can be offered for shortcomings or for successes?
- What lessons from the experiences of others are relevant for policymakers who are considering new initiatives for their nations?

This volume attempts to address these important questions. We believe that the contributions provide useful insights on the strengths and limitations of both government and market mechanisms regarding energy, telecommunications, transportation, water and other infrastructure sectors.

Note that all these sectors involve networks. Most have experienced dramatic technological changes, and their performance is of great interest to individual families and to industries that utilize infrastructure services. The links and nodes that comprise network industries mean that natural monopoly components can justify government oversight in one form or another. However, technological innovations and growth in demand have transformed segments of these industries and made them potentially competitive. More attention is being given to alternative production technologies: small-scale, modular combined-cycle gas turbines and dispersed generation in electricity; radio spectrum, fiber optics and digitalization in telecommunications; less capital-intensive water supply systems;

and substitutes for traditional banking and financial services. Technological change has induced greater liberalization and dependence on market incentives as opposed to government mandates and protections. This trend has resulted in incumbent suppliers losing market share and going to the political process for protection and/or re-regulation. Thus the transition issues are complicated by the fact that some groups may benefit from current production and pricing arrangements. The political economy of rent seeking explains why disruptive changes bring out calls for protection, intervention and social engineering.

STRENGTHS AND LIMITATIONS OF PUBLIC–PRIVATE PARTNERSHIPS

Use of taxpayer money to finance infrastructure investments has resulted in weak performance in a number of situations. A number of the cases described by the Japan team involved poor project selection (excessively optimistic demand forecasts and construction cost projections), inadequate attention to incentives for cost containment and misguided financial structure. Their results suggest that the 'Third Way' (public–private partnerships) joins the weaknesses of both groups. Politicians sought short-term benefits associated with large construction budgets, ignoring the long-term implications of this marriage of convenience. Using 'other people's money' (without accountability or strong incentives for cost minimization) led to short-term employment boosts as a key justification for programs and a license for political pork barrel outlays. Without adequate equity participation, the limited information and passive provision of government support allowed Japan's 'Private Finance Initiative' to become a public drain, with risks borne by taxpayers and benefits accruing to special interests (the construction sector and local project promoters). Lessons outlined by the Japan team may stimulate better project selection, financing, implementation and operation in the future.

An approach that promotes efficiency would evaluate the use of public funds in terms of value for money and incentives for good performance, with a clear allocation of risk and liability among private and public sector participants (see the UK team chapters). While the benefit of these objectives should be obvious, the cultural and political traditions of Japan did not give them high priority until the Financial Structure Reform Act in 1997 and the Central Government Structural Reform Act of 1998. Public expenditure reviews had previously been haphazard at best and totally absent at worst. When short-run macroeconomic objectives drive the process, the resulting policies can waste resources and shrink the production possibilities of the economy. When bankruptcy is delayed, poor projects become enshrined in political rhetoric and protected from needed restructuring. As the Japan team makes clear, the bursting of the bubble economy revealed the vulnerable financial and managerial underpinnings of many projects. Whether the Private Finance Initiative (PFI) becomes a mechanism for true reform or a symbolic gesture is yet to be determined.

The Japan team examines the electricity and telecommunications sectors. While both sectors are in various stages of liberalization, the pace and pattern of entry lag behind developments in other OECD nations (those belonging to the Organization for Economic Cooperation and Development). The team points out the potential advantages of multiple centers of initiative in these sectors traditionally protected from competitive threats. In the case of Japan, the Ministry of Trade and Industry (MITI) performed regulatory functions for the nine regional electricity monopolies without the kind of transparent and participatory processes characteristic in the US and UK. Siting problems, construction lags and high costs finally led MITI to propose a new regime in 1996, one that opened production to independent power producers.

In telecommunications, technological opportunities were a catalyst for changes in industry structure and the extent of private involvement in the sector. Of course digitalization and the convergence of voice, video and data transmission require massive investments for innovations to be brought to the people. Often local governments play a role in funding such investments, the so-called public–public partnerships. Examples of applications to health care and education argue for high involvement by government authorities, since these are so closely linked to fundamental social objectives. However, it is certainly possible to distinguish between conduit and content for the new information industry: the role of government as an innovator might be questioned in both fields. One question is whether public–private partnerships would avoid the mistakes that characterized other infrastructure investments. An even more important question is whether the risks associated with investments in new technologies are best borne by taxpayers, who are then left with no way to mitigate those risks, or by investors, who monitor projects from start to finish since their wealth is threatened by mismanagement and waste. When other people's money is at risk, politicians and bureaucrats may be tempted to go for big projects rather than provide seed money for experimentation, modular development and systematic reviews.

These principles apply to infrastructure creation throughout East Asia. The lessons from Japan can serve as signposts for private and public decision-makers in the region. Emerging nations will be able to attract private capital only if the regulatory rules are clear. Commercial and technological risks are real and will be borne by someone. Political risks are also real and cannot be hidden. The experience of Asian markets indicates that crony capitalism provides a form of public–private partnership where risks are on citizens and returns are provided to favored parties. Historical approaches to granting monopolies and excessively favorable financial support basically privatized the profits when enterprises were successful and socialized the losses when there were mistakes or bubbles collapsed. The political economy of rent seeking played out as expected: when large costs are diffused across the citizenry but benefits are concentrated on the favored, the political process can result in uneconomic projects receiving government protection and/or funding. In good times, the mistakes seemed small, but when conditions changed, the weak economic underpinnings became clear. But then it was too late.

LIGHT-HANDED REGULATION

No nation has ideal policies. What is important is that leaders understand how policies lead to performance outcomes. Just as important is the need to look behind policies to the institutional conditions that lead to particular government initiatives. The UK team provides a useful overview of the declining role of the state in infrastructure investments. After significant privatization of telecommunications, electricity, gas, airports, water and railway sectors in the 1980s, the Conservative government continued to press for a reduced role for the state. It sold off millions of the municipally owned council houses and promoted the creation of housing associations designed to attract public and private capital into the sector. In the early 1990s, the PFI served as the mechanism for raising private capital for health, prisons, transport and defense.

The principles adopted by the UK's PFI have been studied by other nations interested in improving the cost-effectiveness of government activities. The basic issue is how to translate national savings into productive investments and how to meet government concerns about equity while improving efficiency. If projects with low returns are regularly accepted, then neither tax-financed nor privately financed projects will add significantly to the productive capabilities of the economy. Of course when there are social benefits that are difficult to assess in terms of monetary value (health, environmental protection and education), project financing is likely to include some form of government involvement and/or subsidization. Nevertheless, the cost-effectiveness of projects can be measured and compared across investments, and incentives can make managers more attentive to cost containment and quality improvements.

The UK team surveys both the positive and negative experiences of the PFI, using examples to illustrate the innovations that have arisen from promoting multiple centers of initiative. However, bidding procedures take time and involve costs. If there are only a few bidders, the resulting contracts can still be expensive. And without carefully crafted incentive systems, cost overruns can still haunt projects. Finally, the assignment of risk is not handled well in all situations.

With regard to energy, liberalization and deregulation can be viewed as relatively successful to date. Along most dimensions of performance (productivity, price, innovation, service quality) the record is solid. Privatization and the creation of a light-handed independent regulatory system have led to a number of successes. Yet recently the Labour government has stepped in to influence the mix of fuel used in the production of electricity, protecting jobs in the coal industry to avoid excessive dependence on natural gas as a fuel source for new capacity.

The experience in India underscores the importance of independent regulation and getting the industry structure right. There has been some liberalization, but the private sector remains somewhat skeptical of the regulatory system and of the political commitment to get prices to track costs. Citizen expectations for continued low prices (but not for continued low-quality service) are unrealistic. We shall see whether key stakeholder groups can become convinced of the need for reform and significant private participation in energy, telecommunications and water. Unless customers perceive the system as legitimate and investors are convinced that the rules will not change with each election, significant change is unlikely over the next decade.

REGULATION AND DEREGULATION IN MIXED ECONOMIES

A common theme of the papers by the US team is the important role of regulatory governance and incentives in promoting efficient investment in and operation of infrastructure firms. Regulatory governance refers to the principles and procedures utilized by agencies charged with infrastructure oversight responsibilities. Since regulatory agencies are basically setting constraints on corporate behavior, those implementing public policy need to understand what is driving decisions in the marketplace. A brief review of market processes can help identify the challenges facing regulators who are trying to simulate competitive outcomes.

Firms can create value by lowering costs. Valuable resources are freed up for use in other sectors of the economy. Value is also created when product quality improvements or entirely new products better meet the needs of consumers. In competitive markets, firms creating value are able to capture profits from their risk-taking activity. Economic profits represent returns to equity investors who put their capital at risk. Normal returns arise from normal performance. Above-normal returns arise from superior performance, which reflects best practice in operational effectiveness and selection of a strategy that meets the preferences of consumers and builds on the capabilities of the firm.

There are clear links between economic principles and business decision-making. Investors respond to signals provided by the securities markets, and firms enter and exit markets based on profit expectations. These expectations are affected by the governmental track record. Regulatory governance that promotes transparency implies openness to the views of different stakeholder groups. Participation by stakeholders is one way regulators can be held accountable for their actions. In addition, communication and consultation are important principles for infrastructure policy implementation. The process includes stakeholders who contribute to the information-gathering process and are kept informed of developments. Even though legislation establishes broad policy, agencies still have to interpret and apply the law in the context of facts and unanticipated situations. As the number and the diversity of market participants expand, US agencies are supplementing traditional adversarial hearing processes with alternative dispute resolution procedures.

Similarly, incentives established by regulators, including entry policies and access regulation, have significant impacts on what firms do and how they do it. Unless agencies understand the processes underlying decisions in an unregulated setting, they will be unable to do a good job of meeting public policy objectives through appropriate selection and use of policy instruments. In particular, by encouraging firms to create value via cost containment and the introduction of valued new services, regulators can enhance industry performance. However, if poor incentives are promulgated, value can be destroyed as investors withdraw capital from the industry or costs drift upward in response to cost-of-service regulation. Case studies of water systems in South America and telecommunications in Africa illustrate the importance of incentives for production efficiency and product innovation. The art of regulation involves establishing rules that allocate value to consumers and suppliers in a way that maintains political legitimacy in the eyes of consumers and other stakeholders while providing incentives for firms to create value.

SUMMARY

It is not easy for those developing and implementing infrastructure policies to prioritize objectives, design optimal incentives and evaluate performance. However, national leaders must take responsibility for creating and nurturing institutions that promote the citizenry's well-being. Although markets have proven to be relatively robust, some people can be left behind when powerful forces of change alter the ways infrastructure services are delivered. No nation can afford to waste resources; for emerging nations, wise policy implementation can mean the difference between life and death for its people. If we believe that people are precious and that resources should not be squandered, attracting private capital into infrastructure sectors and ensuring that it is utilized in cost-effective ways is surely one of the most important issues for the early decades of this new century.

The public policy problems described here will not be easily resolved. Analysts and policymakers will continue to debate the effectiveness of policy instruments, including the following:

- Techniques for evaluating the performance of publicly and privately owned firms,
- Incentive mechanisms for stimulating efficiency in public–private partnerships,
- Ways to mitigate environmental impacts of production and consumption,
- Approaches to providing universal access to the information economy (for communication, learning and e-commerce),
- The sustainability of independent regulatory agencies that promote credibility for investors and legitimacy for consumers,
- Ways to raise capital and ensure affordability for infrastructure services, and
- The design of government institutions that facilitate transparency in the oversight process.

We hope that this volume will contribute to the policy discussions surrounding these issues.

ENDNOTE

1. In technical terms, consumer surplus is the consumer willingness to pay minus actual consumer outlays. Producer surplus is the revenue received by suppliers minus the opportunity cost of providing the output. The summation of consumer and producer surplus provides an indication of the net benefit of a market to society.

REFERENCES

Kagami, Mitsuhiro and Masatsugu Tsuji (eds) (2000), Privatization, Deregulation and Economic Efficiency: A Comparative Analysis of Asia, Europe and the Americas, Cheltenham, UK and Northampton, MA: Edward Elgar.
North, Doug (1990), *Institutions, Institutional Change and Economic Performance*, Cambridge, UK: Cambridge University Press, vii–152.

PART ONE

Japan: Public–Private Partnerships in Transition

1. Infrastructure building in the Japanese telecommunications sector: From public–public to public–private partnership

Masatsugu Tsuji

Telecommunications infrastructure is fundamental to the information society in the twenty-first century. Remarkable developments in telecommunications technology since the late 1980s, especially in the field of multimedia, allow the transmission of a huge volume of data at high speed, including images, voice, and words through optical fibers. Development of computers, ISDN (integrated services digital network), and ATM (asynchronous transfer mode) switches has made multimedia a reality and the world small enough for face-to-face transmissions in real time.

Telecommunications infrastructure such as the optical fiber network has been deployed extensively in many countries and enables the transmission of a huge volume of information at high speed. This infrastructure makes multimedia and the Internet possible. Both infrastructure and application (in other words, both hardware and software) are essential to the information society, and one without the other is meaningless. In this chapter I discuss the current status of telecommunications infrastructure in Japan and the applications of multimedia based on it, providing examples from the fields of medicine and education.

The traditional fixed telephone network is one example of telecommunications infrastructure. In Japan the penetration ratio is almost 100 percent and so-called universal service is discussed not in terms of promoting telephone service to low-income families but in terms of fairness in the level of charges and the content of services in different regions.[1]

The optical fiber network has been constructed as a part of telecommunications infrastructure, and its deployment in Japan is mainly the responsibility of telecommunications carriers such as NTT (Nippon Telephone & Telegraph) and other non-common carriers (NCCs). These companies have their own schedule for installing optical fibers according to their business strategy, and competition has promoted expansion of the optical fiber network throughout the economy. But because the current areas covered are not satisfactory for fully utilizing multimedia in every region, local governments and agencies that are financially supported by the central government have been constructing their own networks for their own policy purposes.

This chapter presents and explains the Japanese approach to building telecommunications infrastructure. I first focus on the optical fiber network as an example of telecommunications infrastructure and discuss competitive and non-competitive infrastructure building. Local governments all over the world are constructing their own optical fiber networks, and the example of Kobe City shows how different agents in that city collaborated to construct the network. I then analyze the Japanese 'public–private partnership' used to construct telecommunications infrastructure. This differs from the 'public–public partnership' typical in some other economies. Then the necessity for the Private Finance Initiative (PFI) is discussed. In the final section, I propose conditions for further applications of multimedia in the fields of medicine and education.

TELECOMMUNICATIONS INFRASTRUCTURE

In Japan the various agents who deploy optical fiber networks as telecommunications infrastructure include (1) long-distance telecommunications carriers such as NTT Communications and other long-distance NCCs such as KDDI and JT, (2) local telecommunications carriers established mainly by electric companies called local NCCs, including NTT East and NTT West (divested from NTT), TTNet (Tokyo Telecommunication Network, Inc.), CTC (Chubu Telecommunications Co., Inc.), OMP (Osaka Media Port) and QTnet (Kyushu Telecommunications Network), etc., (3) CATV companies, and (4) cellular and mobile phone companies. These agents have been competing with one another while constructing optical fiber networks according to their own business strategies.

Telecommunications infrastructure is, in general, classified into two categories: trunk lines and subscriber lines. As for trunk lines, long-distance carriers have already established their fiber networks among all their nodes (branches) throughout Japan. For example, NTT has about 180,000 km of trunk fiber cables, including a high-speed network completed in late 1999. And the former international carrier KDD deployed a 100 Gbps (gigabit per second) optical fiber network under the ocean surrounding Japan. Called the 'Japan Information Highway', it began operations in April 1999. With the expectation of increased demand for the Internet and electronic commerce, efforts to expand gigabit capacity continue as the result of market competition.

The situation of subscriber lines is quite different.[2] Telecommunications carriers, both long-distance and local, have no intention of deploying optical fibers for individual homes, referred to as 'fiber to the home' (FTTH). Not only is this costly, less demand for high-speed and large-volume communications is expected from households. Instead, telecommunications carriers are planning 'fiber to the curve' (FTTC). CATV companies, however, have networks for individual families, even though these are still mainly based on copper lines and coaxial cable rather than optical fibers. Since CATV and cellular and mobile phone companies have their own network, they are considered an important segment of the telecommunications infrastructure.

Construction of Optical Fiber Networks in a Non-competitive Environment

In a competitive environment, only profitable services are provided to high-demand users or areas. High-cost areas such as sparsely populated regions or isolated islands, for example, cannot receive such services. To remedy this situation, the concept of universal service is brought to bear. That is, telecommunications carriers are said to have an obligation to deploy infrastructure and provide services, with the cost of this universal service to be borne by all telecommunications customers.

Another scheme to construct telecommunications infrastructure other than through the market mechanism is to have local governments deploy telecommunications infrastructure using tax money. This view holds that sparsely populated areas, last on the list for telecommunications carriers deploying optical fibers, should not be expected to wait for such services. According to economic theory, public intervention is one solution to market failure. In the age of an information society, however, this has a much more significant meaning. Telecommunications infrastructure provides the basis of the regional information policy implemented by local governments. The development of information technology makes it possible for even small regions to pursue policy goals, including promoting economic activities as well as increasing amenities and welfare services.

There are many examples of large regions and small-sized cities that have constructed a fiber optics system inside a region, not only for administrative purposes but also for attracting factories, business offices, and big commercial complexes (Longcore and Rees 1996, Grant and Berquist 1998, Sharon and Berquist 1999). Examples of large networks are the North Carolina Information Super Highway (NCIH) and the Iowa Communications Network (ICN). The former was constructed through the collaboration of telecommunications carriers and the state government, and the latter by the State of Iowa. These networks support regional information policies and interconnect administrative offices, schools, educational institutions, libraries, and medical facilities.

Technological Progress and Telecommunications Infrastructure

Because of widespread belief in the theory of natural monopoly in this industry, fixed telephone telecommunications networks in most countries to date have been constructed by either government enterprises or a regulated monopoly. But rapid technological development in the info-telecommunications field, including digitalization and multimedia, has caused the cost of equipment and devices to drop and quality to improve. This lowered the barriers for other firms to enter the telecommunications industry, and thus competition for services and for the construction of infrastructure began.

In Japan competition among carriers was responsible for the replacement of all trunk cables with optical fibers, as will be explained later in more detail. Subscriber lines, in contrast, are still owned by NTT, since the costs to deploy those lines are thought to be high. Again, because of technological development, new networks such as those of CATV and cellular and mobile phones are expected to reach more users. Moreover, a wireless local loop is also expected to be introduced in the near future. In sum, the definition of telecommunications infrastructure is not set, but rather changes according to technological development.

TELECOMMUNICATIONS INFRASTRUCTURE CONSTRUCTION IN A COMPETITIVE ENVIRONMENT

In 1994, the Japanese government set up a schedule to make coverage by optical fibers 100 percent complete by the year 2010 (see Figure 1.1). In 1997, it was decided to speed up the schedule for completion by 2005 with the help of the private sector. At this time, special loans were made available for installing optical fiber to subscriber lines, and the amount has increased year by year. Coverage has increased as well, from 10 percent in 1994 to 13 percent in 1995, 16 percent in 1996, 19 percent by 1997, 27 percent by 1998, and 30 percent by 1999.

The total length of optical fiber networks in subscriber lines deployed by NTT and other NCCs is summarized in Table 1.1. As of the end of March 1999, the total length was 200,000 km; NTT had 80,000 km and NCCs 120,000 km. This table shows that NTT's share is always less than 50 percent, which seems to imply that NTT is not dominant in this market and that NCCs have an advantage in the deployment of optical fiber. NCCs here include companies other than telecommunications carriers, such as CATV and power companies, and all of their networks do not necessarily connect to the telephones or PCs of each household. Competition among different companies in the deployment of optical fiber indicates that carriers recognize optical fiber as the basis of future competitiveness.

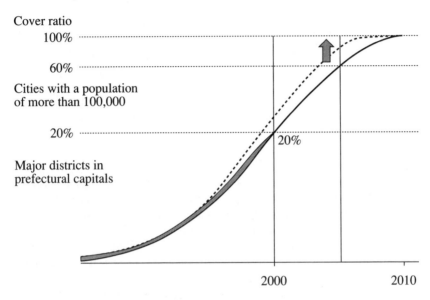

Figure 1.1   Construction schedule for the optical fiber network

Table 1.1   Length of optical fiber subscriber lines (thousand km)

Companies	1993	1994	1995	1996	1997	1998	1999
NNT	15	20	25	40	50	60	80
NCC	25	30	45	70	105	120	140
Total	40	50	70	110	155	180	220

Source: Ministry of Posts and Telecommunications (MPT).

Table 1.2 indicates coverage by NTT optical fibers and shows that most of the business areas of big cities are already covered by optical fibers. Although NTT was divested into four companies, each of these is still big in size and they play important roles in the Japanese telecommunications market. The most important characteristic of the NTT group is that local NTTs such as NTT East and NTT West own subscriber lines. All NCCs have to interconnect with subscriber lines in order to provide services to each customer. In 1997, NTT completed the digitalization of trunk cables and local switches. On the basis of this digitalization, NTT started to offer new services such as a monthly discount for long-distance calls and a fixed monthly rate for a specific time zone, ISDN services, and Internet services.

Table 1.2   Percentage coverage by NTT's optical fibers

Area Type	1994	1995	1996	1997	1998	1999
Business	30	50	70	90	93	95
Residential	7	8	9	10	20	30
Average	10	15	18	20	25	35

Source: NTT.

NTT has also been replacing existing copper networks with optical fibers, and currently the ratio of optical fibers in the network is about 30 percent. Replacement with optical fibers is complete in business districts in prefectural capitals and big cities with a population of more than 100,000, and NTT plans to complete all replacement by the year 2010.[3] NTT's strategy of promoting optical fibers places high priority on metropolitan and business areas by aiming at leased circuits for business users.

Another new technology supporting FTTC called x Digital Subscriber Line (xDSL) utilizes existing metallic lines. This is also called SDSL, HDSL, ADSL, etc., according to the different transmission methods. It enables high-speed transmission such as 50 Mbps and is expected to promote multimedia.[4]

Local Telecommunications Carriers

Local telecommunications carriers base their systems on the networks of electric companies. Electric companies own power plants, distribution networks, and other facilities, and the aim of their networks is to control and operate their systems related to generation, transmission, and distribution of electric power, and so secure a stable supply. The networks are also used for automatic gauging of electric usage. Since these networks have to meet specific purposes and require a certain level of quality and reliability, they can be utilized as the public switched network of telecommunications carriers. The characteristic of this type of network is that it can play the role of subscriber lines, and this is why electric companies have started providing telecommunications service.[5] Table 1.3 shows the total km of optical fiber installed by major power companies in Japan.

Tokyo Electric Company, for instance, currently owns 45,000 km of optical fiber network, and plans to extend this to 80,000 km in five years. The purpose of this expansion is not only to promote the company's telephone services, operated by its affiliated company TTNet, but also to set up a new company with Softbank to provide Internet service at a fixed rate beginning in the summer of 2001. The existing network is too small for starting a new business and expanding the network to FTTC. Tokyo Electric Company will deploy 8,000 km of optical fibers in metropolitan Tokyo and will expand to cities with a population of more than 100,000 within its business area by the end of the year 2004.

Table 1.3   Length of optical fiber deployed by six major power companies

Companies	Length of optical fiber (thousand km)
Tohoku Electric Co.	18
Tokyo Electric Co.	45
Chubu Electric Co.	18
Kansai Electric Co.	40
Chugoku Electric Co.	6
Kyushu Electric Co.	20

Source: MITI.

CATV

CATV has an optic fiber network that also serves as part of the information infrastructure of Japan. With the characteristics of locality and interactivity, CATV is currently at the center of the so-called 'convergence of telecommunications and broadcasting' and has expanded services to telephony and Internet connection. In many countries CATV plays an important role in telecommunications as well as broadcasting, and the number of subscribing households in Japan has been increasing following deregulation that began in 1993. In April 1999, the number of subscribing households was 2.2 billion in Japan and the ratio to total households was 13.4 percent.

The Ministry of Posts and Telecommunications (now known as the Ministry of Public Management, Home Affairs, Posts and Telecommunications) has been revising CATV regulations since 1993 with the aim of making it the core of the info-communications infrastructure, particularly at the regional level. The following items are aspects of this deregulation: (1) abolition of the local operator requirement for CATV operators, (2) lifting restrictions on foreign capital investment, (3) simplification of the application form for obtaining permission to deploy cable TV facilities, (4) utilization of fiber-optic subscriber networks owned by telecommunications carriers (June 1998), and (5) using wireless networks for complementing the CATV network (September 1998).

By abolishing the local operator requirement, CATV operators have been able to expand their business over a wider area. Because of this, capital is entering the CATV market from a variety of sources, including trading companies. CATV businesses covering multiple administrative districts are on the rise, and multiple system operators have started to launch businesses. CATV operators use the fiber-optic subscriber network owned by telecommunications carriers on the condition that fair and effective competition is secured.

With deregulation and technological development, CATV operators have been expanding their business activities into telephony services and Internet access, and preparing for digitalization and full service. CATV can access the Internet much faster (30 Mbps) than the ISDN (64 kbps) of telecommunications carriers, since the former has a broadband network with 750 MHz. In addition, CATV was the first to provide Internet service at a fixed rate.[6] In spite of these advances, interconnections among different CATV networks remain unsatisfactory. Each CATV network is an important local information infrastructure, but networks are still separated from each other and have not reached the level of nationwide infrastructure.

TELECOMMUNICATIONS INFRASTRUCTURE CONSTRUCTION IN A NON-COMPETITIVE ENVIRONMENT

The largest ATM network in the world was constructed in a non-competitive framework that involved collaboration of public and private organizations. Located in the US, the North Carolina Information Super Highway (NCIH) is utilized for tele-education, tele-medicine, and administrative purposes. It is the first broadband ISDN SONET/ATM network to be put to practical use, and the speed of transmission is 155 Mbps.

NCIH is owned by three major regional telecommunications carriers in the state, BellSouth, GTE, and Sprint. Thus it is a commercial network even though the State of North Carolina is its largest user. The benefit for private companies in constructing huge infrastructure lies in their expectation of increased demand and new business from the private sector in future, although the main user is currently the state government. Regional banks such as Branch Banking & Trust and Mercedes Benz are also end users of the network, the latter using it for training automobile mechanics specialists.

In the State of Iowa, the Iowa Communication Network (ICN) is in operation. The construction of ICN was begun in 1991, and the current total mileage of the network is 3,000 miles. ICN also serves tele-education and tele-medicine, and is used by the legal field and leased to private companies such as Sprint and MCI. When the construction of ICN was being planned, private companies were asked to present bids for the project. Since no bids were received, the state government decided to construct the network by itself. The end users of ICN are educational facilities, libraries, state government, the National Guard, clinics and hospitals, federal government, and post offices. The manner in which this infrastructure was constructed is in contrast to that of the NCIH and can be explained by differences in density of population and economic strength between the states.[7]

Regional Optical Fiber Networks: Wide Area Network (WAN)

Projects similar to the NCIH have been discussed in Japan by prefectural governments such as those of Okayama, Oita, Mie, and Kochi. The objective is to construct a broadband optical fiber as the backbone of the Wide Area Network (WAN) in the region. This will connect all other networks in the region, both public and private and including the Local Area Network (LAN) of local governments, regional Intranet, CATV, and telecommunications carriers. All agents such as firms, schools, Internet providers (IP), and individuals can have access. The ultimate aim is for all households in the region to have access to this WAN at high speed on the order of several Mbps. The essential difference between WAN and NCIH and ICN is WAN's incorporation of the Internet as a core factor.[8]

The regional information policies based on WAN are (1) tele-education, which will interconnect all schools in the region and provide study at home as well as lifelong education, (2) tele-medicine, which will provide tele-home care for the elderly and emergency services, (3) volunteer activities, and (4) administrative services twenty-four hours a day.

Regional Information Policy and Telecommunications Infrastructure

Some small-sized local governments have already constructed their own networks, either by themselves or with the collaboration of the central government and private telecommunications carriers. Two examples are Setouchi Town, Kagoshima Prefecture, and Kawai Village, Iwate Prefecture.

Setouchi Town is located at the southern tip of Amami-Oshima Island, Kagoshima Prefecture, and includes three other small isolated islands, namely, Kakeroma, Koishima, and Yoro Island. The population of the town is 12,017 and falling since there is no large industry in the town other than fishery.

The tele-education system of Setouchi Town interconnects elementary schools of the town with the Education Research Center of Kagoshima Prefecture by ISDN (64 kbps and 1.5 Mbps). The main aim of tele-education in this town is to provide the teachers and pupils on the isolated islands with a sense of unity. In this project, NTT constructed an optical fiber for this purpose only. (See Tsuji et al. 1999a for more details.)

In Kawai Village the local authority built an optic fiber network (64 kbps) at its own expense at a cost of ¥7 million (US$70,000), although the total length is about 1.5 km. Kawai Village is located in a mountainous area; it has 4,300 inhabitants and the second lowest income level in Iwate Prefecture. The network interconnects related offices such as those for administration, health, welfare, and medical services. By sharing information, these offices achieve an efficient allocation of caretakers, visiting nurses, medical doctors, and equipment. This network is essential for promoting efficiency and reducing the cost of medicine and home care. (See Tsuji et al. 1999b for more details.)

Tele-Home Care System

An optical fiber network becomes meaningful only when it is actually applied.[9] The tele-home care system connects patients at home with medical institutions through a telecommunications network, which includes public telephone lines of telecommunications carriers, leased circuits, ISDN, and the CATV network. At advanced university hospitals and medical institutions, cellular and mobile phones, the Internet, and even satellite communication are used.

The characteristics of the tele-home care system are real-time, two-way interactive transmission of motion pictures via a videoconference system or videophone. This system makes the greatest possible use of the characteristics of multimedia and is classified into three categories according to the type of network: CATV-broadcast type, CATV-LAN type, and ISDN type.

The CATV network utilized in the first two categories can transmit a high-definition motion picture of 30 cells per second with a color digital camera. Working examples of the CATV-broadcast type are the systems of Goshiki Town in Hyogo Prefecture and Kamaishi City in Iwate Prefecture. The only working example of the CATV-LAN type is the care-at-home support system called 'Anshin-netto' in Minami-Shinano Village, Nagano Prefecture. Both the CATV and LAN broadcast networks were constructed through the so-called 'third-sector method' as a joint venture of local governments and local companies with the financial assistance of the central government.

The ISDN type of tele-home care utilizes 64 kbps of NTT's public telephone lines as its network, and image information is transmitted by the videophone system. As for quality of screen image of videophones, the motion picture is 10 to 25 cells per second and is inferior to that of the CATV type. This type of system is in operation in Bekkai Town in Hokkaido, Mogami Town in Yamagata Prefecture, Ogaki City in Gifu Prefecture, and Mitoyo Region in Kagawa Prefecture.

Table 1.4 provides a comparison of the three systems. Each has advantages and disadvantages in terms of quality of screen image, construction expenses, operating cost, and so on.

Table 1.4   Comparison of systems

Characteristics	CATV Type	CATV-LAN Type	ISDN Type
Number in operation	2	1	4
Location (cost in million yen)	Kamaishi City (20) Goshiki Town (170)	Minami-Shinano Village (100)	Mogami Town (27) Ogaki City Bekkai Town Mihama District
Picture quality	High	High	Low
Privacy	By scramble	Easy	Easy
Telephone bills	None	None	Mogami Town (1 million yen)
Extension of system	Difficult	Easy	Easy and simple

Source: Tsuji et al. (1999b).

The ministries of the central government financed most of these projects, leaving the local governments responsible for maintenance and telecommunications charges. This subsidy policy explains how small and sparsely populated regions have been able to implement tele-home care systems.

INFRASTRUCTURE CONSTRUCTION IN KOBE CITY

To show how different agents collaborated in constructing a network, I present the case of Kobe City.[10] As has been widely reported, the earthquake of January 1995 devastated Kobe City and left more than 6,000 casualties. Since then, Kobe has had the unique opportunity of reconstructing the city by building a telecommunications infrastructure aimed at preventing disasters and promoting economic and social activities.

Optical Fiber Network Constructed by TAO

The Telecommunications Advancement Organization of Japan (TAO), an agency of the former Ministry of Posts and Telecommunications, began construction of an optical fiber network in Kobe City in 1996. TAO, a research organization with an R&D branch institution in Kobe, develops telecommunications technology through experimental activities and constructed the network in Kobe in order to conduct research on network applications for disaster prevention. Although the network will be transferred to Kobe City after a certain period, TAO currently owns and operates the Kobe network in collaboration with the city office.

This network consists of two sub-networks: a trunk optical cable with 622 Mbps and a branch optical cable with 155 Mbps. At a cost of about US$100 million, the total length of the network is about 53 km, which makes it the longest optic fiber network of a local government in Japan. It is an ATM network with seven ATM switches in the network. Five CATV access points allow interconnection with the CATV network. The network is deployed along the subway lines (30 km), along a new urban transportation system called Port-Liner, and along highways such as the Harbor Highway, roads, and underground shopping malls.

The network serves as the city's basic infrastructure and interconnects the city office and its main branch offices, universities, schools, and major hospitals. Many projects involving a regional information policy based on multimedia have been implemented by using this infrastructure.

NTT's Optical Fiber Network

As mentioned earlier, NTT is the biggest agent for deploying optic fibers, and it has its own policy for deployment all over Japan. To support reconstruction in Kobe City, NTT put a high priority on deploying optic fibers. Currently, deployment has been completed in most business districts. For areas outside business districts that were heavily damaged by the earthquake, NTT plans to replace 40–50 percent of the telecommunications network with optic fibers. In other areas, 20–30 percent of the network had been replaced by optic fibers by the year 2000.

CATV

CATV was started in Kobe City in 1973. The five CATV companies now in operation cover most city areas, and all are joint ventures of the public and private sectors. Interconnection of the CATV ATM networks, as mentioned, was attempted by TAO as an experimental project after the earthquake. Yet, these networks remain unconnected with each other or with the Internet. CATV in Kobe is used mainly for broadcasting. Efforts are ongoing to expand the CATV network even more widely and to renovate its technology to provide new services such as Internet connection, TV shopping, video on demand (VOD), and telephony.

TELECOMMUNICATIONS INFRASTRUCTURE CONSTRUCTION IN JAPAN

Japan's unique way of constructing infrastructure is based on the relationship between the central government and local governments, which coordinate with one another from construction to application. Under traditional Japanese jurisdiction, the central government has ultimate power in all policy fields including budget allocation. The ministries set up their plans and strategies, and allocate tax money to realize those policy goals. However, local governments actually implement the policies.[11] I term this relationship a public–public partnership.

This mode of operation can be analyzed using principal–agent theory in that the central government is the principal and local governments are the agents. Local governments such as those of the city, town, and village are responsible for the fields of health, medical care, and education, since these public services are closely related to the lives of all the residents. For services to be adequately provided, it is important for local governments to identify the needs and demands of the residents, and select the most suitable policies. Thus, local governments interested in such related matters proceed with their own policies. So although the central government has the power, it lacks access to information related to different regions. Recognizing this asymmetry of information, the central government selects a local government to implement its policy goals.

The traditional basis for the public–public partnership in Japan is the Fiscal Investment and Loan Program (FILP), which is discussed extensively in Tsuji (1996). The FILP is a general name for government activities related to financing and investing public funds. The total amount of funds associated with this program is so huge, almost half the national budget, that this program is sometimes referred to as 'the second national budget.'

When local governments require funding to improve infrastructure such as roads, parks, and schools, they issue bonds, which the FILP also purchases. In fact, the program buys almost half the bonds issued by local governments. The particular objectives of investment by the FILP are classified into twelve categories: housing, maintaining national land and environment, welfare, education, financing small businesses, agriculture and fishery, preventing natural disasters, roads, transportation and communication, regional development, industrial technology, and trade and overseas cooperation.

Government financial involvement is explained by market failure or market imperfections. Failures arise due to externalities or public goods. Imperfection can occur in the financial market for various reasons, leading to allocation inefficiency. Such inefficiency results mainly from either imperfect information or imperfect competition. As suggested by Ide and Hayashi (1992), the former results in incomplete contracts in the private sector. The resulting sub-optimal level of investment can lead to government provision of funds in risky areas where there is less incentive for the private sector to invest (see Yoshino 1990).

Another reason the public–public partnership is successful in the field of info-communication is competition among government agencies. Because bureaucrats are often eager to expand their power to related areas of their administration, there is competition among government ministries. Now targeting the information society of the twenty-first century, bureaucrats are announcing their own projects in the information industry. The Ministry of Economy, Trade and Industry (formerly MITI), the Ministry of Land, Infrastructure and Transport Construction, the Ministry of Agriculture, the Ministry of Health, Labor, and Welfare, and the Ministry of Public Management, Home Affairs, Posts and Telecommunications have formulated ambitious projects for promoting regional information policies based on multimedia. Even the Ministry of Education has joined this race.[12] This claiming of new territory has the same basis as the government's role in implementing an industrial policy for Japanese economic development.

The 'third-sector method' characterizes projects that proceed through the joint venture of the public and private sectors. This method is usual when the size of the project is such that local governments cannot undertake it by themselves and regional firms are asked to join the project. This scheme itself is quite reasonable, but as Kagami (2002) argues, most projects based on this scheme tend to fail. The main reason for this is 'coordination failure' resulting from lack of leadership and responsibility. It is apparent that regional information policies carried out with the strong leadership and clear vision of the head of local government are successful.

CONCLUSION: FROM PUBLIC–PUBLIC PARTNERSHIP TO PUBLIC–PRIVATE PARTNERSHIP

In the UK and other countries, PFI is utilized for information technology (IT), and this particular kind of PFI is called IT-PFI. It is widely believed that IT-PFI is among the most promising types of projects (see Hidaka 1999). Specifically, it is called System Development and Service Provision, which means that a private contractor designs, builds, and operates an IT system for a particular authority, including construction of a computer system and provision of public service through it. In the UK examples of IT-PFI are the New Insurance Record System (NIRS2) and the Immigration and Nationality Directorate (IND). In the US, there is the SmartTraveler System in Washington, DC.

In Japan, PFI generally refers to investment for hardware, typically physical facilities such as buildings and roads, and it is less concerned with IT and software. From the experience of field research in the areas of tele-medicine and tele-home care, it appears that most projects in Japan proceed more or less by public–private partnership and involve collaboration between local governments and manufacturers of related industries such as those dealing with computers, electrical appliances, and cameras. Since tele-medicine is a new field and there was no ready-made equipment or devices of mass production, these had to be developed. In the case of Goshiki Town and Kamaishi City, for instance, the private sector had already been participating in the tele-medicine projects in this way. Household electric appliance companies manufactured a CATV system working together with the staff of local governments. Computer makers and equipment manufacturers are quite eager to sell their hardware as well as software related to home care, since home care insurance was put into effect in April 2000. They have already started experimental projects to establish the network to exchange and share information concerning home care among the related sections of local governments. As these experiences accumulate, IT-PFI in this field might be successful.

As noted, public- and private-sector collaboration is proceeding, but only in the technological field. To achieve real public–private partnership, more private funds should be directed toward IT-PFI, with attention given to the scope of the project and risks. Scope and risk may be difficult to determine since IT-PFI in the fields of tele-home care, tele-medicine, and tele-education, for example, includes various activities and since the assets on which the services are based are both tangible and intangible (e.g., hardware and software, personnel or staff). Without a clear understanding of the business activities of PFI, success cannot be assured.

The most important issue of PFI in general is how to share the risks among related agents. IT-PFI has risks associated with management and development. Management risk relates to inefficient project management, vagueness of business objectives and scope of projects, and inconsistency of demands by local governments. Development risk is related to the time between contract signing and operation, the period in which projects give rise to concrete effects. In addition, IT-PFI is concerned with the newest available technology, and risks come from the reliability of technology and its completion on schedule.

The examples of actual projects related to telecommunications infrastructure implemented by local governments given in earlier sections highlight certain issues related to IT-PFI. First, project size is rather small. From the business viewpoint, small projects are less attractive for private firms. To make projects more profitable, several nearby local governments need to join together to implement IT-PFI. But projects that require a large investment for infrastructure may not be successful, and the greater the amount of funds required, the more risky projects become. For IT-PFI to be successful, partners must agree on the proper share of responsibility. The proper share in public–private partnerships, for instance, makes the public sector responsible for constructing infrastructure and the private sector responsible for software, which reduces the risks for the private sector. As shown by tele-home care, the central government takes care of infrastructure investment, and the local government manages the costs of maintenance and telecommunications charges. Cost sharing that assigns responsibilities to appropriate groups requires a deep understanding of risk assignment and risk mitigation to avoid having costs going out of control.

ENDNOTES

1. For the current discussion on universal service, see Sugaya (1997) and Tsuji (1999a).
2. Tsuji (1999a, 2000) discusses issues related to the bottleneck monopoly of subscriber lines.
3. The timetable for replacement can be viewed on NTT's web page, http://www.ntt.co.jp.
4. It is reported that NTT has started video on demand (VOD) service by making use of this technology. One shortcoming is the distance of transmission; 7 km is said to be the limit.
5. Gas companies also own networks for the same reason. No gas company operates a telecommunications business, but some provide services such as home security through their networks. An interesting service that is expected to have increased demand is found in the application of a tele-medicine network. One small gas company in Gifu Prefecture has been providing vital sensors to families and they send medical data through its network.
6. In the case of Titus Communications, the ratio of households using CATV telephony is 3.3 percent and that of Internet connection 1.7 percent as of April 1999.
7. For a comparison of NCIH and ICN with Japanese projects, see Tsuji et al. (1999c).
8. Some analysts argue that huge and expensive networks like NCIH and ICN are products of the pre-Internet age and are not necessarily essential.
9. This section is based on Tsuji et al. (1999c).
10. This section is based on Tsuji (1999b).
11. It is said that local governments have only so-called '30% autonomy' in terms of money and power, and most of the power is in the hands of the central government.
12. Another field of competition among government agencies is venture business, and most ministries mentioned also provide financial assistance for promoting venture businesses.

REFERENCES

Grant, A.E. and L.B. Berquist (1998), 'Telecommunications infrastructure and the city: Adapting to the convergence of technology and policy', paper presented at Telecommunications and the Cities Conference, University of Georgia.

Hidaka, N. (1999), *Johotusin PFI* (Telecommunications PFI), Nikkan Kougyo Shinbun Sha.

Ide, I. and T. Hayashi (1992), 'Kinyu chukai ni okeru kouteki bumon no yakuwari' (Role of the public sector in financial intermediation), in A. Horiuchi and N. Yoshino (eds), *Gendai Nihon no Kinyu Sisutemu* (Financial System in Contemporary Japan), Tokyo: University Press, 219–47.

Kagami, M. (2002), 'The Third Sector's Failure in Japan', this volume (Chapter 2).

Longcore, T.R. and P.W. Rees (1996), 'Information technology and downtown restructuring: The case of New York City's financial district', *Urban Geography*, 17 (4), 354–72.

Sharon, S. and L.B. Berquist (1999), 'Telecommunications infrastructure development: The evolving state and city role in the US', *Proceedings of the City in the Information Age Conference*, Newcastle, UK.

Sugaya, M. (1997), 'Advanced universal service in Japan', *Telecommunications Policy*, 21 (2), 177–84.

Tsuji, M. (1996), 'Deregulation and privatization of the fiscal and loan program', Working Paper No. 121, Center on Japanese Economy and Business, Columbia Business School, Columbia University.

Tsuji, M. (1999a), 'Deregulation in the Japanese telecommunications market: New regulatory schemes', in M. Kagami and M. Tsuji (eds), *Privatization, Deregulation and Institutional Framework*, Chiba, Japan: Institute of Developing Economies, 22–49.

Tsuji, M. (1999b), 'Kobe: Rebirth as a multimedia city – Application of the ATM network for regional information policy', *Proceedings of the City in the Information Age Conference*, Newcastle, UK.

Tsuji, M. (2000), 'The new direction of regulation and deregulation in the converging Japanese telecommunications market', in E. Bohlin et al. (eds), *Convergence in Communications and Beyond*, Amsterdam: Elsevier Science.

Tsuji, M., M. Teshima and F. Taoka (1999a), 'Multimedia technology and tele-education: An international comparison', *Proceedings of the International Conference on Distance Education, Distant Learning and 21st Century Education Development*, Tsinghua University, Beijing, China.

Tsuji, M., M. Teshima and S. Miyahara (1999b), 'The economic effect of tele-care at home through the application of multimedia', paper presented at the ITS European Conference, Torino, Italy.

Tsuji, M., M. Teshima and T. Mori (1999c), 'Applications of telecommunications and multimedia technology in the fields of medicine and education: An international comparison based on field research of local governments', *Osaka Economic Papers*, 49 (1), 1–21.

Yoshino, N. (1990), 'Zaisei toyushi no genjo to kadai' (Current situation and issues of the fiscal investment and loan program), in K. Kaizuka et al. (eds), *Henbo suru Kokyo Bumon* (Transforming the Public Sector), Yuhikaku, Tokyo.

2. The third sector's failure in Japan

Mitsuhiro Kagami

The 1999 Act on Promotion of Public Infrastructure Development by Using Private Finance Initiative, hereafter cited as the PFI Promotion Act, is the Japanese version of the British PFI introduced in 1992 (Pollitt 2002, Grout 1997). Japan is now undertaking the actual measures to execute this law. The idea behind its introduction is to reduce governmental intervention and promote private-sector initiative, which will interject market mechanisms into infra-structure services once recognized as public-sector activities.

Public works and public investment have long been considered government activities. The public sector has undertaken responsibility for infrastructure services because of (1) their natural monopoly nature (economies of scale), (2) goals of universal service, and (3) market failures (public goods and external-ities). Therefore, national as well as local budgets have allocated enormous amounts to infrastructure building and related public works in Japan for many years since the Meiji Restoration in 1868. In 1997, for example, Japan spent 16.2 percent of GDP for government expenditures (central plus local governments), of which 41 percent was for public fixed-capital formation (6.6 percent of GDP). In contrast, the US spent 17.1 percent of GDP for government expenditures, of which only 11 percent (1.9 percent of GDP) was for public fixed-capital formation (OECD 1998). This shows that investment expenditures still play a vital role in Japanese government spending.

However, inefficient and sometimes wasteful government investments, and the fact that private sectors can participate in certain public infrastructure services (mainly because of recent technological advances), have changed people's way of thinking. Now it is thought that market forces can enter into many government activities and that smaller government is better for society. Under these circumstances, many innovative ideas dealing with infrastructure businesses are being put forward, such as PFI and various contracting forms between the public and private sectors. In Japan 'third-sector' development was one of these ideas.

Joint efforts by public and private sectors in providing community-based services have long been practiced in Japan. Public services, such as ferry and bus transportation jointly operated by a local government entity and a local private firm, are common. This was particularly true during the 1980s, when ongoing deregulation and the opening up of the Japanese economy stimulated a surge in third-sector development. Regional and resort developments were undertaken enthusiastically with the participation of the private sector. However, these projects encountered serious problems after the economic bubble burst in the early 1990s. Many third-sector corporations had large deficits and faced bankruptcy.

The failures during this earlier period of third-sector development highlight important lessons for Japan as the country embarks on new PFI programs that anticipate private-sector participation in the development of infrastructure businesses. In this chapter, Japan's budgetary system and public investment are briefly explained, then third-sector development is examined, and causes of its failure are illustrated. Finally, some lessons and policy recommendations are pointed out.

BUDGETARY SYSTEM AND PUBLIC INVESTMENT

Both central and local governments execute public investment in Japan. For example, national highways and waterways are constructed and maintained by the central government, while local roads, public housing projects, water and sewage facilities, and urban planning are carried out by local governments. Funding for these public investments involves very complicated procedures, and one needs to understand the Japanese budgetary system, especially mechanisms between central and local governments. Because local governments lack funds, attributable to differences in the tax revenues collected locally, the central government has to defray balances out of the National Treasury as subsidies or tax transfers. Usually more than 40 percent of local government budgets are supported by central government funds in Japan.

Budgetary System

Each ministry begins budget preparation in May for maintaining existing projects and launching new ones for the following budgetary year (April–March). Local governments appeal for more funds for certain projects to the relevant ministries by using politicians or by sending petition missions to related departments of the central government. Politicians who have special connections in certain fields are called '*zoku*' (or clan) congressmen. There are, for example, health and welfare *zoku*, construction *zoku*, and transport *zoku*. These politicians have a strong influence on the relevant ministries because of previous experience as ministers or keen vested interests in their local communities.

In October the Ministry of Finance (MOF) makes a draft of the next year's budget after negotiations with other ministries and sends it to the cabinet. MOF's

Budget Bureau is staffed by the brightest and ablest bureaucrats and wields the most power in Japan since it controls the national purse strings. By the end of December the final budget is determined after adjustments are made, and it is sent to the Diet for approval. At the same time, local governments prepare their own budgets. All budgets are usually finalized by mid-March for the new budgetary year.

The central government has three fiscal measures to support local governments: local grant tax, local transfer tax, and direct subsidies. The local grant tax and local transfer tax come from national tax revenues associated with specific taxes. The local grant tax is linked to such taxes as the local road grant tax, petroleum and gas grant tax, vehicle weight grant tax, aircraft fuel grant tax, and special tonnage grant tax. The local transfer tax is assigned to five national tax revenues. Pre-fixed support ratios allocated to local governments for the 2000 budgetary year are: 3.2 percent of personal income tax revenues, 35.8 percent of corporate income tax, 3.2 percent of alcohol tax, 29.5 percent of consumer tax, and 2.5 percent of tobacco tax. The direct subsidies come from general tax revenues and are determined according to the total demand of the local governments.

The total general budget of the central government amounted to 85,000 billion yen (US$810 billion) in the 2000 budgetary year, while the total local government budget amounted to 88,900 billion yen (US$847 billion) (Local Finance Association 2000). Of this US$847 billion total, US$6 billion or 0.7 percent came from the central government as local grant tax, US$212 billion or 25.1 percent as local transfer tax, and US$124 billion or 14.6 percent as direct subsidies. The remainder of the local government budget came from local tax revenues (US$334 billion or 39.5 percent), local bond issues (US$106 billion or 12.5 percent), and other revenues (US$65 billion or 7.6 percent). To sum up, approximately 40 percent of the total local government budget came from the central government (see Figure 2.1). Looking at local government expenditures, we see that 26.7 percent of the total US$847 billion went to wages and salaries, 22.2 percent to general administration, 31.9 percent (US$270 billion) to investments, 13.6 percent to local bond expenditures, and 1.9 percent to others.

In Japan, there is a special fiscal account called the 'fiscal investment and loan program.' Its funds come mainly from post office savings and pension funds run by the Ministry of Health and Welfare. This account substantially aids public investment under the name of the Fund Arrangement Bureau of MOF. These funds were channeled into local bonds for the local government budget for 2000. More precisely, a local bond plan is approved by the central and local governments each year under the guidance of the Ministry of Home Affairs. In fiscal 2000, a plan amounting to 16,300 billion yen (US$155 billion) was approved to issue local bonds. Of this total, US$106 billion was allocated to local government bond issues and US$49 billion to local public corporation

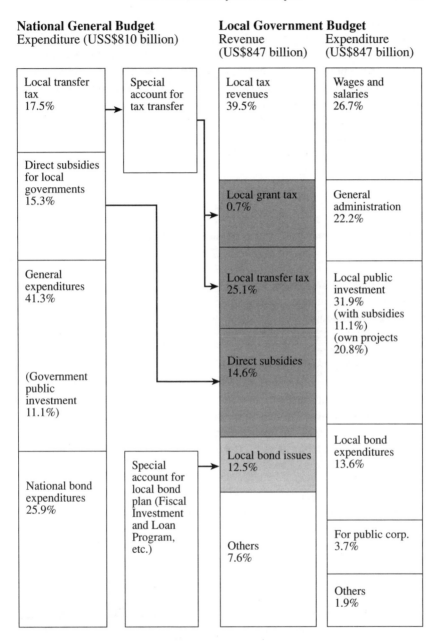

National General Budget
Expenditure (USS$810 billion)

Local Government Budget
Revenue
(US$847 billion)

Expenditure
(US$847 billion)

Local transfer tax
17.5%

Special account for tax transfer

Local tax revenues
39.5%

Wages and salaries
26.7%

Direct subsidies for local governments
15.3%

Local grant tax
0.7%

General administration
22.2%

General expenditures
41.3%

Local transfer tax
25.1%

Local public investment
31.9%
(with subsidies 11.1%)
(own projects 20.8%)

(Government public investment
11.1%)

Direct subsidies
14.6%

National bond expenditures
25.9%

Special account for local bond plan (Fiscal Investment and Loan Program, etc.)

Local bond issues
12.5%

Local bond expenditures
13.6%

Others
7.6%

For public corp.
3.7%

Others
1.9%

Source: Local Finance Association 2000.

Figure 2.1   Local finance plan, 2000 budgetary year

bond issues. In financing these issues, 46.9 percent of the total US$155 billion came from the Fund Arrangement Bureau of MOF, 12.4 percent from the Public Enterprise Finance Corporation under MOF and the Ministry of Home Affairs, and 40.7 percent from private purchases (public subscription associations and closely related banks or 'kin funds'). Therefore, in addition to the 40 percent of the local government budget that comes directly from the central government, a large part of local government bond issues are covered by central government funds.

Public Investment

Public investment is undertaken either by governments themselves or by public corporations, and funds come from either government budgets or bond issues financed by governments as well as public corporations. This can be illustrated as follows:

I. National public investment
    A. Central government
       1. General budget
       Seashore protection works, fishing ports, forest conservation, disaster restoration, etc.
       2. Special budget
       National highways, national rivers, airports, commercial ports, etc.
    B. National public corporations
       1. Japan Highway Public Corporation
       2. Japan Railway Construction Public Corporation
       3. Urban Development Corp. (formerly Japan Housing Public Corp.)
       4. Water Resources Development Public Corporation, etc.
II. Local public investment
    A. Local governments
       General budget (including projects with national subsidies and local government's own projects)
       Civil engineering, public works, education, welfare programs, etc.
    B. Local public corporations
       Sewage, water supply, transport, hospitals, rural development, etc.

In the 1998 budgetary year, a total of 45,838 billion yen (US$350 billion) was spent for public investment, of which approximately US$75 billion or 22 percent was carried out by the central government and national public corporations and US$275 billion or 78 percent by local governments and their public corporations. In terms of payment burdens, the central government and its public corporations spent 35 percent of the total and local governments and their public corporations 65 percent.

Problems

Japan's budgetary system and its public investment face several problems. For example, once a budget is approved, it is difficult to cut or stop it. Politicians want to continue a given project to attract votes in their communities. Bureaucrats want to maintain their power by pouring money into it. Those engaged in a project do not want to be fired. Thus, an approved budget takes on a life of its own.

Difficulties also arise with the introduction of new projects such as IT (Information Technology) that have not had a budgetary base in the past. And local governments' dependence on the central government is not corrected so long as they continue to receive large amounts of money from the central government.

Public investment is used to buoy economic recession as a traditional measure of macroeconomic demand. But in Japan this fiscal policy can create unwanted or excessive infrastructure facilities such as paved roads in remote rice fields and luxurious harbor facilities in run-down fishing villages. Spending cuts and the reallocation of investment funds are needed.

Over-dependence on bond issues creates budgetary deficit problems and leaves a heavy burden on future generations. Japan's total outstanding long-term public debt amounted to approximately US$6,322 billion in 2000. Special accounts such as the fund for fiscal investment and loan program have played an important role in building infrastructure in the past but have also created huge public enterprises and special corporations that continue to survive even after they have become unnecessary.

Among recent movements to reverse these trends and reform the system, the Mori Cabinet (July 2000–April 2001) re-examined public investment programs for 2000 and agreed to halt projects with low feasibility ratings. Special corporations that are semi-governmental organizations established by law for particular purposes (such as construction of public housing and highways, extracting of petroleum, and lending Official Development Assistance money to developing countries) will either be abolished within five years or become independent agencies if they have legitimate reasons to exist. The fiscal investment and loan program is also under scrutiny, and the subsidizing of public corporations is being rechecked.[1] Under Governor Shintaro Ishihara, the Tokyo metropolitan government imposed a new asset-based tax on large commercial banks operating in the capital to increase local tax revenues and thus increase independence from the central government.

Huge public-sector deficits coupled with the recent trend toward 'small government' led governments to promote private initiatives in public activities. Private-sector participation is welcomed in infrastructure building and operation, and PFI is now being eagerly promoted by both business and the public sector. However, there are lessons to learn from third-sector development failures over the last fifteen years.

WHAT IS THE THIRD SECTOR?

In Japan the term 'third sector' refers to joint ventures financed by private and public capital. Central as well as local governments and their related agencies are generally called the 'first sector', while the private sector is termed the 'second sector.' The third sector is seen as a mixture of the two in terms of capital, and it is expected to contribute to public-related activities while remaining financially sustainable and economically efficient. Traditionally, local infrastructure such as railways and ferry services, which are lifelines to local communities, are run by a corporation or agency using both local government and local private capital.

Third-sector development benefits the first sector because funding shortfalls can be remedied by the second sector; know-how, efficiency and better services related to the second sector can be utilized. In addition, job positions can be secured for senior first-sector employees, who are sometimes called '*amakudari*', meaning descending from Heaven.

The second sector benefits because third-sector development allows it to expand business opportunities under the aegis of the first sector. The first sector offers fiscal incentives to the second sector, and in emergencies, the second sector can expect support from the first sector in the form of debt compensation, subsidies, etc.

There are legally binding stipulations for the third sector in Japan. The Act for Local Self-Governing requires that a report be submitted to the local Diet by the local government head (e.g., governor or mayor) when local government's share of a project's capital investment is more than 50 percent, and an audit is required whenever the local government's share exceeds 25 percent.

Background

Since the early 1980s Japan has followed the world economic trend of privatization and deregulation that began with the conservative administrations of Margaret Thatcher and Ronald Reagan (Kagami 2000). The impetus for the trend was to utilize private-sector vitality and market forces. In Japan, the government began supporting the private sector with tax and financial incentives.

Under the Nakasone Cabinet (1982–87) the Act on Provisional Measures for Promotion of the Expansion of Designated Facilities by Using Private Contractors' Ability (known as the Private Promotion Act) was promulgated in 1986. The act provided incentive for the private sector to enter into the development of infrastructure businesses. In 1987 the Special Act for the Promotion of Private Urban Development and the Act for the Facilitation of Integrated Resort (the Resort Act) gave additional momentum to the trend. The latter stimulated private-sector participation in the development of resort areas with the help of local governments. Parks and resort areas sprouted like mushrooms throughout Japan under the third-sector scheme. These projects included Canadian World (Ashibetsu City, Hokkaido), Urausu Resort Development (Urausu Town, Hokkaido), Ohwani Integrated Area Development (Ohwani Town, Aomori Prefecture), Okuni Regional Development (Okuni Town, Niigata Prefecture), Space Neotopia (Nagaoka City, Niigata Prefecture), South Chita Resort Development (Minami-chita Town, Aichi Prefecture), Seta River Resort

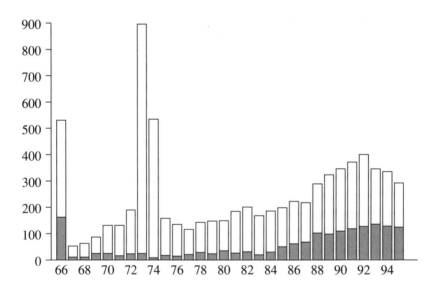

Notes:
(1) For 1966, 525 corporations represent an accumulated number up to the year; the accumulated number by the end of 1995 is 7,580 corporations.
(2) The shaded area represents the number of joint-stock and limited companies.

Source: Ministry of Home Affairs.

Figure 2.2   Evolution of the third sector (local government share exceeds 25 percent)

Development (Ohtsu City, Shiga Prefecture), Tajima Sea Sightseeing Development (Okayama Prefecture), Kure Portpia Land (Kure City, Hiroshima Prefecture), and the Nagasaki Sightseeing Development (Nagasaki City, Nagasaki Prefecture).

This boom followed a development rush that had occurred in the 1970s during Kakuei Tanaka's tenure as prime minister (1972–74). Author of *A Plan for Reconstruction of the Japan Islands* published in 1972, Tanaka promoted frenzied growth coupled with loose monetary policies (see Figure 2.2).

After the Plaza Accords of 1985, the Japanese yen rapidly appreciated against the US dollar, and this trend did not cease. The US economy at that time plunged into a serious slump and suffered from fiscal and trade deficits. The rapid depreciation of the US dollar, however, did not have an immediate impact on the US trade deficits, especially against Japan, and the US stock market experienced a major crash in 1987 known as Black Monday. In response to the ongoing economic turmoil, the Japanese government followed loose monetary policies by cutting interest rates to give incentives to the domestic market (partly) in order to stimulate the US economy. The immediate outcome however was the

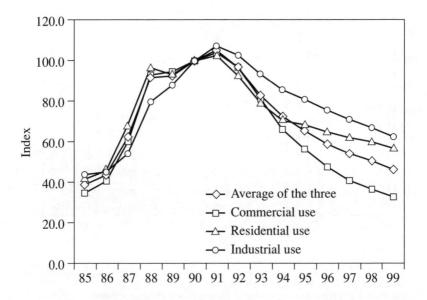

Note: Measured in March of each year; 1990 equals 100.

Source: Japan Real Estate Institute.

Figure 2.3   Urban land price index of the Tokyo metropolitan region

creation of the bubble phenomena. Land and housing prices soared, and financial assets such as stock prices rocketed upward.

In the case of land prices in the Tokyo metropolitan region, the average index jumped from 39.1 in March 1985 to a peak of 104.7 in March 1991 (2.7 times as high). The largest increase was recorded in 1988, a yearly increase rate of 48.3 percent. After this peak the price gradually dropped back to 47.3 in March 1999, close to the pre-bubble level, particularly in the price of land for commercial use (see Figure 2.3).

Third-sector development was generally perceived as a good idea by local governments because they could utilize private-sector initiative for regional development and to develop local infrastructure. Banks vied for lending opportunities while construction companies eyed increased business chances. With the opportunities possible under this scheme many new corporations were established. In 1995 there were 7,580 local public agencies and corporations with a capital share of more than 25 percent provided by the local government. Of these, 1,668 were joint-stock and/or limited companies (Figure 2.2). About 40 percent of these companies were said to be involved in urban/rural developments or leisure/resort developments. After the bubble burst these corporations faced serious problems because of demand contraction, bad debt problems, asset price declines, and shrinkage of bank loans. Many corporations suffered problems from accumulated red tape and some faced bankruptcy.

Third-Sector Failures

According to an investigation by the *Nihon Keizai Shimbun* (Japan Economic Daily) published 29 December 1997, 50.8 percent of 389 third-sector companies surveyed that had been established since 1985 and that had capital of more than 100 million yen (about US$0.8 million) and local government participation of more than 25 percent said they faced serious loss of capital and either had no plan to solve their accumulated deficit problem or faced serious difficulties if they were to reduce their deficits. The main reasons given for the deficits were: (a) unexpectedly low sales in the severe recession after the bubble burst, (b) depreciation that had not yet been completed, (c) existence of many unexpected constraints such as delays in project developments, and (d) the lack of professionals and/or poor managerial know-how.

The Tokyo metropolitan government (www.metro.tokyo.jp) has fifteen companies classified as third-sector. Four of these, examined below, showed severe accumulated deficits in 1998 and were listed as red-card companies for their excessive losses (losses carried over plus present losses). According to Sakata (1998) these difficulties are explained by (a) an unexpectedly low number of entrants as tenants/users following the end of the bubble period, (b) lower lease charges because of fewer tenants/users, (c) modifications and delays in the development projects, and (d) increases in labor costs (number of directors, etc.).

1. Construction of Tokyo Sub-center at the Waterfront (accumulated loss, US$382 million as of 31 March 1998). The company was established in 1988 to construct such infrastructure facilities as water supply and sewerage, garbage collection through pipe networks, and parks in the Tokyo Sub-center at the Odaiba Waterfront, Tokyo Bay. Its capital was registered as US$168 million. The Tokyo metropolitan government participated with a 52 percent capital share. In 1998 the current deficit was US$63 million.
2. Takeshiba Area Development (accumulated loss, US$356 million as of 31 March 1999). The company was established in 1987 to redevelop the Takeshiba region, which had once prospered as a port area. The plan included the construction of a shopping mall, hotels and lease buildings after demolition of old storehouses. The capital was US$132 million, with the Tokyo metropolitan government's share at 50.5 percent. The current deficit in 1999 was US$16 million.
3. Tokyo Tele-port Center (accumulated loss, US$221 million as of 31 March 1998). The company was established in 1989 to construct a telecommunications center as an information-transmitting base for the twenty-first century in the Tokyo Sub-center at the Odaiba Waterfront. The capital was US$134 million, with the Tokyo metropolitan government share at 51.5 percent. The current deficit as of 1998 was US$33 million.
4. Tama New Town Development Center (accumulated loss, US$63 million as of 31 March 1998). The company was established in 1988 to develop the Tama area (west side of Tokyo) as a new residential town. The capital was US$14 million, with the Tokyo metropolitan government's share at 51.2 percent. The current deficit in 1998 was US$10 million.

Case Studies of Bankruptcy

According to Tokyo Industry and Commerce Research, ninety-nine companies went bankrupt (including bankruptcy, liquidation, special liquidation, etc.) between 1996 and 2000 (six in 1996, nine in 1997, twenty-five in 1998, twenty-six in 1999, and thirty-three in 2000).[2] Seven major projects are shown in Table 2.1, and three of these are examined in more detail below.

Japan–Korea High Speed Ferry
The company was established in November 1990, initiated by the mayor of Shimonoseki City. Yamaguchi Prefecture and Shimonoseki City invested 10.25 percent each with private companies such as Osaka/Mitsui Commercial Liners. The first hydrofoil boat started sailing between Shimonoseki Harbor and Pusan

Table 2.1 Representative cases of bankruptcy in the third sector, 1996–98

Company	Capital (US$millions)	Public-Sector Participant	Percentage Share	Liability (US$millions)
Japan–Korea High Speed Ferry	3.4	Yamaguchi Prefecture Shimonoseki City	10.25 10.25	16.5
Akita Wood Housing	0.6	Akita Prefecture	25	138.9
Okuni Regional Development Corp.	0.5	Town of Okuni	70	2.6
Urausu Resort Development Corp.	0.6	Town of Urausu	40	103.1
Kure Portpia Land	17.2	Kure City	20	87.6
Izumisano Cosmopolis	6.9	Osaka Prefecture Izumisano City	16 16	463.4
Obihiro Station	0.6	Obihiro City	24	3.2

Source: Excerpted from Matsumoto (1999, p. 24).

Harbor in Korea in July 1991. However, frequent suspension of services because of bad weather, especially in winter, and low user demand resulted in an accumulation of deficits. The ferry stopped service in November 1992 after operating only one year and four months. Shimonoseki City gave a subsidy of US$8.3 million to save the company in 1994, but the company went bankrupt in March 1996 with a debt of US$17 million.

When a group of Shimonoseki citizens sued, claiming that the subsidy for the company did not fall within the criterion of public purposes, the Yamaguchi local court admitted that the subsidy was illegal and ordered the then-mayor to return US$8.3 million to the municipal coffer. This judgment stimulated subsequent civil movements in Japan to sue the third sector for damages, auditing, and disclosure of its balance sheet (Matsumoto 1999).

Akita-ken Wood Housing
The company was established in 1982 to promote the use of Akita cedar for housing with funding by the Akita Prefecture government (25 percent) and two local banks. At first the company performed well, marketing high-quality wood houses in the Tokyo metropolitan area, but demand for housing fell after the bubble burst. Prices for land that had been purchased at exorbitant prices during the bubble also fell, precipitating bankruptcy of real estate companies and the emergence of bad debts.

A total of 1,646 houses were sold. In 1997 several of these were found defective because of their soft groundwork and poor structural design. According to a TV program some houses sank and subsided because they had been constructed on swampland. Walls developed cracks, and other defects were found in roofs and below the floorboards. A group of residents who bought houses in Chiba Prefecture sued the company and its related organizations for constructing and selling defective houses. The company declared bankruptcy in February 1998 with total debts amounting to approximately US$139 million. The court case is ongoing. Akita Prefecture government has decided to cover minor repair work for defective houses but has refused to make full reimbursement.

Izumisano Cosmopolis
The development corporation was established in 1987 with the Osaka metropolitan and the Izumisano city governments each contributing 16 percent of the US$6.9 million in total capital. The project included the development of the hinterland of the Kansai International Airport in Izumisano to attract high-tech industries and research institutes. The company bought land, and total investment was estimated at US$759 million. However, during the following years of recession enterprises declined to move to the area and only losses accumulated.

In 1998 the Osaka metropolitan and Izumisano city governments decided to buy back land that the corporation had bought at a cost of US$108 million and appealed to the court for the corporation's dissolution. The accumulated losses were estimated at US$463 million, the largest amount among the bankruptcy cases of the third sector by 1998. The corporation is now under special liquidation.

CAUSES OF FAILURES

Several reasons for the failure of the third-sector projects are apparent. Project plans were based on a bubble economy and were not fully examined. Feasibility studies were not thorough, and demand projection was incomplete and often wrong. Revenue estimates based on erroneous demand projections undermined the projects.

Even without the distortions of a bubble economy, some plans were defective from the beginning. Responsibility was not clearly defined among entities. Governors and mayors change every three or four years. Senior bureaucrats (*amakudari*) also move. With the private sector anticipating financial rescue packages by the public sector in case of emergency, a moral hazard in the minds of many directors and a spoiled and dependent culture were created.

Banks, construction companies and consulting (or design) companies made profits while the welfare of users and persons living in the project areas was ignored. Concepts pertaining to third-sector projects were vague. Third-sector developments were supposed to be 'publicly useful' projects, but instead leisure development such as ski resorts or seashore sightseeing developments competed directly with the private sector. Such projects needed no public sector participation at all.

The bubble mentality had a strong influence on projects. During the bubble period, prices of land, properties and stocks soared. This caused project planners to consider expansionary developments. When the bubble burst and many real estate companies went bankrupt, banks and the third sector held bad debts or time-expired liabilities. Third-sector asset value shrank and companies faced payment difficulties. Wounded banks also cut lending for borrowers, including the third sector. Local governments suffered from smaller tax revenues.

Rescue scenarios were also confusing. The majority of projects should have been stopped immediately and liquidated. Postponement and slow decision-making processes caused further damage and increased costs. Sometimes local governments paid subsidies or provided new loans for dying projects, thus deepening the damage by throwing good money after bad. It is problematic for the public sector to guarantee debt compensation for third-sector projects; such behavior raises a legal issue about the extent local governments can guarantee third-sector development. Information disclosure was incomplete, and when the local government's participation was less than 25 percent of total capital, there was no obligation for disclosure by third-sector corporations.

LESSONS FROM FAILURES

Several lessons can be drawn from Japan's experiences in third-sector failure. For example, complete cost and benefit analyses of every project are indispensable. In the British PFI, this principle is called 'value for money.' Accurate demand forecasts are especially important. Accountability and information disclosure are necessary. Public-related business activities should have an obligation to report to the local Diet because of its budgetary approval and should be open to public scrutiny. A credible auditing system must be available at all times, and careful monitoring of the intermediate processes of the project is also necessary.

Responsibility should be clearly defined to avoid moral hazard among directors. This means that risks and obligations should be transparently shared among participating agents. If something goes wrong, reconstruction plans should be designed without expecting local governments' financial support. And local governments should not routinely guarantee covering bad financial situations with such measures as debt compensation, subsidies and special loans. Decisions regarding whether a project continues or shuts down should be quick; otherwise, pouring public money into a hole will further burden taxpayers.

Evaluation of assets needs reform in Japan. Land and property prices are often valued in traditional ways that create violent fluctuations of asset values, rather than being based on project evaluations or the present value of future profit. Since land is used as collateral for bank lending, projects can become unstable. Construction and real estate companies in Japan also need reform because of their heavy bad-debt problems. In particular, land bought at high prices in the past has become deadweight with sharp price declines. The Japan Official Accountant Association has declared that the asset value of real estate should be evaluated at current prices in the balance sheet beginning March 2001 (*Nihon Keizai Shimbun*, 19 January 2000). This change will accelerate reforms in this sector. In this context, the new PFI in Japan should not be utilized to save sinking shipwrecked construction and real estate companies. Such a strategy is an expensive way to save local jobs.

The post-bubble credit crunch ended third-sector activities in Japan, at least for the time being. Sound banking is necessary to avoid a repeat of history. In this connection the coming financial and banking reforms in Japan (the so-called 'big bang') are welcome policy initiatives.[3]

ENDNOTES

1. Japan established a mechanism for infrastructure building through post-office savings. Through a nationwide network of post offices, small amounts of money are collected from individuals. The amount collected through such post-office savings (US$2,167 billion) is almost equal to the deposit amount collected by all Japanese private banks (US$2,367 billion). Together with pension funds, the post-office savings funds go to the fiscal investment and loan program of MOF and then are distributed to infrastructure investments through government agencies and/or special public corporations. This corpulent system is the center point of a heated discussion under the new Junichiro Koizumi administration (from April 2001).
2. The largest failure, a theme park called Seagaia in Miyazaki Prefecture, filed for court protection under the Corporate Rehabilitation Law in February 2001. Seagaia was the project that was the first approved under the Resort Act in 1988. Since then the operators, Phoenix Resort Ltd. and its two affiliates with participation of the Miyazaki Prefecture government and Miyazaki City, have accumulated debts totaling US$2.72 billion. A US-based investment firm, Ripplewood Holdings, was finally chosen to support revival of the project (*Nihon Keizai Shimbun*, 14 May 2001).
3. Japanese banks finally realized that their size and number could not compete with world-class commercial banks and their subsequent mergers resulted in four major groups by 2001: Mizuho Holdings Inc. (Daiichi Kangyo Bank, Fuji Bank, and Industrial Bank of Japan), Mitsubishi Tokyo Financial Group Inc. (Tokyo Mitsubishi Bank, Mitsubishi Trust Bank, and Japan Trust Bank), UFJ Holdings Inc. (Sanwa Bank, Tokai Bank, and Toyo Trust Bank), and Sumitomo Mitsui Banking Corp. (Sumitomo Bank and Sakura Bank). The bad-debt problems of these banks (more than US$250 billion as of March 2001) have yet to be solved because of delayed reforms.

REFERENCES

Grout, Paul A. (1997), 'The Economics of the Private Finance Initiative', *Oxford Review of Economic Policy*, 13 (4): 53–66.
Kagami, Mitsuhiro (2000), 'Privatization and Deregulation: The Case of Japan', in Mitsuhiro Kagami and Masatsugu Tsuji (eds), *Privatization, Deregulation and Economic Efficiency: A Comparative Analysis of Asia, Europe and the Americas*, Cheltenham, UK and Northampton, MA: Edward Elgar.
Local Finance Association (2000), *An Outline of Local Bonds* [in Japanese], Tokyo.
Matsumoto, Yoshihiro (1999), 'Trend of the Third Sector's Bankruptcy' [in Japanese], *Kinyu Homu Jijo*, 1536 (Jan. 25): 23–5.
OECD (1998), *National Accounts: Detailed Tables 1960–1997*, vol. 2, Paris: Organisation for Economic Co-operation and Development.
Pollitt, Michael G. (2002), 'The Declining Role of the State in Infrastructure Investments in the UK', this volume (Chapter 4).
Sakata Tokio (1998), 'The Suffering Third Sector: Present Situations and Issues' [in Japanese], *Chihou Zaimu* (Local Financial Affairs), 525 (Feb.): 25–44.

3. Regulatory reform of the electricity industry in Japan: An overview of the process

Toru Hattori

Regulatory reform of the electricity industry has become an important policy issue in many parts of the world, particularly in the US and European countries.[1] In most developed countries, the industry had typically been characterized as a regulated monopoly, and reform has opened the industry to competition, whether full or partial. In some countries, the industry was also characterized as a vertically integrated structure, which reform has separated into generation, wire (transmission and distribution), and retail supply to secure competition on equal terms. In the UK, for example, the Central Electricity Generating Board (CEGB) was privatized and vertically separated in 1990, and the retail market was fully liberalized in 1998. In some states in the US, such as California, investor-owned electric utilities divested their generation assets, and the retail markets in the state were opened fully.

In Japan, ten privately owned, vertically integrated utilities dominate the electricity industry.[2] They are regulated regional monopolies, and only these ten utilities are allowed to sell electricity directly to customers. The government and large customers, as well as potential entrants, have argued for deregulation of the industry, principally because the price for electricity in Japan is the highest among OECD member countries.

Since Japan's major utilities are already privately owned, the reform effort has focused on how to introduce competition into a traditionally regulated industry. The tentative conclusion reached by the policymakers is that 'partial' liberalization is the proper course of action. That is, initially, only large customers who consume about 28 percent of the utilities' total sales will be able to choose their electricity supplier directly.[3]

As the phrase 'partial liberalization' suggests, reform in Japan at present is less drastic compared to reforms that have occurred in other developed countries. The existing electric utilities remain vertically integrated. An electricity pool will not be mandated. A spot market to facilitate open and transparent competition will not be established. The possibility of further

46

opening remains, but it depends on the assessment of the partial liberalization three years after implementation.

The pace of reform may be a reflection of the commitment by government and the existing utilities to Japan's energy infrastructure policy. Although aware of the importance of introducing competition to gain more efficiency, they recognize the public interests associated with energy infrastructure, such as energy security, environmental protection, universal service, and reliability of supply. Some of these public interests involve country-specific factors, and this at least partly explains the cautious step toward liberalization of the electricity industry in Japan.

This chapter is an overview of regulatory reform in the Japanese electricity industry since the mid-1990s and considers how Japan's energy infrastructure policy may be constraining reform. The recent investment behavior of the new entrants and existing utilities is also discussed.

PROCESS OF REFORM

In 1997, the Electric Utility Industry Council, an advisory panel to the Minister of International Trade and Industry, established the Basic Policy Committee to consider industry reform to reduce the cost of electricity to an internationally comparable level by the year 2001. This implied a 20 percent reduction from the current level. The prime motivation for liberalization in Japan, therefore, is to lower electricity prices. Table 3.1 compares international electricity prices for households and industry.

Several factors might be contributing to Japan's high price of electricity, many of them not directly controlled by the utilities.[4] The prices of inputs, including fuel, land, equipment, and structure, are high because of various taxes, safety standards (e.g., earthquake resistance) and environmental regulations at local and national levels. Japan's low load factor (the ratio of average demand to the annual peak demand), usually caused by use of air conditioning during the summer, also increases the cost of extra capacity. In some years, the exchange rate has further exacerbated Japan's price disadvantage. In fact, the real electricity price has continuously fallen since the second oil shock at the end of the 1970s, as shown in Figure 3.1. Nonetheless, it is critical for large industrial customers that the price of electricity in Japan be as low as in other countries so that Japanese industry can stay competitive in the midst of a long economic recession.

It should be noted that while electricity prices are high compared to those of other countries, Japanese electric utilities have maintained a high reliability of supply, a low level of emissions, and a diverse energy mix.[5] Although it is controversial whether any of these aspects justify the high price of elec-

Table 3.1   International comparison of electricity prices (US$ per kWh)

Customer	1994	1995	1996	1997	1998	1999
Household						
OECD	0.116	0.127	0.121	0.114	0.110	NA
OECD Europe	0.135	0.150	0.147	0.131	0.131	NA
France	0.150	0.167	0.164	0.134	0.129	NA
Germany	0.178	0.203	0.180	0.159	0.159	0.152
UK	0.122	0.127	0.125	0.125	0.121	0.117
US[1]	0.084	0.084	0.084	0.084	0.083	0.081
Japan	0.250	0.269	0.230	0.207	0.187	0.212
Industry						
OECD	0.073	0.079	0.074	0.068	0.063	NA
OECD Europe	0.071	0.077	0.074	0.065	0.065	NA
France	0.053	0.060	0.057	0.049	0.047	NA
Germany	0.089	0.100	0.086	0.072	0.067	0.057
UK	0.067	0.068	0.065	0.065	0.065	0.064
US[1]	0.047	0.047	0.046	0.044	0.040	0.039
Japan	0.172	0.185	0.157	0.146	0.128	0.143
Exchange rate[2]	99.83	102.91	115.98	129.92	115.20	102.08

Notes:
(1) Price excluding tax.
(2) Yen per US dollar. Inter-bank rates US dollar spot closing, end of year.

Source: International Energy Agency.

tricity in Japan, they should not be forgotten when electricity prices are compared internationally.[6]

Among the many reasons for high electricity prices in Japan, however, the most popular appears to be the alleged inefficiency of the current electricity supply system of local monopolies. This naturally motivates regulatory reform to introduce competition and lower price.[7]

Wholesale Generation Market Opening

A step toward reform in the wholesale generation market preceded discussion of retail market liberalization. In 1995 the Electric Utilities Industry Law was amended to allow independent power producers (IPPs) into the wholesale electricity-generation business by means of a competitive bidding system organized by existing electric utilities.[8] The original purpose of this liberalization was to

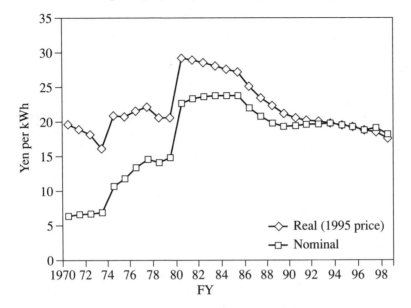

Source: Federation of Electric Power Companies and Bank of Japan (for CPI).

Figure 3.1   Electricity price in Japan (system average rate)

utilize decentralized generators that were highly efficient. To facilitate entry by new generators, a competitive bidding procedure was institutionalized to ensure transparency and equal access for potential entrants (Maruyama 1996).

The Ministry of International Trade and Industry (MITI) required the use of the competitive bidding system whenever a utility had an incremental need for capacity that could be developed in a short time. Specifically, a thermal power plant with a development period of less than seven years would be a candidate for the competitive bidding system, while a utility with sufficient prospective capacity under development would not have to resort to competitive bidding.[9] Thus, although entry into the generation business has been liberalized, the utilities do not necessarily have to face direct competition from IPPs, and in fact a few utilities had not solicited bids from IPPs as of 1997.[10] However, utilities can solicit additional generating capacity from IPPs when they think this would be cheaper than constructing their own new generating plant, the costs of which have been increasing with the growing lead times for construction. Perhaps this is why some utilities have actually considered postponing some of their investment plans. The IPPs can enter into long-term power purchase contracts with the utilities (for fifteen years, in principle) as they are supposed to substitute for part of the long-term power development by the existing utilities.

Competitive bidding during the first two years (1996 and 1997) was generally successful. The utilities solicited bids from various types of companies for both peak load and base load. Steel companies and oil refineries, which have access to cheap fuel and knowledge of electricity generation from their experiences with self-generation, were the main subscribers.

The electricity supplied to the utilities as a result of competitive bidding is only 3–5 percent of the utilities' total output. Furthermore, the earliest IPP contracts began only in 1999. Therefore, the direct impact on electricity prices is apparently very limited in the near term. However, the potential generation capacity of IPPs revealed by the process of the competitive bidding was beyond the expectation of the utilities. As shown in Table 3.2, subscribers for the capacity produced by the IPPs exceeded the utilities' solicitations by more than three times in 1996 and more than four times in 1997.[11]

Table 3.2   Solicited and subscribed capacity with cost differences for IPPs

Location	Solicited (MW)		Subscription (MW) (# in parentheses)		Rate of deviation below avoidable cost	
	1996	1997	1996	1997	1996	1997
Hokkaido	100	100	345 (6)	455 (7)	NA	30%
Tohoku	155	155	850 (10)	1,250 (14)	20%	30%
Tokyo	1,000	1,000	3,860 (31)	6,800 (35)	25%	40%
Chubu	200	400	1,153 (13)	1,327 (10)	10%	25%
Kansai	1,000	700	3,580 (29)	2,560 (11)	25%	30%
Chugoku	NA	200	NA	2,229 (16)	NA	40%
Kyusyu	200	300	1,025 (10)	1,500 (9)	35%	NA
Total	2,655	2,855	10,813 (99)	16,121 (102)		

Note: The figures for avoidable cost are approximate. When there was only one IPP in the bidding, figures are not available (NA).

Moreover, the winning bidders appear to be efficient. After a utility has entered into a power purchase contract with a winning bidder, the rate of deviation of the successful bids from the utility's average avoidable costs is made public unless there is only one winning bidder. The reported differences in costs for the utilities and the winning bidders are substantial in some instances. Some winning bids were 30–40 percent lower than the utilities' avoidable cost, mainly because of unused land and cheap fuel. Still, these reported cost differences gave the impression that the existing utilities' costs were high, and this increased the pressure for further cost reduction and has facilitated the process of liberalizing the retail market.

Outline of the Partial Liberalization of the Retail Market

When the Electric Utility Industry Council began considering a framework for the liberalization of the electricity retail market in 1997, two competing positions became apparent. Members of the council, including economists, and representatives of industrial and commercial customers generally called for liberalization of the electricity retail market so that customers could directly access different suppliers. Various proposals referred to the ongoing liberalization processes in other countries, the extent of market openings and structure of the industry, including establishing a power pool market. In contrast, electric utilities were generally cautious about changing the current system of electricity supply by vertically integrated and regulated monopolies. A wide gap existed between the two positions, and it seemed that it would be difficult to reach an agreement.

In the course of discussions, however, the electric utilities proposed to open their transmission lines to large customers but continued to strongly resist full liberalization of the retail market and formation of a power pool market. The basis for their opposition was their belief that it might endanger their 'public service obligation', such as maintaining reliability of supply. Their proposal provided a mutually agreeable point for a framework to liberalize the retail market. At least some customers would be able to choose different suppliers, and the utilities could largely maintain the current structure to supply electricity.

In the interim report presented in May 1998, the council decided to adopt the principle of partial liberalization and to maintain the vertical integration of the incumbent electric utilities. It also decided not to establish an electricity pool. Full liberalization and the electricity pool were left for future consideration, as they were thought inappropriate and premature at that time. As a result, initial restructuring of the Japanese electricity industry allowed only large customers to have retail choice. Some see this as a cautious step toward liberalization compared to other countries and regions where electricity prices are relatively high.

The next section discusses in more detail the factors that have made Japan so cautious about liberalizing its electricity industry, but several observations are worth noting here. First, the restructuring plan had to be implemented by the year 2000, so the time to prepare for drastic restructuring was limited. Consequently, partial liberalization was more realistic than more drastic reform options. Concerning the electricity pool, there seemed to be suspicion about the functioning of pools, as indicated by a substantial increase in pool prices in the UK followed by regulatory price caps.

The council also decided on the set of characteristics that would make a customer a candidate for retail choice. Eligible customers were determined to be those with an independent power demand of at least 2,000 kW that receive power from an extra high voltage system of not less than 20 kV. These extra high voltage customers' annual consumption amounts to about 7 GWh (gigawatt-hours), representing about 28 percent of the total electricity consumption in Japan. This degree of market opening is comparable with the EU deregulation schedule for 2003 (Wohlgemuth and Asano 1999).

The regulatory framework for liberalizing the sector was designed to minimize the role of regulation. There is no entry regulation, no rate regulation, and no obligation to supply. Each existing utility is also able to sell to eligible customers in other supply territories. However, the existing utilities are responsible for supplying power to eligible customers unable to negotiate contracts with alternative suppliers, and the utilities must publish the tariff for this service (provider of last resort). To prevent adverse effects on non-liberalized customers and anti-competitive cross-subsidies, accounting separation is obligatory for existing utilities.

One of the most difficult tasks facing the council was how to design the wheeling system. Because new entrants had been granted the right to use transmission networks owned by existing utilities, rules had to be established as to the proper use of the network for 'wheeling.' The council decided that wheeling charges should be determined consistent with two principles: fair recovery of wheeling costs and fair dealings between competitors. Existing utilities, therefore, must provide alternative suppliers with information on available capacity to help assure fair dealing. The utilities also must execute contracts with network users that describe the retail wheeling service that the utilities are supplying pursuant to rules approved by regulators. MITI serves as the final check of the rules and wheeling charges with respect to their fairness and transparency. It has the authority to order a change of the rules, if necessary in its opinion.

The government decided to evaluate the results of partial liberalization after three years of implementation, and to make revisions if further liberalization is deemed necessary. There is strong pressure for further liberalization from outside Japan as well as from domestic customers. International organizations, such as the International Energy Agency, have already made recommendations for further reform, namely, enlarging the number of eligible customers and the functional separation of existing utilities.

Important discussions in the Joint Committee on Basic Policy and Rate System focused on specific issues that included wheeling rules and charges, provider of last resort issues, and guidelines for fair transactions.[12] Although controversies remained in many areas, the report of the joint committee, revised after a public comment period, was finalized in October 1999. Partial liberalization with the wheeling system was subsequently implemented as scheduled in March 2000.

Development of Rate Regulation

Introducing workable competition into the wholesale and retail markets enhances the efficiency of power producers and retailers, but the wire businesses, namely, transmission and distribution, should still be regarded as natural monopolies and should remain regulated. Efficiency of operations and maintenance as well as investment in the wire businesses is ensured by regulation. Many countries have introduced some form of incentive regulation as the means for setting electricity transmission and distribution rates. In Japan, since electric utilities are vertically integrated, any form of incentive regulation would apply to the electric utility as a whole.

In 1995, MITI introduced yardstick regulation in the context of traditional rate-of-return regulation for electric utilities. By benchmarking and penalizing relatively inefficient utilities, this new regulatory mechanism was expected to facilitate inter-utility competition and to encourage utilities to reduce costs. Although price-cap regulation was also suggested as an alternative to traditional rate-of-return regulation, it was not considered appropriate for the Japanese electricity industry. The feeling was that price caps would discourage new investment while the demand for electricity grew. Then the Electricity Rate Committee decided to introduce yardstick regulation as piecemeal reform. Its reasoning was that yardstick regulation represented an incremental change to the existing regulatory environment because competition had been working implicitly among electric utilities and had effectively reduced the price differentials among the supply territories. Yardstick regulation was considered appropriate for encouraging a kind of incentive regulation with less confusion.

Yardstick regulation is applied to three cost categories: the capital cost of generation, the capital cost of the network (transmission and distribution), and general and administrative expenses. The fact that two of the three yardstick indices refer to the cost of capital reflects the original intention of MITI to restrain the capital costs of electric utilities.

Yardstick regulation has led to two rate revisions so far. Although generally considered insufficient to facilitate cost reductions, it has resulted in an accelerated decline of the average electricity rate in Japan. In 1996, the electric utilities proposed an average rate reduction of 3.09 percent, but the approved average rate reduction was 3.9 percent. In 1998, the average proposed rate reduction of 3.41 percent was further reduced to 4.6 percent as a result of yardstick regulation.

Japan's version of yardstick regulation has been criticized by the utilities because it uses book value per kWh (kilowatt-hour) as a performance (yardstick) index. The problem is that book value per kWh is a poor indicator of the utilities' capital costs. An electric utility investing in a large-scale plant in the year of yardstick assessment will surely receive a flawed score with respect to a performance index that is weighted by electricity consumption. This is because the utility's book value increases substantially while its electricity production does not increase proportionally. Therefore, when a large-scale plant such as a nuclear power facility starts operating, the performance index of book value per kWh significantly deteriorates. As a result, the electric utility adding a large-scale plant to meet growing demand is penalized under yardstick regulation.

The rate system developed in 1996 was revised in 1998 when the Electricity Rate Committee decided to leave rate cuts to the electric utilities' discretion. Yardstick regulation would apply only when the utilities sought to raise rates. Moreover, the electric utilities were allowed to determine the portion of their profits they would retain to lower their debt costs.

ENERGY INFRASTRUCTURE INVESTMENT AND REFORM OF THE INDUSTRY

Large-scale energy infrastructures made up of power plants and transmission grids have public interest implications associated with energy security, environmental protection, universal service, and reliability of supply. It is the shared objective of both government and industry to accomplish reform without compromising these public interests. Additionally, a strong public sentiment supports careful reform of the electricity industry so that the utilities continue to be responsible for these public interests.[13] The adoption of partial liberalization with retention of vertically integrated utilities reduces transitional costs by minimizing the need for new rules and institutions. However, these transitional cost savings limit the potential efficiency gains from competition and create some distributional issues between liberalized and non-liberalized customers.

Starting a liberalization effort by partially opening the retail market is common in many countries. Although liberalization in Japan started later than in some other countries, the extent of market opening with the first step is indeed significant. An important point to remember with respect to Japan's liberalization effort is that the current policy does not state the final extent of market opening, leaving this to future consideration beginning in three years.

Electric utilities have insisted that only large users be given a choice among suppliers, claiming that it is necessary to restrict eligibility to those who can be monitored and controlled in order to maintain reliability of supply. Even though it is technically feasible to permit choice among medium-size users, the utilities believe that would generate more uncertainty regarding sales, which would make it difficult for them to commit to long-term power development to ensure system reliability and energy security.

In most developed countries where the liberalization of the electricity industry began early, vertical separation was assumed to be a precondition for workable competition between existing operators and new entrants. Influenced by the international trend in electricity restructuring, Shinji Sato, a minister for international trade and industry at the time, said that vertical separation, although long a taboo in Japan, was a policy option to lower the cost of electricity supply. This was before the Electric Utility Industry Council had begun its discussion of the liberalization of the retail market, and no consensus had been established within the MITI. The comment was a cause for concern with respect to the more-or-less cooperative relationship between government and the industry in pursuing the national energy policy.[14] The utilities strongly opposed vertical separation, insisting that they would be unable to pursue their obligations regarding electricity supply and other public interests. Furthermore, the government knew that it would be an extremely difficult policy to force on the privately owned utilities. Although the minister's comment heated the discussion of the industry's restructuring, the issue of vertical separation was not raised again after Mr Sato left the ministry. The government's view was that the vertically integrated structure is better suited to achieve public interests.

Other countries facing similar problems adopted more aggressive liberalization and structural reform efforts. It was argued that vertical separation and the subsequent deregulation of some markets would not necessarily conflict with public interests. However, this is a difficult argument to make in Japan, a resource-scarce country concerned with energy security. Japan's dependence on primary energy imports is very high, about 80 percent counting nuclear power as domestic energy. Consequently, the attention of government and industry has been focused on the national energy-security issue, particularly after the first oil shock. In addition, electricity consumption in Japan continues to grow at a rate of 2 percent yearly. Given these facts, diversification of fuel sources (energy mix), adequacy of capacity, and energy conservation have long been crucial components of Japan's energy policy. In fact, Japan has realized steady development of nuclear power plants over the past two decades, while other countries have seen only a few or no new nuclear capacity additions in the 1990s (see Figure 3.2).

Nuclear power is expected to play a significant role in Japan's pledge to the Kyoto Protocol regarding climate change. Even though Japan already relies on nuclear power for about 35 percent of its total electricity consumption, MITI has promoted construction of another twenty nuclear reactors to reduce fossil-fuel consumption.[15] Although this policy has been questioned and is subject to criticism, it is clear that government and industry have made a strong commitment to promote nuclear power.

The key question in Japan is how to liberalize the electricity industry while ensuring development of nuclear power (Park and Schreurs 1998). In a liber-

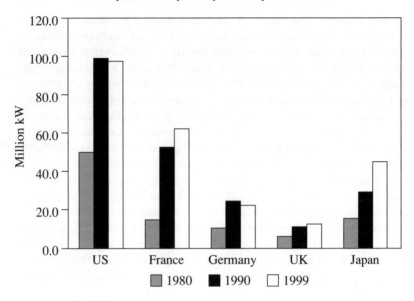

Source: International Energy Agency.

Figure 3.2   Comparison of international nuclear capacity

alized electricity market, investment in nuclear power projects will be very difficult (Yajima and Hensing 1997). In countries where the electricity market is completely liberalized or is scheduled to become so, few investors seem interested in new nuclear power projects for reasons related to construction costs. There are, of course, other difficulties associated with nuclear power projects, and they are not necessarily caused solely by liberalization. In fact, many developed countries have tried to reduce their dependence on nuclear power generation even before liberalizing the electricity industry. It seems to be true, however, that the more complete the industry's liberalization, the more difficult it is to attract investment in new nuclear power plants.

Deregulation proponents have argued that public interests in general and energy security in particular are used as excuses to protect the utilities. Thus there is a difference of opinion as to why government should take an active role in energy security. Deregulation proponents insist that the energy markets would provide a solution to energy security if the energy industries were fully open. The definition of energy security and the corresponding role of government are ambiguous, and more discussion is needed on this issue.[16]

Even if energy security and environmental concerns are accepted as national policy objectives, emphasis on nuclear power by government and the industry has been criticized by many because other energy sources are under-emphasized. There was a technological shift toward gas by IPPs in the UK after restructuring (McDaniel 2002). Demand for gas is expected to increase in Japan also, but whether it will become the dominant fuel source is open to question. Access to gas is limited since no pipelines exist. A pipeline from Sakhalin in Russia is still in the planning stage and progress has been slow because of the huge initial investment cost and political risks anticipated in Russia. A company selecting liquefied natural gas must enter into a long-term take-or-pay contract, which can be a risky business. As a matter of fact, most competitive IPPs entering the wholesale generation market select coal or oil as their fuel. An option to coal and oil is renewables. Although a necessary step on the road to tackling environmental problems and effective in the long run, renewables are unlikely to become a major energy source, particularly in the short run (see Matsui 1998).

Discussion concerning the liberalization of the Japanese electricity industry so far seems to be an attempt to balance the arguments of public interest advocates and deregulation proponents. Such discussion is no doubt important, but the dynamic aspect of the reform process should be emphasized more strongly. Because of the sunk cost associated with infrastructure investment in the electricity industry, regulatory reform may well be constrained by decisions made in the past.

In Japan, both government and industry have already made a commitment to nuclear power development. Although the history of Japanese energy policy is too involved to be treated here in detail, without government support and efficient management by private utilities, Japan would not have seen steady nuclear power development. The huge sunk cost as well as the back-end cost of nuclear power development requires a long-term commitment. It is also important to note that once the commitment is made it is quite costly to change the regulatory framework and structure of the industry that supported the commitment. Moreover, development discontinued because of liberalization would be very difficult to resume again when or if needed. In other words, decisions regarding the liberalization of the industry will have irreversible effects on energy infrastructure investment. A further difficulty arises not only as to the choice of policy objectives but also in their timing with respect to implementation. Piecemeal reform or a wait-and-see policy may be justified in light of the timing issues. Although the pace of reform should not necessarily be slowed by country-specific factors, it should be determined by careful con-sideration of such factors, and the reform itself need not be done all at once.

The situation facing nuclear power development in Japan at present is severe from the viewpoint of promoting new investment, aside from liberalization. There have been several accidents in nuclear power plants in recent years. In 1999, Japan's worst accident occurred at a nuclear fuel processing plant in

Tokaimura, Ibaragi Prefecture. To ensure the safety of nuclear-related facilities, the utilities, companies and research institutes engaged in nuclear operation established the 'Nuclear Safety Network', an organization to monitor and inspect nuclear operations for safety. The latest accident, however, has delayed current plans for the construction of new nuclear power plants by electric utilities.[17] Unlikely to change its promotion of nuclear power, the government has been forced to reconsider its energy policy on long-term nuclear power development: public trust will be difficult to restore.

THE CHANGING ELECTRICITY INDUSTRY

Newcomers to the Power Market

Several newcomers have entered the retail electricity market. As eligible large users, central and local governments solicit bids for long-term electricity supply for their office buildings to facilitate workable competition. New entrants were able to successfully coordinate excess supply of self-generators and win some of these solicitations.

Some entrants that are joint ventures with foreign companies plan to build their own power plants. In fact, quite a few companies have shown an interest in entering the retail supply business. Oil refiners and trading houses are actively planning to begin retailing power, and other companies have shown an interest in electricity trading. Presumably, these firms are aware that the retail supply business is riskier than the wholesale supply business because payment for wholesale supply is guaranteed by the existing utilities for a long time period. A recent survey by Shishikura and Makino (1999) shows that newcomers in retail supply are likely to begin by selling power to companies with whom they have financial or business relationships.

Obviously, the level of the wheeling charge set by utilities and reviewed by regulatory authorities is crucial for effective competition. The wheeling charges were first estimated at 3–4 yen per kWh by the utilities, but industrial companies wanting to enter the market asked them to reduce it to 1 yen. In response, the utilities announced that they would charge less than 3 yen. During this period MITI assessed the rules covering wheeling charges and confirmed that they were appropriate. Nevertheless, entrants' demand for lower charges is unlikely to dissipate.

There is another cost difficulty for entrants that should not be ignored. Two prospective IPPs gave up their plans to supply electricity to an existing utility because they had underestimated the costs of pollution control. Concern over the impact of liberalization on the environment has become an issue because entrants are likely to use fossil fuels.[18] A growing number of IPPs could have a significant impact on the global environment. An increased awareness of this factor on the part of government may weaken the ability of IPPs to enter the market by using cheap fuel. The recent rise in oil prices has also made many business plans less attractive.

New Direction for Electric Utilities

To prepare for a more competitive environment in their industry, incumbent electric utilities have been trying to improve their financial health. Partly as a result of this effort, investment in power plants has decreased over the past few years, as shown in Figure 3.3. Although the decrease in investment can be explained by the expectation of slower growth in demand, regulatory reform in Japan seems to be accelerating the reduction of investment. Some major utilities recently announced that construction of new power plants is being postponed.

While making continuing efforts to reduce the cost of electricity supply and to introduce discounts for large customers, existing utilities are now moving in a new direction in response to liberalization and have begun to be actively involved in overseas power production, particularly in Asia. In May 1996, MITI indicated that it would support overseas business by electricity and gas utilities.

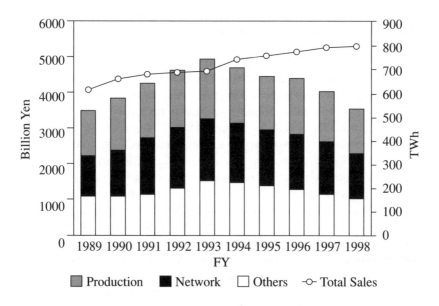

Source: Federation of Electric Power Companies.

Figure 3.3   Gross investment of the ten Japanese electric utilities (nominal)

Since Japanese utilities are less experienced in overseas business, they initially sought joint projects, consulting or participating in collaboration with trading houses. Some utilities have invested in the energy infrastructure of China and South East Asia. As the demand for electricity in Asia is expected to increase rapidly, US and European companies have also actively invested in this region's energy infrastructure. Therefore, Japanese utilities will be competing with more experienced international competitors and will have to evaluate project risks accurately, including country risk.

With liberalization, Japanese electric utilities are no longer subject to regulation that prohibits them from business other than electricity supply.[19] Fearing some loss of customers, existing utilities are looking for new business that is profitable. The largest electric utility, Tokyo Electric Power Co., has been very actively investing in new business.[20] It has expanded to other energy-related business, such as gas supply,[21] and also to Internet-related business and even care for the elderly. Needless to say, success in new ventures totally unrelated to their core business, such as the Internet, depends on how well the utilities manage the risks involved.

CONCLUDING REMARKS

As was the case in other developed countries, high electricity price motivated liberalization of the electricity industry in Japan, which has the highest price among OECD countries. Although Japanese electric utilities have used highly advanced technology to control costs and maintain a high reliability of supply, customers have become more sensitive to prices during the long economic recession. There is need for regulatory reform of the industry, but the reform effort at present is rather cautious compared to other countries. Japan's energy infrastructure policy, which takes into account public interests, has determined the extent of liberalization, at least tentatively. In particular, a need for the steady development of nuclear power plants for energy security and global environmental protection seems to be the major constraint on further liberalization. While 'partial liberalization' is unlikely to be the final answer for the Japanese electricity industry, provision for further liberalization is not yet clear. Although consideration of public interests associated with energy infrastructure does not necessarily imply that the reform should be slowed down, the sunk cost associated with infrastructure might well pose a problem for radical reform. Japan is in a position to learn valuable lessons from the experience of other countries where the industry went through a more drastic reform. It is always important, however, to take into account country-specific factors of energy infrastructure.

While the debate over future liberalization continues, the industry has already moved toward a new direction in a changing environment for energy infrastructure. This change certainly gave non-utility generators an opportunity to sell directly to customers, but it is uncertain whether this changing environment will enhance economic efficiency without adverse effects on the public interests associated with energy infrastructure. In spite of the cautious approach, 'partial liberalization' will have a significant impact on the structure of the industry. It is evident that existing utilities have reduced their investment in electric utility plants. For the future, it is apparent that evaluation of the Japanese reform effort must take into account the impacts on the public interests as well as the impact on economic efficiency.

The key policy issue is how to address energy security, environmental protection, universal service, and reliability. Should these objectives continue to be the responsibilities of regional, vertically integrated monopolies? Or should policymakers develop specific public policies that transparently target each 'public interest' in order to use competition in electricity generation as the mechanism for promoting cost-containment? The latter strategy, at least in theory, allows the opportunity costs associated with achieving each objective to be identified and balanced against perceived benefits.

Of course benefits from competition are realized only if the competition is properly introduced and the generation market is workably competitive. Experiences in the UK and US seem to have created confusion about the benefits of competition in the electricity industry. This challenges the fundamental motivation of liberalization of the industry, which is to lower prices.

ACKNOWLEDGMENTS

The author wishes to thank Masayuki Yajima, Robert Graniere, Ken Costello and the editors for valuable advice, although of course I am solely responsible for any errors. The views expressed herein do not necessarily state or reflect the views of CRIEPI (Central Research Institute of Electric Power Industry).

ENDNOTES

1. See Yajima (1997) and Pollitt (1997) for an international overview of regulatory reforms in the electricity industry.
2. For an historical overview of the industry, see Navarro (1996).
3. The Electric Power Development Company, a quasi-government-owned wholesale generator, will be privatized in the year 2003. It is worth noting that since the major electric utilities are already privately owned, the process of reform is quite different from that in the UK and other European countries where privatization of the industry is involved in the reform process.

Japan is more or less comparable to the US electricity industry with its vertically integrated private local monopolies.

4. See also International Energy Agency (1999) for more information.
5. International comparisons on these aspects are available from Japan's Federation of Electric Power Companies (FEPC) at http://www.fepc.or.jp/english/data/index.html.
6. International Energy Agency (1999) ignores these aspects in discussing the high price of electricity in Japan.
7. It should be noted that the regional price differential is very small in Japan. The ratio of the highest electricity price to the lowest has been about 1.1 to 1.2 in recent years. In contrast, in the US there have been large price differentials among the states. The ratio of the highest price to the lowest was almost 3 in 1998. Such a price differential was one motivation for introducing market competition in the US electricity industry, but it is not at all an issue in Japan.
8. The amendments also created 'special supply utilities' able to supply electricity directly to customers at a specified point. However, only a few instances of this system exist, and their impact has been small. For more information, see Matsuo (1996) and Asano and Tsukamoto (1997).
9. A thermal power plant can be built in two to five years, assuming no serious difficulty with siting, such as in negotiation with neighboring residents. The period of seven years is determined by considering that an additional few years may be necessary for subscribing bids and entering into contract.
10. To introduce complete competition in capacity procurement, the Electric Utility Industry Council later proposed to mandate competitive bidding whenever the utilities need new thermal capacity. Even if the utilities have a plan to build their own thermal plants, they must be subject to competitive bidding.
11. According to a survey conducted by MITI, the potential IPP capacity would be about 30 GW or more, given the current condition of the bidding system.
12. As a consequence of liberalization, special exemptions for electric utilities in the anti-monopoly law were abolished. MITI and the Fair Trade Commission (FTC) then jointly announced guidelines on transactions for utilities to protect new entrants.
13. 'Electric Power Reformers Should Step Carefully Toward Free Market', *Nikkei Weekly*, 9 March 1998.
14. 'Tokyo Ponders a Power Split-up', *Japan Times*, 18 February 1997.
15. 'MITI to Promote More Reactor Construction', *Nikkei Weekly*, 18 May 1998.
16. Toman (1993) discussed several possible externalities of energy security that may justify government intervention in the energy market.
17. 'Tokaimura Accident Delays Plans for New Nuclear Plant', *Nihon Keizai Shimbun*, 1 November 1999.
18. 'Cheaper Power Bills May Exact Toll', *Japan Times*, 21 October 1998.
19. They had previously been allowed to enter other businesses only through subsidiaries.
20. 'Power Utility Embraces Change, Reduces Rates', *Nikkei Weekly*, 10 January 2000.
21. The retail market for gas supply was partially liberalized for large customers in 1995.

REFERENCES

Asano, H. and Y. Tsukamoto (1997), 'Transmission pricing in Japan', *Utilities Policy*, 6 (3), 203–10.

International Energy Agency (1999), *Energy Policies of IEA Countries: Japan 1999 Review*, Paris: OECD.

Maruyama, M. (1996), 'Saikin-no denryoku oroshi kyoukyuu ni tuite' [On the recent auctions for wholesale power], *Koueki Jigyou Kenkyuu* [Journal of Public Utility Economics], 48 (3), 1–9.

Matsui, K. (1998), 'Global demand growth of power generation, input choices and supply security', *Energy Journal*, 19 (2), 93–107.

Matsuo, N. (1996), 'Deregulation of Japan's electric utility and its prospects', *Energy in Japan*, 142 (Nov.), 33–45.

McDaniel, T. (2002), this volume (Chapter 5).

Navarro, P. (1996), 'The Japanese electric utility industry', in R. Gilbert and E. Kahn (eds), *International Comparisons of Electricity Regulation*, Cambridge, UK: Cambridge University Press.

Park, J. and M. Schreurs (1998), 'Power industry confronts jolt of deregulation', *The Nikkei Weekly*.

Pollitt, M. (1997), 'The impact of liberalization on the performance of the electricity supply industry: An international survey', *Journal of Energy Literature*, 3 (2), 2–31.

Shishikura, Y. and T. Makino (1999), 'Partial liberalization of electricity retailing and a new power market. How should consumers and suppliers take this opportunity?', *Energy in Japan*, 160 (Nov.), 19–33.

Toman, M.A. (1993), 'The economics of energy security: Theory, evidence, policy', in A.V. Kneese and J.L. Sweeny (eds), *Handbook of Natural Resource and Energy Economics*, vol. 3, Amsterdam: Elsevier Science.

Wohlgemuth, N. and H. Asano (1999), 'The regulatory environment for electric utilities in the European Union and Japan', paper presented at the 22nd IAEE International Conference, Rome.

Yajima, M. (1997), *Deregulatory Reforms of the Electricity Supply Industry*, Westport, CT: Quorum Books.

Yajima, M. and I. Hensing (1997), 'Liberalization of the electricity supply industry and nuclear power development', CRIEPI Report EY97002, Central Research Institute of Electric Power Industry, Japan.

PART TWO

UK and India: Declining Role of the State

4. The declining role of the state in infrastructure investments in the UK

Michael G. Pollitt

A massive reduction in government control of infrastructure investments in the UK began in 1979 under Margaret Thatcher and continued under John Major. This trend has continued since Tony Blair became Labour Prime Minister in 1997 following eighteen years of Conservative government.

This trend has been manifest in three major ways. First, the program of privatization of government-owned commercial enterprises has resulted in the transfer of as much as 15 percent of gross domestic fixed-capital formation from the state to the private sector, notably with the privatization of telecoms, gas, airports, water, electricity and railways.[1] Second, the government has sold off millions of council-owned houses and encouraged the formation of housing associations that attract public and private money to support new social housing. Since 1986 more than £10 billion has been raised from the private sector to support such housing, while the share of private house building in total new building has increased sharply.[2] Third, in the early 1990s the government launched the Private Finance Initiative (PFI) in an attempt to attract private-sector support for a wide range of government projects in such sectors as health, prisons, transport and defense. To date this initiative has raised around £24 billion of capital investment from the private sector and raises 15–20 percent of the government's capital budget each year. Total government commitments to future payments under 350 contracts are estimated at £94 billion over 25 years.[3]

The current UK Labour government has retreated a long way from the 'old' Labour policy of seeking to control the 'commanding heights' of the economy and from the traditional view that investment has to be significantly socialized to stabilize fluctuations in overall economic activity. Indeed, the current administration did not seek to reverse any of the privatizations of the previous two administrations and has part-privatized air traffic control and has plans to privatize the London Underground and the Post Office, specifically to attract the sort of investment these businesses require for expansion. The government recently (June 2001) announced plans for an extension of private-sector involvement in the provision of government-funded health and education services.[4]

Meanwhile, the sale of council houses has largely run its course and is no longer a political issue. The PFI has become so mainstream that it is no longer thought of as 'an initiative' but as part of the government's policy of public–private partnerships (PPPs). The rate at which new deals are being signed under the PFI has actually increased significantly since the Labour government came to power. There has been a quiet revolution in the way socially desirable investments are funded in the UK.

The UK trends in private involvement in infrastructure investments are not unique. Privatization is a global phenomenon in many countries and industries. The PFI has been copied all over the world. For example, South Africa is among those countries seeking to attract private capital into its prison-building program, following the British (and earlier US) model. Such models appeal to developing countries because they attract foreign multinationals with access to superior management techniques and international capital markets to initially finance and then run essential public-sector investments with high up-front costs.

In this chapter I survey the current UK scene on such private-sector involvement in infrastructure investments and present lessons for other countries embarking on a path of increased private-sector financing of investments traditionally in the public sector. In the next section I briefly review the impact of the privatization program on infrastructure investment, then shift the focus to the PFI. I also examine the theory of private finance for public goods and provide details of five PFI case studies based on independent National Audit Office reports.

PRIVATIZATION AND INFRASTRUCTURE INVESTMENT

In Pollitt (1999), I comprehensively reviewed the UK's liberalization of public enterprises, concluding that the deregulation and privatization process yielded considerable benefits to consumers, shareholders and the government. Although the number of employees fell sharply, most who left went voluntarily to other jobs or to retirement, while those who remained enjoyed higher pay. In sum, all the major groups in society seem to have benefited from the process. This assessment has been qualified somewhat following a recent rail crash that revealed the poor condition of large sections of railway track subsequent to privatization. There has been widespread disruption to the railway network as repairs take place and recent placing into administration of the responsible privatized company, Railtrack.[5]

The sale of public enterprises in the UK transferred at least 7 percent of GDP from the public sector to the private sector. The government sought this outcome primarily to reduce its public-sector borrowing requirement (PSBR) by asset sales, and so remove the investment programs of the firms involved from the budget deficit. Most utility privatizations came at a time when the physical infrastructure was beginning to crumble (especially in water and railways), European Union (EU) directive compliance costs were rising (particularly in water), and rapid technical progress was leading to new investment require-ments (notably in electricity and telecoms). Indeed, for both the water and telecom sectors, privatization reflected government's desire to shift investment requirements to the private sector. A detailed account of the effect of privati-zation on investment in the electricity industry is given by McDaniel (2002). This pressure to reduce the government's borrowing requirement is still a major factor behind continuing moves to privatize the few remaining significant public enterprises. The London Underground is estimated to require £7 billion of improvement investment in the near future.[6] The 2000–2001 capital budget of the Department of Environment Transport and the Regions was just £6.3 billion.[7] Political pressure not to appear to favor the capital city and normal budgetary constraints make it difficult for the government to find this sort of money within the public-sector budget.

The National Air Traffic Control System is currently suffering from a huge cost-and-time overrun on the installation of new computer systems. The perceived failure of the upgrade project in the public sector and the need for additional finance has led the government to carry out plans to privatize air traffic control in part in 2001 in spite of widespread opposition inside and outside Parliament on the grounds of safety.[8] The Post Office has been the focus of continuing privatization pressure since a failed attempt to privatize it in 1994. The main reason advanced for privatization is that only in the private sector will the Post Office be free to raise the capital it requires for new investment in service improvement and for potential merger activity. It seems likely that EU plans to liberalize the postal market in Europe will eventually pre-cipitate privatization (see Bergman et al. 1999, p. 12).

Thus the need to raise funds for investment has been a primary reason for pri-vatization since the privatization of British Telecom in 1984. In 1983 the pre-privatization telecoms, gas, airports, water, electricity and railways companies invested £7.6 billion (at 1995 prices); the same sectors invested £9.7 billion in 1995 when the railways were in the process of privatization and all others had been privatized. Figure 4.1 shows the real amounts of investment in the different industries. Strikingly, privatization seems not to have much effect on the aggregate amount of investment in these industries. This observation is remarkable because the transfer of so much of the responsibility for investment from the public to the private sector might have been expected to create some disruption in the pattern of investment activity. Privatization has not been accompanied by the sort of fluctuations in investment activity that followers of Keynes (1936, p. 164) might have predicted.

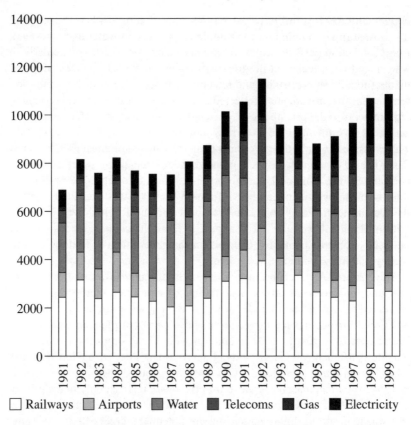

☐ Railways ▧ Airports ▨ Water ▦ Telecoms ■ Gas ■ Electricity

Note: Electricity, Gas, Water = Census of Production Industry; Airports = BAA plc; Telecoms = BT and Mercury; Railways = DETR figures. Current prices deflated by GDFC deflator in ONS *UK National Accounts*. Electricity, Gas and Water calendar years; Airports, Telecoms, Railways financial years.

Sources: ONS Business Monitor PA 1002; Company Accounts; DETR; CRI (1996).

Figure 4.1   Investment in UK utilities, 1981–99 (£m 1995 prices)

The reason for the apparent smoothness of the transfer of large investment obligations to the private sector lies in the fact that all of the industries are subject to RPI-X regulation (see Pollitt 1999), which involves a four- to seven-year review period over which prices are set. Allowed prices are set with reference to the detailed investment plans of the regulated companies. Paradoxically, the need to submit medium-term investment plans subject to ex post explanations when goals are not met has led to highly smoothed and predictable patterns of investment in these industries. Investment has not fluctuated as it might do in an unregulated environment in the private sector, or equally as it might do in response to short-term government budgetary constraints. It may be the case that 'gold plating' of assets (following the Averch–Johnson effect, 1962) may be encouraged by utility regulation. However, the statistics do not suggest a large surge in the amount of investment occurring in privatized industries.

Table 4.1 gives some information on what has happened to the sources of finance for investment in privatized industries. It was suggested above that privatization would free companies from government budgetary constraints and allow them to borrow more freely on the capital market by issuing share capital and through debt financing. Electricity and airports have increased gearing (financial leverage), taking advantage of opportunities for expansion as profitable enterprises constrained from borrowing in the public sector. The initially highly geared water and rail industries have reduced gearing and increased equity holdings. The highly profitable British Telecom has been able to expand while reducing gearing as it has accumulated retained profits. Thus, while some companies have been able to expand by borrowing on the capital markets, improved efficiency has improved profitability such that most new investment can be financed from retained profits. The message from the UK privatization of utilities is that well-regulated companies have no difficulty in financing their investments efficiently.

Table 4.1   Gearing ratios in selected privatized firms

Company	Gearing ratio	
	Before privatization	After privatiztion
Electricity — CEGB	17.9 (1982)	57.4 (Powergen)
		57.0 (National Grid, 1998)
British Telecom	50.0 (1983)	17.0
British Rail	50.1	25.4 (Railtrack)
Anglian Water	92.3	44.7
British Gas	3.6 (1982)	0.7 (Centrica, 1997)
British Airports Authority	16.7	32.0 (1998)

Note: Gearing ratio = long-term borrowings/total assets less current liabilities.

Source: Group Accounts.

THE DEVELOPMENT OF THE PRIVATE FINANCE INITIATIVE

The PFI is 'one of the main mechanisms through which the public sector can secure improved value for money in partnership with the private sector. Through

PFI, the private sector is able to bring a wide range of managerial, commercial and creative skills to the provision of public services, offering potentially huge benefits for Government' (Treasury Task Force Private Finance, *Partnerships for Prosperity — The Private Finance Initiative*, p. 2).

Characteristics of PFI projects

There are currently three types of PFI projects. In the first instance, the public sector buys services from the private sector. The private sector is responsible for the capital investment and the public sector pays only for the delivered product. This is the most widespread form of PFI investment and has been used for new roads and prisons. Financially freestanding projects are the second type. The private sector designs, builds, finances and operates an asset, recovering costs through direct charges to users rather than from the public sector (e.g., toll bridges such as the Second Severn Bridge and the Dartford River Crossing). The public involvement is in securing the planning and licensing in order to effectively create a state-regulated private monopoly. Joint ventures, the third type, occur when the entire cost of a project cannot be recovered from users and the government offers a partial subsidy to enable the project to go ahead (e.g., Manchester's Metrolink, a light railway, and the Docklands Light Railway Extension).

The PFI allows several types of payment contracts with different combinations of risk and incentive for private-sector contractors. Thus there may be *long-term service contracts* based on service availability (e.g., prison contracts). These encourage firms to minimize lifetime costs in balancing capital costs with maintenance costs. *Trigger mechanisms* may involve payment only when a service is actually supplied. This type of contract provides strong incentives to avoid delays, especially where the contract termination date is independent of when service actually commences. *Payment based on availability* gives good incentives to maintain assets.

The PFI works under a number of core principles. First, the private sector should genuinely assume risk. Second, projects undertaken with the private sector should deliver value for money.[9] Third, private-sector partners should be selected through a process of open competition.[10] The final decision rests largely on the consideration of value for money.[11]

The process of signing a PFI project is potentially lengthy and involves a number of steps. First, the public-sector body concerned must define its service requirements, appraise the options and make the case for change in an Outline Business Case. It then obtains approval from the Treasury Task Force, which is now in the process of being replaced. Once a fully detailed specification of the outputs, outcomes and desired allocations of risks is prepared, the government body undertakes a procurement process, beginning with identification of suitable providers for the best obtainable privately financed solution. This part of the process usually begins with an advertisement in the *Official Journal of the European Communities*. In negotiation with the preferred bidder, the definitive investment appraisal and Full Business Case must be completed and approved by the contracting agency before the contract is finalized, awarded and implemented.

The Evolution of the PFI

Pressure for the PFI arose in the recession of the early 1990s. At that time the UK government was apparently caught between the demands for public-sector investments and the limited capacity of current taxation to meet those demands. At that time the PSBR and fiscal deficit were increasing and private-sector investment in the public sector was seen as a way of improving the government's finances (see Clark and Root 1999).

The PFI is not a new idea. Italy, France and Spain have used private finance for building motorways for many years (see Public Services Privatisation Research Unit 1997). For many years Australia, New Zealand and the US have used private finance to build prisons, roads and hospitals (Terry 1996). According to the National Housing Federation (1997), the concept of a UK Housing Association that combined public and private finance in the provision of social housing dates from 1986. Terry (1996) discusses the financing of the Channel Tunnel as a freestanding private project in 1987 and notes that the Manchester Metrolink system was proposed in 1985. Blyth (1987) notes the influence of the General Agreement on Tariffs and Trade (via the Government Procurement Code) and the EU (via directives relating to government pro-curement) in making the solicitation and award of government procurement contracts more open and competitive. The advertising of contracts in the *Official Journal of the European Communities* is an example of this influence.

Until 1989 the UK public sector had operated under the Ryrie Rules (named after a Treasury civil servant). These prescribed the limits of private-sector involvement in the financing of government projects (see McCarthy 1995). Specifically, private investors in public projects could not be offered favorable risk terms, and projects were expected to yield benefits in terms of improved efficiency and profit commensurate with the cost of raising risk capital from financial markets. Under these rules, private-sector capital could not be offered fair terms when invested in government-sponsored projects because the risk-transfer aspect was not valued by the public sector. The aim was not to prevent private-sector involvement but to stop ministers from posting financial oblig-ations into the future in order to get around budget constraints. In 1989 the Ryrie Rules were 'retired' by John Major while he was Chief Secretary to the Treasury.

The PFI formally began in 1992 when the Chancellor, Ken Clarke, announced significant changes to the role of privately raised finance in the public sector (see Grout 1997 and Kerr 1998). The main changes were that self-financing projects could go ahead without the need to compare them to similar projects in the public sector and that leasing could be used to purchase services without the discounted value of the lease being counted against the public expenditure limits.

To stimulate a flow of projects, the Private Finance Panel Executive, the Private Finance Office within the Treasury and Private Finance Units within individual government departments were created in the autumn of 1993. The objective was to 'increase the quality and quantity of the nation's capital stock' (HM Treasury 1993). In November 1993 the Parliamentary Under Secretary of State for Health announced that National Health Service (NHS) bodies would not be given government funding for capital projects unless they had explored PFI options first. In the November 1995 budget the Chancellor cut the NHS capital budget by 16.9 percent, implying that the NHS was expected to attract £700 million in PFI funding over three years.

Although the initial take-up of projects was slow, in November 1994 the PFI became the preferred option for the funding of capital projects. No public-sector funding for a capital project would be approved unless the private-sector alternative had been explored and found uneconomic. A private accountancy firm, Price Waterhouse, was appointed to train 5,000–10,000 civil servants in how PFI projects were to be prepared. The PFI handbook *Private Opportunity, Public Benefit* (Private Finance Panel/HM Treasury) appeared in November 1995.

In 1996 the House of Commons Treasury Committee expressed doubts about the PFI. It questioned whether risk had been transferred to the private sector through the PFI and whether management of projects had improved, highlighting the fact that the Treasury did not appear to know what its total financial commitments were under PFI projects. The Treasury itself responded to concerns of private-sector bidders about the cost of bidding and the length of the process with the publication of *Private Finance Initiative: Guidelines for Smoothing the Procurement Process* (HM Treasury 1996). In October 1996 the Environment Minister granted local councils new freedoms to enter into PFI schemes and promised £250 million of revenue support over two years for those that did so.

As Figure 4.2 shows, the value of signed PFI projects began to accelerate toward the end of the Major administration. By the end of 2000, PFI projects with a capital value of around £24 billion had been signed (see Table 4.2). The private sector is investing around £3.9 billion in 2000–2001 in projects, and the government is paying out around £2.8 billion under existing PFI deals. This represents less than 0.5 percent of the total government budget and around 10 percent of government capital spending. Payments are projected to rise to a peak of £4.6 billion by 2006–07 but will still be £2.6 billion in 2025–26.[12]

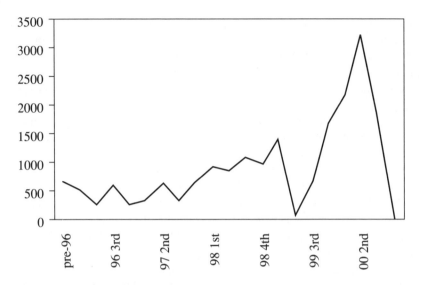

Figure 4.2   Value of PFI projects signed (£m)

Table 4.2   PFI deals signed by the central government to fourth quarter 2000

Department	Number of signed projects	Value (£m)
Defense	36	4,678
Social Security	3	670
Education and Employment	66	1,369
Environment, Transport and Regions	84	11,537.4
Health	108	3,027.7
Home Office	34	1,422.3
Other	33	1,658.5
Totals	364	24,362.4

Source: PFI Report, November 1999, p. 19.

After the election of the Labour government in 1997 the new administration announced a review of the PFI under the chairmanship of Malcolm Bates, chairman of Pearl Assurance. Following his report a number of changes were made to the PFI.[13] The Private Finance Panel Executive and the Private Finance Office were replaced with a Treasury Task Force. This body confirms the viability of all significant projects before the procurement process in an effort to minimize procurement costs and speed up the procurement process. Small projects can be grouped, and only projects in priority-listed areas are required to test against privately financed options. Compensation may now be paid to bidders if a project is cancelled at a late stage by the purchasing department. New legislation removed some initial legal uncertainties about whether contracts between public-sector bodies and private-sector contractors could be enforced (particularly between contractors and NHS Trusts). However, the PFI remains embodied in the rules of different government departments rather than in a single piece of legislation.

A second Bates review of the PFI completed in March 1999 led to the creation of Partnerships UK, which employs City experts to help the private sector get the best deal from the PFI and other forms of public–private partnerships.[14] This was set up after certain large computer contracts were signed under the PFI without a proper assessment of risk, apparently because the Treasury lacked the necessary in-house expertise.

Partnerships UK succeeded the Treasury Task Force and became a partnership with a minority government stake (49 percent) in March 2001. It will seek to win business from the public sector by offering high-quality expertise on PFI contracts. It may provide some development funding to public-sector bodies in order to get partnerships off the ground. Similar expertise is offered to local government bodies through 'the 4ps' of the Public Private Partnership Program, an agency set up by local authority associations in April 1996.[15]

In a parallel development, the government instituted a review of government procurement policy in 1999 led by Peter Gershon, the CEO of BAE Systems. He concluded that widespread inefficiency and lack of coordination in purchasing policy caused large variations in the prices government departments pay for the £13 billion of goods and services purchased annually.[16]

His report led to the merger in April 2000 of several agencies previously involved in procurement into the Office of Government Commerce, a new Treasury department.[17] With respect to PFI projects, the new office is responsible for overall contract strategy and the spread of best practice within the public sector. Partnerships UK will provide 'hands-on implementation, skills to bear on individual PPP projects.'[18]

THE THEORY OF PRIVATE FINANCE FOR PUBLIC PROJECTS

The theoretical basis for the increasing private involvement in infrastructure projects considers the effects of liberalization – the introduction of market-based incentives into industries where they did not exist previously (see Pollitt 1997). First, property rights theories suggest that creating a market for ownership rights means that assets tend to get allocated to owners who can exercise them most efficiently (see Alchian 1965). Second, bureaucracy theories suggest that government officials tend to focus on objectives such as maximizing the size of their budget rather than on efficiency maximization (see Niskanen 1968). If this is true, liberalization can improve efficiency. Third, liberalization may reduce lobbying by reducing the likelihood that government policy can be influenced (Milgrom and Roberts 1990). Fourth, liberalization affects the nature of regulation relating to an industry, and this may affect the efficiency of production. The Averch–Johnson effect (1962) occurs under rate-of-return regulation, while misrepresentation of costs may occur under British RPI-X price control. Fifth, liberalization may increase the cost of subsequent government interference and hence lead to a reduction in it (Willig 1994).

On balance, these effects seem to favor moves toward privatization of state-owned assets. Hart et al. (1997) go as far as to suggest that state ownership is superior to private ownership only under a narrow range of circumstances: when opportunities for cost reductions that lead to non-contractible deterioration of quality are significant, when innovation is relatively unimportant, when competition is weak and consumer choice is ineffective, and when the reputational mechanisms affecting private firms keen to win additional government contracts are also weak.

Privatization of utilities in the UK was reasonably straightforward because a large number of representative consumers already paid for commercial services from companies that were financially viable. The transfer of these companies to the private sector could be undertaken without the need for increased charges, and regulation could uphold public-service obligations such as supplying remote customers at subsidized prices. Telecoms, gas, airports, water and electricity thus passed to the private sector without continuing implications for the PSBR.

Some activities that are not capable of being privatized can be financed by the private sector. The railway operation is an example of this. The privatization of the UK's train-operating companies conformed to the mold of the PFI, with private companies being asked to bid for the right to operate a rail franchise. The bidders had to specify the minimum subsidy they would accept to run the part of the network they were bidding for. The government offered 25 train-operating company franchises with declining subsidy levels, from £2,037 million in 1996–97 to £729 million in 2003–04 (see Kain 1998).

The railways-operating companies highlight one of the three reasons for continuing state support for certain activities – the fact that although the activity is commercial there are considerable *external benefits* to rail travel. These include the reduced environmental impact of rail travel and its importance in providing smaller local communities with access to the public transport network. The second reason for state finance is that some goods are *public goods*. This means the benefits are shared across the community in such a way that those who do not wish to buy the service cannot be excluded from the benefits created by those who do buy the service. A prison is a good example of this. The final reason for state support is the *undesirable distributional consequences* of charging for a potentially chargeable service. A hospital is an example. The state funds the NHS to maintain equity of access to health care that is independent of financial circumstances.

The above reasons for state financing of certain services do not constitute reasons for the state to act as a monopoly in deploying the assets required to deliver those services. Thus, railways, prisons and hospitals can be built, designed and operated by the private sector even if the state provides some or all of the finance for them. It is this fundamental distinction that lies behind the theoretical appeal of the PFI. It seems entirely reasonable to suggest that the government should always investigate the possibility that the private sector may be able to provide cheaper and/or better quality services when there is increased private-sector involvement in the assets that produce those services.

PFI projects may pass the responsibility for the production process behind services to the private sector in a number of areas. First, *project management* may become the responsibility of a private contractor charged with delivering a product or service at a fixed price. This has the effect of creating powerful incentives for cost minimization on the part of the company. This is in sharp contrast to many state-managed projects, such as nuclear power station building, which come in substantially over budget. Second, the government shifts its focus to the service provided and away from the *design of the delivery*. This leads to private-sector innovations in design that can improve quality and reduce cost. It also leads to less risky designs that are more likely to work. In the past the UK government has tended to use big capital projects to subsidize speculative innovation, greatly adding to the cost, rather than accept tried and tested designs.

Third, when the *operation of a created asset* remains the responsibility of the private contractor, strong incentives to cut costs can yield cost reductions. This may be important when the contractor is not paid until the asset has been made operational (as with large computer projects) or when ongoing operation remains the responsibility of the contractor (as with private prisons). Fourth, the payment schedule offered by the government typically has the result of smoothing the government's payments relative to a project's capital cost, which leaves the private sector to finance the capital cost. This has the advantage of allowing the private capital market to value the *financial risk* involved in the project. The relationship between the cost of a project and its financial risk creates strong incentives for private contractors to efficiently minimize risk.

These incentives are absent when finance comes from the government budget, where the price of finance (the interest rate on government bonds) does not reflect risk on individual projects.

Each of the above ways in which the private sector can improve efficiency is enhanced by the fact that the private sector can involve specialist project managers, designers, operators and financial risk managers, which may not be available within the public sector. This process is facilitated by bidding for projects by different private-sector contractors who 'compete for the field' (Demsetz 1968). Such competition should lower prices. However, in a repeated-bidding game dominated by a few large contractors the process may become collusive and some of the potential benefits of the PFI may be lost.

Private finance for public services gives rise to a number of issues that individual projects must address (see Brealey et al. 1997, Grout 1997, and Hall 1998). These include the following.

1. *Measurement.* The PFI can work only if the outputs and inputs specified in a contract can be measured accurately. This is problematic for public services because they are often multi-dimensional and quality is difficult to assess. Thus the 'output' of a prison or hospital represents a measurement challenge. Similarly it is not easy to assess a created asset's quality (as distinct from the service that it provides). For example, can the quality of a road be measured easily?
2. *Incentives.* The most desirable aspect of the PFI is that it introduces private incentives into areas of public-service delivery where they did not exist previously. However the extent to which this occurs depends on how well the terms of the contract are written. This may be a function of measurement. For instance, failure to specify that all of the equipment in a privately built and financed hospital must actually work when it is handed over to an NHS Trust would give the contractor a strong incentive to economize by not spending money getting the equipment operational.
3. *Public-sector comparator.* An important issue in evaluating PFI contract bids is the comparative cost of doing the project in the public sector. Cross-sectoral comparisons pose three issues. First, interest rates used in the private sector are higher than in the public sector because the private sector accounts for risk while the public sector does not. This tends to inflate the financial cost of the private sector even though the cost to society may be the same. Second, private contractors will have to pay tax on profits, and this inflates their bids relative to the public sector. Third, no accurate public-sector comparator may exist for big projects, and thus the system may be biased toward PFI solutions to the funding of capital projects.
4. *Risk.* A number of different risks are associated with PFI projects, and these need to be efficiently allocated between the parties. Risks associated

with building an asset, such as strikes, technical problems and poor management, can affect cost. Service risks affect the cost of operating the asset once it has started to deliver services. These may arise because of fluctuations in the price of materials and labor. Volume risks are a particular service risk relating to the amount of service demanded by the government. These costs may be affected by government actions such as a change in sentencing policy that affects prison occupancy. Residual risk is the risk associated with the terminal value of the asset at the end of the contract. Because physical assets last longer than contractual obligations, fluctuations in the terminal value of the asset may significantly affect the price of a PFI contract.

5. *Flexibility.* The major disadvantage of PFI contracts is their relative inflexibility. This poses the problem that government will find it expensive to break PFI contracts if these subsequently prove not to be meeting social needs. Thus, private prisons and hospitals with PFI contracts can be shut down only if significant compensation is paid. It may also be difficult to renegotiate service-delivery terms. Both the private sector and the government face potential hold-up problems when one party can take advantage of changing circumstances to increase the cost to the other party if situations arise that are not specified carefully in the original contract.

6. *Mortgaging the future.* A major advantage of the PFI is that it allows the fiscal-deficit implications of large infrastructure projects to be smoothed, but this comes at the cost of transferring claims to future governments. While the current total value of these claims in the UK is currently only 0.5 percent of total government expenditure on PFI projects, the figure is nearer 10 percent for the transport budget. What is an acceptable level of PFI commitments? The degree to which future budgets should be pre-allocated by earlier administrations is clearly an important political issue.[19]

7. *Safety and security.* There has been significant use of the PFI in transport and defense projects. In transport, questions have been raised about incentives to compromise safety that may be present in the private sector, as highlighted by the debates around the proposed partial privatization of the National Air Traffic Control System and the failings of the rail industry. In defense, the government has signed a PFI contract to undertake the building of a new top-secret intelligence-gathering center at Cheltenham. Contracts such as these can have security implications. Indeed the center was financed on the basis of much less information than would normally be available to investors.[20] It is important that PFI contracts with public safety and security elements be very well-specified with respect to the allocation of risks. The additional danger inherent in such contracts is the likelihood that the public will unfairly blame the private sector if something does go wrong.

PFI EXPERIENCE

In this section I draw together some of the main observations to arise from the PFI program as a whole, noting both positive and negative aspects. Among the positive outcomes are the lifting of financial constraints, the enthusiastic response of the private sector to the PFI, and stimulation of innovation. On the negative side, the bidding process under PFI can be very lengthy, bidding costs are high, and there are often only a small number of bidders. In addition, PFI contracts often have questionable risk properties, and cost overruns can be substantial. A detailed list of signed PFI projects up to mid-1999 is given in the Appendix.

Positive Experiences

The PFI has been successful in lifting financial constraints by attracting significant amounts of private-sector capital spending. While the overall figures show that PFI expenditure by the private sector is ahead of PFI payments by the government, it is possible to identify several large projects that probably would have been seriously delayed if they had not been financed by the PFI. These include the Channel Tunnel Railways Link and the Skye Bridge (see National Audit Office 1997a). The PFI seems well-suited to handle the high up-front capital costs of transport projects that yield extended streams of benefits. If conventionally financed, these projects would have absorbed a large percentage of their relevant budgets while they were being built.

The private sector has responded enthusiastically to the PFI. As experience with the PFI process has grown, private contractors have come forward to provide services to the government. These companies include significant numbers of foreign companies, which can bring new ideas and technology into the UK public sector.

Innovation has been substantial as well as varied, from the types of contracts private-sector bidders have offered to the physical assets that have been installed. The National Audit Office (1997c) noted the innovation in design and operation of prisons in the winning bidders' plans for the new Fazakerley and Bridgend prisons. There have also been financial innovations with development of extended maturity bank loans for PFI projects and uninsured PFI bond issues.[21]

Negative Experiences

The bidding process under PFI can be very lengthy. From the initial phase of public-sector assessment to the signing of a contract takes up to two years. The process of inviting, preparing, assessing and refining bids and negotiating contracts is complex and procedural. This process certainly delayed the initial flow of signed contracts (see Cutler 1997 and Gaffney and Pollock 1999 for experience in the NHS). A survey of investors and non-investors in urban regeneration (Royal Institution of Chartered Surveyors 1998) revealed criticism of the PFI as speculative, time-consuming and overly bureaucratic, with too high a risk transferred over to the private sector. Recently, the length of time in commissioning PFI projects has been blamed for the relatively low levels of public-sector investment in 1999 and 2000 and the failure to meet targets for PFI investment.[22]

The bidding costs are high. The detailed and lengthy nature of the bidding process naturally implies increased transaction costs under the PFI (Hewitt 1997), and these can be substantial for each bidder. Initial bids may cost £0.5 million per bidder to prepare; the final bid costs for a winning hospital-building project may total £3 million (Kerr 1998). Wilkins (1998) estimates the tendering costs for all PFI projects in the pipeline in 1998 may finally total £500 million. These costs are eventually reflected in the cost of contracts signed and are significant for most projects.

There are often only a small number of bidders for PFI projects, and the statistics on which companies are actually involved in PFI deals reveal that a small number of firms act as legal advisors, financial advisors, contractors, funders, technical advisors, property advisors and facilities managers to PFI projects.[23] This has given rise to the suspicion that competition is more apparent than real in the bidding process. On large individual projects there may be, even initially, only two or three serious bidders. For example, the Dartford and Gravesham Hospital (National Audit Office 1999b) had only one bidder at the final bid stage.

Cost overruns can be substantial for PFI projects, and there is often considerable scope for cost inflation through the bidding process. The initial evaluation of the viability of PFI funding may be based on calculations that are massively exceeded by the final contract stage. Even after the contract has been signed, contract terms may leave much of the cost risk with the government, which leaves considerable scope for cost inflation. The initial project to computerize payments at post offices, a £1.5 billion project dating from 1996, has now been partially abandoned at a cost of £620–940 million to the government.[24] According to the British Medical Association (1997) capital costs for 14 prioritized hospitals had increased 72 percent by the tender stage.

PFI contracts often have questionable risk properties. On the one hand it is not clear to what extent the government can shift risk to the private sector, given the fact that its policies can affect the returns to contractors. Thus the government may have ended up paying for the high price of financing investments that its actions make more risky. In this case it may be sub-optimal for the private sector to bear the risk. On the other hand it may have proved too easy for the private sector to argue that it needed to be compensated for potential risks at the same time as ensuring that those risks remained with the government. The private sector's relative advantage in risk management may have facilitated this.

Overall Opinions of the PFI

The government view of the PFI since 1992 has been extremely positive. This is striking because there have been high-profile problems with individual projects such as the Skye Bridge and a series of reviews of the PFI under both Conservative and Labour administrations. Yet the view taken has been to streamline the process and to expand its size and scope. The willingness of the Labour administration to embrace 'privatization' of public services can be seen in the wider context of its willingness to accept most of the pro-market policies of the previous Conservative administration.

One obvious explanation of this government enthusiasm for the PFI stems from the experience under the previous system of government procurement. A National Audit Office report on the price of road contracts (National Audit Office 1992a) showed that the Department of Transport was paying an average of 28 percent more than the originally agreed price. A major problem was the unwillingness of the department to transfer project risks to the contractor, something which the PFI aims to do. The National Audit Office also unearthed problems with contracting out by the Ministry of Defence (National Audit Office 1992b). The ministry was accused of failing to keep records over the thirteen years of the contracting-out process and of not having the expertise to assess contractors' bids. Serious problems with government procurement *before* the PFI put isolated problems with the PFI in context.

Unions have been critical of the PFI. In 1996 the public-sector trade union Unison called on Scottish councils to boycott the PFI because it was a way of making 'cash strapped councils open up to public services for exploitation and commercial gain' (see Kerr 1998). The 1998 Trade Union Congress backed a motion against the PFI to reinstate 'proper capital funding to ensure the future infrastructure of the public services in a way which does not damage jobs and services' after the GMB union changed its previous policy of supporting the PFI.[25] The British Medical Association, the doctors' union, recently stepped up its opposition to the PFI in the NHS following evidence that PFI schemes are costing more than traditional schemes.[26]

In January 2000 a report commissioned by the Treasury Task Force analyzed the outcome of 29 PFI projects with a net present cost of £5 billion[27] and found a cost saving relative to the public-sector comparators of just over £1 billion. This figure was dominated by two large projects, but the unweighted average saving was 17 percent, with individual savings varying between 0.7 and 45 percent. These figures are estimates and the true value to the public sector depends on the value of risks transferred and on actual future payments. The report identified six key elements for success: risk transfer, long-term contracting, output-based project specification, competition, performance measurement and private-sector management skills. The report recommended more sharing of experiences, more centralized monitoring of PFI project performance, transfer of experienced staff between departments, use of ongoing benchmarking to ensure continuing value for money from existing projects and more careful assessment of the value of the risks transferred to the private sector.

The NAO has assessed a number of large PFI projects in terms of value for money. On the basis of this ongoing experience, the National Audit Office (1999a) highlights four key aspects of successful PFI projects: clear objectives, application of proper procurement processes, getting high-quality bids and ensuring that the final deal either makes sense or is dropped or re-tendered. The results of ten NAO reports summarized in Table 4.3 reveal that the planning of PFI projects within the government authority involved is not always good, and this often results in long delays. The process of soliciting bids and specifying the contract is similarly mixed, although authorities usually selected the best available deal. Finally, in several cases there remains considerable doubt as to whether the final contract actually represented value for money relative to a conventionally funded scheme. Overall the picture is of mixed success.

An influential report from the Institute for Public Policy Research (IPPR 2001) concluded that the PFI had been successful for prisons and roads but of limited value to date in hospital and school projects. It highlighted two key determinants of this. First, more control of service provision by the private sector further encouraged cost reduction. An example is the transfer of all operation and management of services for prisons to the private contractor, rather than distinguishing between core and ancillary services and having core services remain the responsibility of the public sector, as was done for hospitals. The second determinant was the successful role of a centralized procurer in prison building and road construction, in contrast to lack of experience in the case of individual health authorities commissioning hospitals. The report further noted that value-for-money calculation was sensitive to the choice of discount rate, with higher discount rates (6 rather than 5 percent) favoring PFI schemes over public-sector comparators because costs are shifted into the future by PFI. The report highlighted the work of Boyle and Harrison (2000) in hospitals. They found that gains from eleven PFI hospitals were positive but small and more than explained by the valuation of risk transfer. However, it was noted that around 40 percent of personal social services, such as those provided by care homes, are provided by the private sector, which means that private-sector involvement in health care in the UK is already significant.

Table 4.3 The summary NAO evaluation of ten major PFI projects

PFI project	Planning	Process	Best deal	Value for money
Skye Bridge	Good	Probably all right	Yes	Very dubious
National Insurance Co.	Bad	Good	Very good	Probably
Four road schemes	Good	Probably all right	Yes	Probably
Immigration/nationality computer	Good	Very good	Yes	Probably
M74 road scheme	Good	Probably all right	Yes	Yes
Privatization of social security offices	Good	Good	Yes	Yes
Dartford and Gravesham Hospital	Poor	Poor	Yes	Probably
RAF non-combat vehicles	Bad	Bad	Probably	Yes
DSS Newcastle Estate	Bad	Bad	Yes	Dubious
Prisons	Good	Good	Probably	Yes

Source: Nicholas Timmins, 'The £84bn question', *Financial Times*, 15 December 1999, p. 20 (from NAO).

CASE STUDIES OF FIVE PFI PROJECTS

The Skye Bridge (National Audit Office 1997a)

This project involved building a toll bridge to the Island of Skye, off the Scottish coast, to reduce congestion and delays associated with the existing ferry service. The project needed to take account of the sensitivity of the environment, the cost of the existing ferry crossing, and value for money.

The Scottish Office Development Department first advertised the competition to design, build, finance and operate the Skye Bridge in October 1989, before the formal start of the PFI. The department did not assess a public-sector comparator because they had no intention of funding the project except through private finance. There were six initial bidders with ten designs. Three preferred bidders were chosen, and two submitted qualifying bids. The contract was awarded in April 1991 to Skye Bridge Limited, a joint venture between Miller Civil Engineering, Dyckerhoff and Widman AG and Bank of America Financial Corporation. The nature of the original contract allowed the company to recover a fixed discounted sum of £24 million from users before the contract is terminated, over a maximum 27-year period, subject to increasing the price by a maximum of 30 percent in real terms.

The bridge was completed after a local public enquiry that resulted in delays and design changes costing £3.8 million (to protect a local otter population). The total cost of the project was £39 million (constant 1991 prices discounted at 6 percent): £24 million to be paid by users of the bridge, £12 million paid to Skye Bridge Limited by the department and £3 million counted as the department's direct cost of advice and staff costs. The out-turn departmental contribution to Skye Bridge Limited was 48 percent higher than originally expected because of compensation for delays and extra costs.

The bridge opened in 1995 with charges of £5.40 for a single car trip in high season and £4.40 in low season. Ten tickets averaging £2.51 could be purchased in bulk. This compared to £1 for the Dartford Bridge and £3.90 return for the Severn Bridge.

The NAO identified gains to the users from (1) relatively low tolls since all but one of the categories of fare were lower in real terms than with the ferry, (2) improved reliability and (3) the expectation of complete elimination of charges when the contract terminates after 14 to 18 years. The department gained by reducing its peak financing requirements and by transferring risks in building and operation to the developer. The NAO's advisors were satisfied that the project finance terms obtained by the developer were competitive (see Table 4.4).

The tolls for the Skye Bridge have proved controversial. In 1997 the Secretary of State for Scotland announced that the tolls would be cut by up to 50 percent, with the reductions to be financed by the taxpayer. This is estimated to have cost the government another £3 million. It now appears that the PFI has proved expensive as a way to borrow more for a public project.[28]

Table 4.4 How the Skye Bridge was financed

Type of finance	Amount (£m)	Interest rate	Term
Commercial bank debt	Up to 6.0	LIBOR+1.25%	14 years
European investment bank loan	13.01	Fixed at 10%	18 years, including a 7-year grace period
Index-linked loan stock	7.5	RPI+6%	20 years, including a 14-year grace period
Sponsored capital: Equity and equity-like index-linked convertible loan stock	0.5	Estimated at 26.4% (18.4% in real terms)	Estimated at 18 years

Note: The interest rate and terms estimated for the sponsored capital are dependent on the financial performance of Skye Bridge Limited rather than being fixed. The actual returns depend on a range of variables, including actual traffic flows, inflation, etc.

Source: National Audit Office (1997a).

National Insurance Recording System (National Audit Office 1997b)

This project was to replace the computerized National Insurance records held by the Contributions Agency by April 1997, at which time new and more complex pension arrangements were due to come into effect. The NIRS-2 project as it was known became a PFI project in July 1994, and a seven-year contract providing for 15 different types of transaction was awarded to Andersen Consulting in April 1995. The contract involved replacing the previous NIRS-1 system, implementing new procedures before April 1997, converting all existing data to the new system, training users and ensuring that back-up procedures existed.

This project became part of the PFI in spite of warnings that inviting bids would add six months to the delivery date and that private-sector computer projects had a history of overrunning. In the event the bid process was completed quickly with expressions of interest from 34 companies. Andersen Consulting made the cheapest bid by a large margin, a mere £45 million against rival bids of £125 million and £146 million. At the end of the contract there may be a new competition with a compensation payment due from another supplier taking over the existing system; if the Contributions Agency decides it no longer needs the system it will compensate the contractor directly.

The initial cost of the procurement exercise was estimated at £473,000 plus external advisors' fees; the amount actually expended was £1.23 million in 1994–95, including £325,000 for advisors' fees. The project had not been completed by the time of the NAO report, which was critical of the lack of detail in the contract concerning service quality and which noted that most of the risk of delays or non-completion lay with the Contributions Agency. However the contract does not pay anything to Andersen Consulting until the system is working. The NAO described the price paid as 'strikingly good value' because the Andersen bid was so low and because the cost of a public-sector comparator was estimated at £329 million.

The reason for the underbidding appears to have been Andersen's intention to build a reputation that might gain them other contracts – their valuation of this project took £100 million off the price.[29] Andersen had paid £3.1 million in compensation by mid-1998 and their total costs have been estimated at £135 million by mid-1999. The contract has now been delivered two years late.[30] The government has announced that such underbidding would not be accepted in the future, while an NAO spokesman recently declared that, given the delays, NISR-2 'can scarcely be regarded as a successful project.'[31]

Bridgend and Fazakerley Prisons (National Audit Office 1997c)

The Prison Service sought private finance for two facilities: an 800-place prison at Bridgend, South Wales and a 600-place prison at Fazakerley, Merseyside. These were to be designed to accommodate prisoners on remand, awaiting sentence, serving short sentences or awaiting transfer to another prison (Category B prisoners) and also for a small number of Category A (maximum security) prisoners. After a 17-month process the contracts to design, build, finance and maintain the prisons were awarded in 1995 to Securicor/Costain for Bridgend and Group 4/Tarmac for Fazakerley.

An engineering firm will monitor construction performance, and each prison will have a Prison Services' Controller who will monitor service provision against the contract, with financial penalties for lapses. There were ten initial pre-qualification bidders, six were invited to tender bids and five submitted bids for both prisons. Three of the five bidders had overseas partners in their consortia. The Prison Service decided against awarding both contracts to the same bidder, even though the Securicor/Costain bid was the lowest combined bid by 10 percent. They did this to stimulate competition in the sector and because of worries about the consortia's ability to handle two prison projects at once.

The contract transferred the risk of time and cost overruns to the contractors. The contract payment mechanism gives no payment until the prisons are operational. The contractors are paid for availability rather than actual usage. The contract price contains a fixed element relating to construction costs, some operating costs (non-salary costs) are fixed in real terms and further costs (relating to salaries) are indexed to 2 percent above the RPI (retail price index). The contract, which runs for 25 years, allows for some risk sharing of cost increases beyond the contractors' control, some benefit sharing if contractors' profits are higher than anticipated, and additional fees are payable if the specified number of prisoners is exceeded. An identified shortcoming in the pricing is a lack of benchmarking of costs against other prisons at periodic intervals.

The NAO estimated that the prison contracts represented good value for money. Bridgend is expected to cost £266 million over its contract life (against £319 million in the public sector); Fazakerley is expected to cost £247 million (against £248 million). The contract-letting costs were £1.55 million (+140 percent over the original estimate). There has been significant risk transfer, additional funding was secured and there was innovation in building, design and operational methods. The financing arrangements for the projects are in Table 4.5. The prisons are now operational, having been built 45 percent faster than the average for public prison projects.

The companies involved in the deal recently caused controversy by subsequently refinancing their debts associated with the projected savings of £9.7 million after the prisons opened. This saving was added to the direct gains of £3.4 million from opening the prisons ahead of schedule. Only £1 million of this gain was returned to the public sector. This has allowed firms to increase their projected rate of return from 12.8 percent to 39 percent and has led to calls by the NAO to require sharing of refinancing windfalls on PFI projects through contract terms. The reason for the significant saving on financing costs is attributable to the decline in perceived risk of PFI-backed bond and debt issues.[32]

M74 Road Schemes (National Audit Office 1998)

From December 1993 to March 1996, the Highways Agency sought and negotiated four contracts for designing, building, financing and operating roads. The contracts were awarded for 30 years and involve government payment of a shadow toll based on actual road use (the number of cars and other vehicles using the roads). Table 4.6 shows roadway features and gives the estimated contract price and the price of a traditionally financed public road. The public-sector comparator cost is the sum of the NPV (net present value) of the construction cost plus the operation and maintenance costs plus the NPV of the risk transferred to the consortia. As shown in Table 4.6, all but one of the roads is expected to yield considerable benefits.

Table 4.5 The financing of the Bridgend and Fazakerley prisons

Type of finance	Amount (£m)	Interest rate	Term
Bridgend			
Base loan facility	72.0	9.6235% to date of operation, 9.4735% first five years and 9.5735% for remainder	15 Nov 2013
Standby loan commitments	5.0	LIBOR+1.65% until operational, LIBOR+1.5% first five years and LIBOR+1.6% for remainder	15 Nov 2013
Equity/subordinated debt	15.6	Projected 19.4% after tax	
Fazakerley			
Base loan facility	92.5	£82.6 million at 9.05945% until operational, 9.5945% until 15 Dec 2015 and LIBOR+1.5% thereafter Balance: LIBOR+1% until operational, LIBOR+1% thereafter	15 Dec 2015
Working capital facility	3.0	LIBOR+1.5%	15 Dec 2015
Equity/subordinated debt	8.1	Projected 12.8% after tax	

Source: National Audit Office (1997c).

Table 4.6 The first four PFI roads

	Type	Length	Expected NPV of shadow tolls	Public-sector comparator
M1–A1 Link (Yorkshire)	2 to 5-lane dual carriageways	30 km+22 km side roads	£232 million	£344 million
A1(M) Motorway (Alenbury/Peterborough)	all motorway	21 km	£154 million	£204 million
A419/A417 (Swindon/Gloucester)	single/dual carriageway	52 km	£112 million	£123 million
A69 Carlisle/Newcastle DBFO Project Road	single/dual carriageway	84.3 km with 3.2 km bypass	£62 million	£57 million

Note: All monetary values are excluding value-added tax.

Source: National Audit Office (1998).

The NAO was critical of the cost of the bidding process, which was delayed because of the complex information required. Bidding costs were reckoned at more than £11 million for the four winning bidders, and unsuccessful short-listed bidders incurred substantial costs as well. The NAO pointed out that the wrong discount rate had been used in comparing the bidders' prices with the public-sector comparator cost – if the correct figure had been used, the A419/A417 assessment would have yielded negative benefits for a PFI project.

The Highway Agency can terminate the contract if performance criteria are not met, and a department representative monitors the operation and mainte-nance of each road. The roads must revert to the public sector in good condition. The residual life of a road is ten years for 85 percent of the pavement on hand back. Payments are based on complex audits of traffic flows, and there are clauses that allow for additional payments if a road is upgraded.

The Dartford and Gravesham Hospital (National Audit Office 1999b)

This was the first major PFI hospital deal and involved a 400-bed facility that became operational in 2000. The construction time of 38 months compares favorably to an average 66 months for publicly built hospitals. The project has an NPV of £177 million.

Under the terms of the 1997 contract, Pentland (the contractor) will receive an inflation-indexed fee of £1.32 million per month (1996 prices), which includes an availability payment and a performance-related element. Pentland is responsible for seven facilities services, including building management and maintenance and catering, while the NHS Trust is responsible for clinical services. The contract for 25 years from the date of opening required Pentland to bear the construction risk, but the cost of legislative changes are shared with the Trust.

The bidding process involved 13 initial expressions of interest and four indicative bids. One of the two final bidders selected dropped out and did not submit a final bid. Pentland's final bid was 33 percent higher than its indicative bid, which reflects changes made by Pentland and the Trust. The NAO noted significant benchmarking by the Trust in its evaluation of the sole final bid and in the terms of the final contract, which allow performance-related fee increases subject to Pentland's carrying out benchmarking against costs in other hospitals.

The final savings from the project were estimated to be around 3 percent (£5 million) relative to traditional procurement. This small expected saving means that the final cost could turn out to be higher than under traditional procure-ment. The Trust bears the volume risk. At £2.8 million, the cost of external advice to the Trust was substantial, though much of this reflected the fact that this was the first major hospital deal under the PFI.

CONCLUSIONS

There has undoubtedly been a huge transfer of control of the financing, building, operation and management of investment projects from the public to the private sectors in the UK since 1979. This has occurred without a noticeable reduction in the quantity and quality of investment or of the associated services. With the notable exception of Railtrack, it is difficult to argue against the observation that privatization of utilities has resulted in considerable benefits for customers, shareholders, the government and, in many cases, workers. The investment programs of the utilities have continued to be financed, and there has been significant new entry and innovation in most sectors. The PFI attempts to extend privatization to services that continue to be purchased by the government.

The assessment of the PFI is more difficult than that for privatization because the PFI involves many different deals, most of which are at early stages and many of which have involved significant learning curves for the civil servants and contractors involved.[33] The NAO assessment of ten major projects (Table 4.3) suggests that the PFI can yield big savings but that some deals have been bad value. The PFI is heavily concentrated in a few government departments, with differing amounts of success. The NHS seems to be struggling to make it work consistently while the Prison Service and the Highway Agency seem to have mastered the process.

At its best, however, the PFI provides finance for cash-strapped departments, saves time and money, stimulates innovation and efficiently allocates risk. At its worst it leads to unreasonable future claims, costs money and time, and ineffectively and expensively allocates risk. It remains to be seen how the balance between the best and the worst scenarios will change over time as experience with the PFI grows and as projects mature. As public-sector comparators cease to be available, it will be more difficult to assess the comment that 'many of the assumed benefits of the PFI would appear to be available to better managed and controlled conventional procurement.'[34]

The PFI raises a number of issues that are still up for discussion. First, in what areas are PFI projects appropriate vehicles for publicly desirable investment? PFI involvement in defense raises national security issues; safety fears surface in the case of air traffic control. Second, what improvements are possible to the system? Improved project measurement and specification and a standardizing of the process will yield significant benefits. The recent placing of Railtrack into administration has, for instance, raised questions about the considerable level of risk that contracting with the government can involve. Third, to what extent will claims set up under the PFI prove a burden to future generations? The issues of a lack of bidders, long contracts that are costly to alter and mortgaged budgets may prove bigger issues in the future than at present (see Heald and Geaughan 1997). Finally, to what extent can the lessons of the PFI be transferred to developing countries? If relatively well-trained British civil servants and a relatively transparent public procurement system struggle with the PFI, it seems unlikely to be a good option in countries where the PFI may involve increased scope for corruption and expensive contracting and processing mistakes by civil servants.

ACKNOWLEDGMENTS

The author acknowledges the generous financial support of IDE-JETRO for this research. He thanks Ronald Bachmann for his excellent research assistance. David Newbery and participants at an IDE-JETRO workshop in Tokyo provided helpful comments.

ENDNOTES

1. Central Statistical Office (CSO) and Office of National Statistics (ONS) *UK National Accounts*.
2. See National Housing Federation (1997).
3. See Table C18 at www.hm-treasury.gov.uk/budget2001/fsbr/chapc.htm (accessed 13 September 2001).
4. 'Leader: Private finance, public gain', *Financial Times*, 22 June 2001.
5. Christopher Adams, 'Rail repairs will take up to 6 months', *Financial Times*, 3 November 2000, p. 1, and Juliette Jowit, 'How the rail privatization experience went wrong', *Financial Times*, 7 October 2001.
6. 'Tube PPP plans', *PFI Report*, July/August 1999, p. 5, and Industrial Society (2000).
7. See Table C13 at www.hm-treasury.gov.uk/budget2001/fsbr/chapc.htm (accessed 13 September 2001).
8. See www.detr.gov.uk for details.
9. This is not straightforward. See Mayston (1999) and Broadbent and Laughlin (1999) for accounts of some of the issues in project evaluation.
10. PFI contracts are advertised and details of offers are made known. This contrasts sharply with the previous procurement system (described in Blyth 1987), where often a restricted bidding process involved direct contract with 'qualifying' firms by departments and details of offers were not made known.
11. See HM Treasury (1996).
12. Figures from HM Treasury (2000), *Financial Statement and Budget Report, March 2000 – The Public Finances*. Available at www.hm-treasury.gov.uk/budget2000/fsbr/chapc.htm.
13. See HM Treasury (2000), *Public Private Partnerships – The Government's Approach* at http://www.hm-treasury.gov.uk/pdf/2000/ppp.pdf.
14. See www.partnershipsuk.org.uk/puk/index.htm.
15. See www.4ps.co.uk/the4ps/what.htm.
16. Peter Gershon, 'Review of civil procurement in central government', April 1999. Available at www.ogc.gov.uk/gershon/pgfinair.htm.
17. See www.ogc.gov.uk.
18. OGC press release, 13 June 2000.
19. There has been an ongoing debate about how PFI projects should be accounted for in government budgets. The Accounting Standards Board (ASB) standards apply only to the private sector, but the government announced in 1997 that it would comply with ASB's

standard for PFI accounting when this was issued. The ASB ruling was that PFI payments need not be capitalized if it could be established that substantial risk in the capital behind the service lay with the private sector. If this could not be established or if the contract looks too much like a lease, PFI payments should appear in accounts at their full net present value. (See 'PFI accounting amendment goes ahead', *Accountancy International*, October 1998 and Nicholas Timmins, 'Agreement reached on balance sheet regulations', *Financial Times*, 25 June 1999, p. 10).

20. Rebecca Bream, 'Bonds gain in popularity', *Financial Times*, 29 November 2000, Survey p. 2.
21. A. Warner, 'PFI spotting: the PPP track', *The Banker*, 148 (871): September 1998.
22. Peter Robinson, 'Private finance comes up short', *Financial Times*, 29 November 2000, p. 27
23. For details of the most successful firms involved in the PFI, see 'The PFI report database: Leading players', *PFI Report*, November, p. 18.
24. Nicholas Timmins, 'An explosive mixture: Britain's attempts to involve the private sector in designing and operating technology for public services have resulted in some costly failures', *Financial Times*, 27 July 1999, p. 23.
25. 'PFI gets the thumbs down from trade unions', *Supply Management*, 3 (19): September 1998.
26. Nicholas Timmins, 'Health service medical association to step up opposition to PFI', *Financial Times*, 5 July 1999, p. 8.
27. Arthur Andersen and Enterprise LSE, 'Value for money drivers in the Private Finance Initiative', January 2000. Available at www.ogc.gov.uk/frame.home.htm.
28. James Buxton, 'Skye bridge toll cuts will be subsidised', *Financial Times*, 5 July 1997, p. 4 and Nicholas Timmins, 'The pounds 84bn question', *Financial Times*, 15 December 1999, p. 20.
29. Nicholas Timmins, 'Andersen takes the pain for long-term gain', *Financial Times*, 3 June 1997, p. 11.
30. Nicholas Timmins, 'An explosive mixture: Britain's attempts to involve the private sector in designing and operating technology for public services have resulted in some costly failures', *Financial Times*, 22 July 1999, p. 23.
31. Nicholas Timmins, 'Companies warned over public sector IT contracts', *Financial Times*, 4 November 1999, p. 3.
32. See Nicholas Timmins, 'Taxpayers should share fat PFI profits', *Financial Times*, 29 June 2000, p. 2.
33. House of Commons Committee of Public Accounts (1999).
34. House of Commons Treasury Committee (1996).

REFERENCES

Alchian, A.A. (1965), 'Some economics of property rights', *Il Politico*, 30, 816–29.
Averch, H. and L.L. Johnson (1962), 'Behaviour of the firm under regulatory constraint', *American Economic Review*, 52, 1052–69.
Bergman, L., G. Brunekreeft, C. Doyle, N. von der Fehr, D. Newbery, M. Pollitt, and P. Regibeau (1999), *MED2: A European Market for Electricity*, CEPR: London.
Blyth, A.H. (1987), 'Government procurement in the United Kingdom', *George Washington Journal of International Law and Economics*, 21, 127–49.
Boyle, S. and A. Harrison (2000), 'PFI and health: The story so far', in G. Kelly and P. Robinson (eds), *A Healthy Partnership: The Future of Public Private Partnerships in the Health Service*, Institute for Public Policy Research (IPPR): London.
Brealey, R.A., I.A. Cooper, and M.A. Habib (1997), 'Investment appraisal in the public sector', *Oxford Review of Economics Policy*, 13 (4), 12–28.
British Medical Association (1997), *Can the NHS Afford the Private Finance Initiative?*, BMA: London.

Broadbent, J. and R. Laughlin (1999), 'The Private Finance Initiative: Clarification of the research agenda', *Financial Accountability & Management*, 15 (2), 95–114.

Clark, G.L. and A. Root (1999), 'Infrastructure Shortfall in the United Kingdom: The private finance initiative and government policy', *Political Geography*, 18 (3), 341–65.

CRI (Centre for Regulated Industries) (1996), *The UK Regulated Industries Financial Facts 1994/95*, CIPFA: London.

Cutler, P. (1997), 'Can use of the PFI be healthy?', *New Economy*, 4 (3), 142–6.

Demsetz, H. (1968), 'Why Regulate Utilities?', *Journal of Law and Economics*, 11, 55–65.

Gaffney, D. and A.M. Pollock (1999), 'Pump-priming the PFI: Why are privately financed hospital schemes being subsidised?', *Public Money and Management*, 19 (1), 55–62.

Grout, P.A. (1997), 'The economics of the Private Finance Initiative', *Oxford Review of Economic Policy*, 13 (4), 53–66.

Hall, J. (1998), 'Private opportunity, public benefit?', *Fiscal Studies*, 19 (2), 121–40.

Hart, O., A. Shleifer, and R.W. Vishny (1997), 'The proper scope of government: Theory and application to prisons', *Quarterly Journal of Economics*, 112 (4), 1127–58.

Heald, D. and N. Geaughan (1997), 'Accounting for the Private Finance Initiative', *Public Money and Management*, 17 (3), 11–16.

Hewitt, C. (1997), 'Complexity and cost in PFI Schemes', *Public Money and Management*, 17 (3), 7–9.

HM Treasury (1993), *Breaking New Ground: The Private Finance Initiative*, HMSO: London.

HM Treasury (1996), *Private Finance Initiative: Guidelines for Smoothing the Procurement Process*, Private Finance Unit: London.

House of Commons Committee of Public Accounts (1999), *Getting better value for money from the Private Finance Initiative*, HC 583, 1998–99 Session, HMSO: London.

House of Commons Treasury Committee (1996), *The Private Finance Initiative*, 1995–96 Session, HMSO: London.

Industrial Society (2000), *The London Underground Public Private Partnership: An Independent Review by the Industrial Society*, The Industrial Society: London.

IPPR (2001), *Building better partnerships: The Final Report of the Commission on Public Private Partnerships*, Institute for Public Policy Research: London.

Kain, P. (1998), 'The reform of rail transport in Britain', *Journal of Transport Economics and Policy*, 32 (2), 247–66.

Kerr, D. (1998), 'The PFI miracle', *Capital and Class*, Spring (64), 17–28.

Keynes, J.M.K. (1936), *The General Theory of Employment, Interest and Money*, London: Macmillan.

Mayston, D.J. (1999), 'The Private Finance Initiative in the National Health Service: An unhealthy development in new public management?', *Financial Accountability*, 15 (3/4), 249–74.

McCarthy, U. (1995), *The Private Finance Initiative: Policy and Practice*, London: Chartered Institute of Public Finance and Accountancy.

McDaniel, T. (2002), this volume (Chapter 5).

Milgrom, P. and J. Roberts (1990), 'Bargaining activity, influence costs, and the organization of economic activity', in J.E. Alt and K.A. Sheple (eds), *Perspectives on Positive Political Economy*, Cambridge, UK: Cambridge University Press.

National Audit Office (1992a), *Department of Transport: Contracting for Roads*, London: HMSO.

National Audit Office (1992b), *Ministry of Defence: Competition in the Provision of Support Services*, London: HMSO.

National Audit Office (1997a), *The Skye Bridge*, HC 5, Parliamentary Session 1997–98, London: HMSO.

National Audit Office (1997b), *The Contributions Agency: The Contract to Develop and Operate the Replacement National Insurance Recording System*, HC 12, Parliamentary Session 1997–98, London: HMSO.

National Audit Office (1997c), *The PFI Contracts for Bridgend and Fazakerley Prisons*, HC 253, Parliamentary Session 1997–98, London: HMSO.

National Audit Office (1998), *The Private Finance Initiative: The First Four, Design, Build, Finance and Operate Roads Contracts*, HC 476, Parliamentary Session 1997–98, London: HMSO.

National Audit Office (1999a), *Examining the Value for Money of Deals under the Private Finance Initiative*, HC 739, Parliamentary Session 1998–99, London: HMSO.

National Audit Office (1999b), *The PFI Contract for the New Dartford & Gravesham Hospital*, HC 423, Parliamentary Session 1998–99, London: HMSO.

National Housing Federation (1997), *Private Finance Initiatives in Social Housing*, London.

Niskanen, W.A. (1968), 'The peculiar economics of bureaucracy', *American Economic Review, Papers and Proceedings*, 58, 298–305.

Pollitt, M.G. (1997), 'The impact of liberalisation on the performance of the electricity supply industry: An international survey', *Journal of Energy Literature*, 3 (2), 3–31.

Pollitt, M.G. (1999), 'A survey of the deregulation of public enterprises in the UK since 1979', in M. Kagami and M. Tsuji (eds), *Privatization, Deregulation and Institutional Frameworks*, Tokyo: Institute of Developing Economies, 120–69.

Public Services Privatisation Research Unit (1997), *PFI — Dangers, Realities, Alternatives*, London: PSPRU.

Royal Institution of Chartered Surveyors (1998), *Accessing Private Finance — The availability and effectiveness of private finance in urban regeneration*, London.

Terry, F. (1996), 'The Private Finance Initiative — Overdue reform or policy breakthrough?', *Public Money and Management*, 16 (1), 9–16.

Wilkins, N. (1998), 'The Private Finance Initiative', *Business Economics*, 29 (1), 21–9.

Willig, R.D. (1994), 'Public versus regulated private enterprise', *Proceedings of the World Bank Conference on Development Economics*, Washington, DC: World Bank, 155–80.

APPENDIX

List of Major PFI Projects to Mid-1999

Department	PFI Project	Contractor	Date signed	Capital value £m
DCMS	British Library Bibliography		1996	22
DCMS	Royal Armouries Museum, Leeds		1996	42
Defense	Armed Forces Personnel Administration Agency	EDS	Nov–97	150
Defense	Army White Fleet Germany	Ryder	Feb–96	52

Department	PFI Project	Contractor	Date signed	Capital value £m
Defense	Attack Helicopters – Apache Simulator Training	McDonnel Douglas/GKN	Feb–98	250
Defense	Cosford and Shawbury – Accommodation		(1–)4/99	15
Defense	Defense Fixed Telecommunications System	Inca	Jul–97	70
Defense	Fire Fighting Training for the Royal Navy		Apr–99	20
Defense	Hawk Synthetic Training Facility	Reflectone	Dec–97	10
Defense	HMS Nelson	Amey FM	Sep–96	20
Defense	Joint Services Command and Staff College		(10–)12/1998	88
Defense	Lyneham Sewage Treatment	Wessex Water	Aug–98	5
Defense	Material Handling Equipment	Cowie Interleasing plc	Sep–96	18
Defense	Medium Support Helicopter Aircrew Training Facility		Oct–97	100
Defense	Naval Recruitment and Training Agency	Flagship	Aug–96	100
Defense	RAF Fylingdales (Power Station)		(1–)4/99	6
Defense	RAF Light Aircraft – Bulldog Replacement		Oct–97	30
Defense	RAF Lossiemouth (Family Quarters)		(10–)12/98	34
Defense	RAF White Fleet	LEX Service	Jul–96	35
Defense	RNAS Yeovilton (Family Quarters)		Aug–98	8
Defense	Services Defense Helicopter Flying School		1996	118
Defense	TAFMIS	EDS Defense	Aug–96	14
Defense	Tidworth Water and Sewage	Thames Water	Feb–98	10
Defense	Tornado Simulators		(5–)8/99	77
DfEE	Clarendon College, Nottingham	Morrison	Sep–97	16.5
DfEE	Dorset CC – Colfox School		before 2/98	12
DfEE	Dudley MBC – Schools IT Network		(1–)4/99	10
DfEE	ESCOM (Employment Service Communications & Guidance System)	Siemens	Feb–97	5
DfEE	Greenwich University		Oct–97	11
DfEE	Hillingdon School (Barnhill Community High)		(1–)4/99	25
DfEE	King's College London & UMOS	European Land and Property Corporation	Dec–97	142
DfEE	LB of Enfield – School		(1–)4/99	25
DfEE	Leeds LEA – Cardinal Heenan High School		(5–)8/99	10
DfEE	Portsmouth CC – Secondary School		(1–)4/99	14
DfEE	University College London – Cruciform		Dec–97	31
DfEE	University of Brighton (2 projects)		(5–)8/99	14
DSS	Benefit Payments – BAPOCL (withdrawn?)	Pathway (ICL)	May–96	1400 total
DSS	DSS Longbenton Offices	Newcastle Estates Partnership	Jan–98	160
DSS	NIRS	Andersen Consulting	?	150
DSS	PRIME	Partnership Property Management	Apr–98	4000
Environment	Brent Council – Chalkhill Estate		(10–)12/98	100
Environment	Brent Street Lighting		(1–)4/99	10
Environment	Docklands Exhibition Centre	Light Rail Group	Sep–96	100 + total
Environment	Docklands Light Railway		1995	200
Environment	Harrow Office IT		?	8.5
Environment	Hereford & Worcester Waste Management		(1–)4/99	70
Environment	Isle of Wight Waste Management	Island Waste Services	Oct–97	13
Environment	Islington Depot and Vehicle Services		(10–)12/98	29
Environment	Kirklees Waste Management	United Waste Services	Mar–98	41.6
Environment	Lambeth Contract Services	Lambeth Service Team	Oct–97	350
Environment	Millennium Tower		?	?
Environment	North East Derbyshire DC – Property Management		before 2/98	?
Environment	North Wiltshire DC – Property Rationalization		(1–)4/99	10
Environment	QE2 Conference Centre Catering Project		Feb–97	20
Environment	Sheffield CC – Office Accommodation		(5–)8/99	110
Environment	South Gloucester Council – Integrated Waste		(1–)4/99	?
Environment	Surrey CC – Lifestyle Centre		(1–)4/99	16
Environment	West Silvertown Urban Village	East Thames Housing Group	before 10/97	100
Foreign & Commonwealth	Berlin Embassy		(10–)12/98	25

Health	Queen's Medical Centre Nottingham University NHS Trust – IT		(5–)8/99	18.5
Health	Queen's Medical Centre NHS Trust, Nottingham		(5–)8/99	11
Health	Lancaster Priority Services NHS Trust		(5–)8/99	6.5
Health	Hereford Hospitals NHS Trust		(5–)8/99	62
Health	Black Country Mental Health		(10–)12/98	6
Health	Bromley Healthcare		(10)12/98	118
Health	Calderdale		Jul–98	63
Health	Carlisle	Health Management Group	Nov–97	60
Health	Chelsea and Westminster Healthcare NHS Trust	Kensington Housing Trust	Mar–98	7
Health	Chelsea and Westminster Healthcare NHS Trust		(10)12/98	8.5
Health	D'ford & Gr'sham		before 01/03/1997	150
Health (W)	Glan Hafren NHS Trust – Chepstow Community Hospital	KINTRA	Feb–98	10
Health	Leeds Community & Mental Health Services Teaching NHS Trust – 'Omnibus' Project	Revival Properties Ltd.	Sep–98	40
Health	Mayday Healthcare		1997	8.5
Health	NHS Strategic Tracing Service		(1–)4/99	12
Health	Norfolk and Norwich Hospital	Octagon Healthcare	1997	193
Health	North Durham Acute Hospitals NHS Trust	Consort Healthcare	mid–1997	96
Health	North West London Hospitals NHS Trust		(1–)4/99	18
Health	Northallerton Health Services NHS Trust	Primary Medical Property Investments	1997	8.5
Health	Northwick Park & St. Mark's Hospital NHS Trust	London Financial Group led consortium	?	25
Health	Northwick Park & St. Mark's Hospital NHS Trust: Maternity Unit		?	21
Health	Nottingham Health Authority	Mill Group	Nov–97	15
Health	Oxfordshire Mental Health NHS Trust		1998	18
Health	Oxleas		1997	45
Health	Queen Elizabeth Hospital, Greenwich		?	84
Health	Queen Mary's Sidcup NHS Trust		Sep–97	5.7
Health	South Buckinghamshire		Dec–97	29
Health	South Durham NHS Trust – Bishop Auckland Hospital		(5–)8/99	41
Health	South Manchester University Hospital		Sep–98	100
Health	Sussex Weald & Downs NHS Trust		(5–)8/99	23
Health	St. Peter's Hospital NHS Trust		(10)12/98	5
Health	Stockport Healthcare NHS Trust		Aug–98	8
Health	Surrey County Council – Residential Homes		Mar–98	29
Health	Thames Gateway NHS Trust Acute Psychiatric Unit		?	60
Health	University Hospital Wales – Cardiff	Britannia Impreglio/ APCOA	Jun–96	20
Health	Wellhouse NHS Trust – Barnet Hospital		(1–)4/99	5
Health	Westminster CC – Residential Home		May–98	5 +
Health	Worcester Royal Infirmary NHS Trust		(1–)4/99	80
Health	Wythenshawe Hospital – South Manchester		Aug–98	70
MAFF	Broadland Flood Alleviation		(5–)8/99	135
Home Office	Agecroft Prison, Salford	UK Detention Services	Jul–98	74
Home Office (W)	Ammanford Police Station		(10)12/98	25
Home Office	Bridgend Prison	Securicor Custodial Services	1996	74
Home Office	British Transport Police (London) HQ		(1–)4/99	50
Home Office	Fazakerley Prison/HMP Arcourse		1996	88 (?)
Home Office	Greater Manchester Fire Station		before 01/06/1997	5
Home Office	Home Office Pay Service		(10–)12/98	60
Home Office	IND: Gatwick		?	12
Home Office	IND: IT	Siemens Business Services	Apr–96	41
Home Office	Lowdham Grange Prison	Premier Prison Services	Jan–97	32
Home Office	Norfolk Police Authority		(10)12/98	26
Home Office	Police Authority Divisional Headquarters – Derby		Dec–97	16
Home Office	Prison Service Agency – Telecoms	Racal Managed Services	before 01/03/1997	6
Home Office	Prisons Energy		(10)12/98	36
Home Office	Pucklechurch Prison		(10)12/98	30

Department	PFI Project	Contractor	Date signed	Capital value £m
Home Office	STC Cookham Wood	Tarmac/Rebound	Mar–97	10
Home Office	STC Hassockfields – Medomsley		(10)12/98	5
Home Office	STC Rainsbrook Onley	Group 4/Tarmac	Jul–98	10
Home Office	Thames Valley Police Southern HQ		1999	30
Home Office	United Kingdom Passport Agency (2 contracts)		Jul–97	15
Horne Office	Welsh Office – Osiris (IT)	Siemens Business Services	Jun–96	13
Home Office	West Dorset Divisional Police Headquarters		(10)12/98	15
Home Office	Wiltshire Constabulary Police Air Support		?	?
Inland Revenue	IR Bootle		(10)12/98	15
Inland Revenue	IR Manchester & Stockport		Feb–97	32
Inland Revenue	IR Office Accommodation, Edinburgh		Oct–97	6
Inland Revenue	IR Office Accommodation – St John's House Boode		?	12
Inland Revenue	Newcastle Estate (L'benton)		?	120
Inland Revenue	Glasgow		Oct–97	10
Lord Chancellor's	Local County Court System – LOCCS	EDS	Sep–96	14
Lord Chancellor's	Magistrates' Courts' Committees (LIBRA)	ICL/Unisys	Dec–98	183
Lord Chancellor's	Resource Accounting – ARAMIS	CSL Group Ltd/Unisys/ Deloitte and Touche	Feb–98	30
Lord Chancellor's	Northern Ireland Courts		?	30
MAFF	Broadland Flood Alleviation		1999 (?)	135
NI – Crown Prosecution Service	Northern Ireland Court Service – Belfast		?	35
NI – Education	Dept of Education for NI – Drumglass High School		(5–)8/99	5
Post Office	Pathway (formerly BA/POCI)		(5–)8/99	120
Serious Fraud Office	Docman		Jan–98	15
Trade & Industry	Coal Authority		1996	5 +
Trade & Industry	DTI IT – ELGAR		(1–)4/99	26
Trade & Industry	Engineering and Physical Sciences Research Council		(10)12/98	18
Trade & Industry	RA Strategic Partnership		1999	14
Trade & Industry	National Physical Laboratory		(10)12/98	82
Transport	Birmingham Northern Relief Road	Trafalgar House & Tritecna	before 2/98	300
Transport	Channel Tunnel Rail Link			4300
Transport	Croydon Tramlink		1996	200
Transport	Dartford Bridge		1987 (!)	150
Transport	DLR Extension	Tramtrack Corydon Ltd.	Sep–96	200
Transport	Escalators		(1–)4/99	80
Transport	Islington (LA)		1999	22
Transport	Kent IT		1999	7
Transport	Lambeth		1999	10
Transport	LU Power Supply	Powerlink	Aug–98	250
Transport	Luton Airport Parkway		?	20
Transport	Manchester Metrolink	Altram	Apr–97	125
Transport	Midland Metro Line One	Altram	before 3/97	145
Transport	Northern Line Trains		(10)12/98	400
Transport	Oceanic Flight Data Processing System (OFDPS)		before 2/98	30
Transport	Prestige Ticketing – London Underground	Transys	Aug–98	197
Transport	Second Severn Crossing		1995	330
Transport	Tranche 1: A1(M) Alconbury to Peterborough		before 10/97	128
Transport	Tranche 1: A417/A419 Swindon to Gloucester		before 10/97	49
Transport	Tranche 1: A69 Newcastle to Carlisle		1996	9.4
Transport	Tranche 1: MI–A1 Link Road		before 10/97	214
Transport	Tranche IA. A30/ A35 Exeter to Bere Regis		before 10/97	75.7
Transport	Tranche 1A: A50/ A564 Stoke to Derby Link	UK Highways M40	before 6/97	20.6
Transport	Tranche 1A: M40 Junctions 1–15	Autolink	Oct–96	37.1
Transport	Tranche Al: A19 Dishforth to Tyne Tunnel		1996	29.4
Transport (W)	A55 Road		(1–)4/99 (?)	132
Transport	Bute Avenue, Cardiff	Citylink	Apr–98	120

Source: PFI Report and *Private Finance Quarterly*, Summer 1997, pp. 41–8.

5. Private initiatives in the England and Wales electricity industry

Tanga McDaniel

One difficulty in writing about the electricity supply industry (ESI) is deciding where to begin. Much has been written on the England and Wales market. For example, Surrey (1996) and Green (1998) give in-depth accounts of the industry's history since privatization. In this chapter I focus more on investment decisions and the financing of projects since privatization. An obvious difference between the industry of the 1980s and that of the 1990s is the change in technology mix on the network; today, new plant is more likely to be gas-fired than coal-fired. While this shift may have eventually occurred under public ownership as well, records of the industry's investment plans just prior to privatization indicate that the growth of gas-fired generation would not have begun so early. Moreover, one can estimate from the recent political debates about the rapidity of capacity expansion that the growth of gas-fired generation would have occurred more slowly in a nationalized industry.

To date, liberalization in the ESI of England and Wales has led to few public–private collaborations, as much of the new investment has arisen from independent power producers (IPPs). This is partly a consequence of the availability of a relatively low-cost generation option (i.e., combined cycle gas turbines or CCGTs) combined with an environment of surplus capacity. In the future, political objectives such as maintaining a diverse technological mix on the network[1] or the need to meet stringent environmental obligations may boost the appeal of public-sector cooperation with private industry.

In the next section I describe some of the investment and planning decisions undertaken by the nationalized electricity industry under the Central Electricity Generating Board (CEGB). The subsequent section looks at changes in the generation sector since privatization and the types of generators that have emerged. This is followed by a short discussion of recent legislative events that have been affecting the industry since 1998.

THE NATIONALIZED INDUSTRY

Investment

Between 1948 and 1990, decisions relating to generation and transmission in England and Wales were the obligation of the vertically integrated CEGB. The duties of the board are described in the 1957 Electricity Act as follows:

> ... to develop and maintain an efficient, coordinated and economical system of supply of electricity in bulk for all parts of England and Wales. For that purpose they are enjoined to generate or acquire supplies of electricity and provide bulk supplies to [supply companies] (Select Committee Report on Nationalised Industries, p. 11).

In the early 1960s, the CEGB's capital investment amounted to approximately 5 percent of the nation's total. The board was pouring large amounts of money into the industry's infrastructure, though not always prudently, and investment decisions were often closely linked to the political agenda. Irrespective of the perceived autonomy of public companies, the hand of government is neither invisible nor soft, and politically salient issues often take precedence over sound economics and best practice in management.

At the time of nationalization in 1948 the generation assets of the industry totalled 11,680 MW (gross capability). Plant capacity steadily increased throughout the following decades, reaching a high of 62,523 MW in 1975. However, for some time after WWII the industry was plagued with systematic underestimations of demand growth, particularly for the domestic sector. Consumption for domestic consumers was predicted to increase approximately 57 percent between 1957 and 1965, but by 1961 the increase was already 64 percent. Table 5.1 shows the magnitude of the underestimation problem throughout this period.

It was also during this time that economies of scale for larger power stations were being recognized. Whereas generation units in 1947 were limited to 60 MW,[2] technological advancements led to approval of 500 MW units by 1960. For manufacturers, three specific problems led to serious construction backlogs. The first relates to the timing between the testing and ordering of successive capacity increases; instead of a policy whereby a generator of, say, 120 MW was perfected and tested before orders were given for 200 MW sets, the CEGB placed successive orders before the previous, smaller stations had been tested. Such developments challenged manufacturers. Second, essential components such as boilermakers and turbogenerators were being produced by a myriad of companies, thereby increasing the occurrence of design flaws. Third, following the realization of demand forecast inaccuracies, plant orders along with their unit

Table 5.1   Estimated and actual demand for electricity (1958–63)

Year	Estimated Demand (MW)	Actual Demand (MW)
1958–59	20,800	21,000
1959–60	22,200	22,900
1960–61	23,500	25,000
1961–62	25,000	27,200
1962–63	26,400	29,600
1963–64	27,900	29,800
1964–65	29,500	31,400

Source: Reproduced from paragraph 95 of the *Report from the Select Committee on Nationalised Industries: The Electricity Supply Industry*, vol. 1 (1963, Her Majesty's Stationery Office, London) and supplemented from *Handbook of Electricity Supply Statistics* (1968) for the last two years' actual demand.

sizes were increased in 1959. In a committee report on the CEGB's commissioning delays, the Minister of Power summarizes the situation as follows:

New boiler designs depend largely upon empirical correlations and extrapolation of existing design data to larger sizes and more exacting steam conditions. In retrospect, the extrapolations were in many cases found to be unsatisfactory, and the situation was exacerbated by the shortage of good designers, who were spread too thinly over too many firms, and furthermore the productive capacity of the industry was violently overstretched (*Report of the Committee of Enquiry into Delays in Commissioning CEGB Power Stations*, Cmnd. 3960, 1969, p. 16, Her Majesty's Stationery Office, London).

The CEGB's purchasing strategies increased the onus on manufacturers, and in subsequent years the ESI struggled with various forecasting techniques that integrated estimates from the Electricity Council, the CEGB and the area boards. The direction of demand estimation error reversed in the 1970s, and this resulted in a capacity surplus that still exists. 'The CEGB's plant margin ... rose from 21 per cent in 1970–71 to 42 percent in the period 1973–76' (Chesshire 1996, p. 27). The surplus was aggravated by sequential increases in the CEGB's planning margins and the government's aggressive intentions to substantially augment existing nuclear capability.

The British experience with nuclear generation is well documented, so I will give only a brief account of it here.[3] Although the CEGB was in favor of expanding nuclear capacity significantly, defending such a hugely expensive program might have been more difficult were it not for the Conservative

Government's own enthusiasm for the nuclear program as well as its hopes for reducing the nation's dependence on the National Coal Board.[4]

The nuclear program consisted of two distinct phases, the first of which began in 1955 with the commissioning of Magnox reactors. Throughout the following five years, the size of the program and anticipated date of completion were often modified. The ten-year plan in 1955 called for completion of 1.5–2 GW of nuclear capacity. This number went as high as 6 GW in 1957 before being scaled back to 5 GW in 1960. The first Magnox stations were completed at Berkeley and Bradwell in 1962. The last station at Wylfa was not commissioned until 1971 — five years after the adjusted target date announced in 1960. Total capacity for the Magnox program reached approximately 4.8 GW.

The government's target for 8,000 MW by 1975 under the second nuclear program was also not met. In this case, the industry's financial outlays were significantly increased because of the insistence on using the latest British technology. In the mid-1960s several prototypes became available internationally, including a heavy-water reactor in Canada, two light-water reactors in the US, and the advanced gas-cooled reactor (AGR) in the UK. The CEGB chose the AGR design for the first station envisioned under the new program. In the event, the winning company's bid price was not achievable, and the government's exhortation that the new AGRs would produce power at costs significantly below the US alternative was 'founded on speculations from a year's operating experience of the pilot project [the prototype at Windscale in Cumbria], then scaling up size by a factor of twenty, increasing the operating temperature by more than 100°C, and increasing the circuit pressure by two thirds' (Henney 1994, p. 131).[5] Using 1985 prices, Green (1995) estimated that the Magnox stations were £9.7 billion more expensive than the cost for building 4.5 GW of coal-fired stations instead. Henderson (1977) produced a 'mid-term' cost–benefit analysis of the AGR program had the CEGB chosen a light-water reactor instead. His estimates suggested a loss from the AGR program of £2.1 billion (in 1975 prices). A straight summation of these figures would suggest a joint loss of £16.1 billion in 1985 prices, given the alternatives.

Government involvement in the industry, particularly with policies such as 'Buy-British', affected capital investment costs in other ways, as can be seen in the heavy electrical industry. The special relationship between the ESI and the heavy electrical industry was aided by the sheer size of the ESI along with the immensity and consistency of power demand. That is, the ESI relied on the availability of building materials to ensure security of supply, but because of the magnitude of its demand the electricity industry could be expected to receive priority over smaller customers. Additionally, the specificity of designs and the need for research into design improvements provided an incentive for close liaisons between the two industries. A downside of this association was that the CEGB was required to spread its orders over all of the heavy electrical companies. This lack of competitive bidding for projects gave little encouragement for cost-minimization, and because use of the import market for capital supplies was frowned upon, the CEGB could not benefit from lower international prices or competing technologies. Later, the international mergers and more liberal trade policies occurring outside of Britain necessitated movement away from such strict nationalistic buying policies: '[t]he whole ethic of the new industry was based around market forces, and any process of supplier choice which did not involve open bidding would have been unthinkable' (Thomas 1996, p. 273).

Another constraint on the CEGB was governmental supervision of its finances.[6] The board was charged with maintaining an efficient supply of electricity, but expenditure plans had to meet government approval. The board was limited in what it could borrow, and increases in borrowing limits required parliamentary legislation. Beginning in the mid-1950s there was a shift in thinking about the objectives of the electricity industry. Seeds of the idea that the industry should operate 'commercially' were planted, but were slow to take root. Two white papers in 1961 and 1967 show this change in thinking. In 1961, the obligation of meeting costs year by year (without specific penalties for losses) was replaced with a more forward-looking strategy whereby balance was to be achieved over five-year periods. Furthermore, companies began to partially fund their investments through retained profits.

The 1967 paper went a bit further in increasing commercial objectives: by raising the required rate of return on investment projects to 8 percent, 'a figure broadly consistent in real terms with the average return on low-risk projects in the private sector of industry at the time' (Tivey 1973, p. 188), by discouraging cross-subsidization, and by drawing attention to the desirability of long-run marginal-cost pricing. Nevertheless, it was stressed that the industry had non-economic objectives as well, and even the economic objectives were under the influence of government direction.

Independent Generation

Some use was made of private generation in the nationalized era, but very little of this was supplied to the grid. A 1956 government report examining the ESI recommended that the installation of private generation be left to the discretion of industrialists and that arrangements between area boards and industrialists for negotiated use of private supply be allowed without approval from the CEGB.[7] Still, the amount of production from private sources was small (see Figure 5.1). Moreover

... the number of industrialists who could justify generating for themselves was thought to be falling because of the improved economics of modern plant. On the other hand,

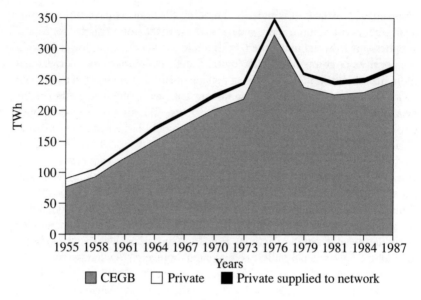

Source: Handbook of Electricity Supply Statistics (1966–1988).

Figure 5.1　Public and private generation, 1955–87

at least one Area Board considered that unless the prices they quoted were as tight as they could possibly manage, large industrial consumers might decide to generate for themselves (1956 Select Committee, p. 359).

THE PRIVATIZED INDUSTRY

New Entrants

A look at some of the earliest stations built post-privatization illustrates the speed with which private enterprise was able to advance new projects. Henney (1994) gives a brief synopsis of the planning and construction time lines for several of the earliest CCGT stations. Two examples include the Roosecote project – planned and constructed in just three years, with actual construction time being less than two years – and Teesside. The time between planning and commissioning of Teesside was just over four years, with construction taking less than three. The momentum of these projects was aided by circumstances that made financing easier. Because the industry environment of the time was amenable to long-term power purchase agreements and fuel contracts, new entrants faced few commercial risks. As Henney discusses, Lakeland Power, the owners of Roosecote, arranged power purchase agreements with one of the supply companies and much of its financing with the Swiss Bank Corporation, all before the industry was privatized.

Like most independent power schemes, many of these new stations were undertaken on a project finance basis by project companies or through joint ventures. The ownership and equity interests for several of the newer stations are shown in Table 5.2 in the Appendix. Joint ventures include (1) Seabank, owned by Seabank Power Ltd., a joint venture between Scottish Hydro-Electric PLC[8] and British Gas PLC, (2) Fellside Heat and Power, a joint venture between Scottish Hydro-Electric PLC and publicly owned British Nuclear Fuels PLC,[9] and (3) SELCHP, another public/private venture. In contrast, Corby illustrates ownership by an independent private generation company.

The merits of project financing can be found in, for example, Finnerty (1996) and Daniel (1997). The advantage to developers is their limited financial exposure; i.e., debt is serviced by the cash flow generated by the project, and risks are usually shared with equity partners. There is the associated disadvantage that project financing can take longer to secure than traditional corporate financing, as the lender must be satisfied that sales risks have been sufficiently mitigated and that the expected revenue is adequate to cover the debt.

Two features of the industry environment post-privatization helped to make project financing attractive and to speed the entry of new players. First, at the time of privatization (1990) the regional electricity companies (RECs) were given monopoly rights over supply to the domestic and small-business customers in their respective areas for a period of eight years. The regulated tariff for these 'franchise' customers included the cost of generation, which the RECs were permitted to pass on in full. New generators were therefore able to negotiate long-term contracts with suppliers and satisfy lenders that the market for their output was secure. Second, their supply licences allowed RECs to own generation assets totalling a specified fraction of their total demand. The licence originally limited this fraction to approximately 15 percent, but the regulator allowed more flexibility beginning in 1995. By 1994 eleven of the twelve RECs had signed long-term contracts with an IPP to build nearly 5 GW of CCGTs. As fuel sources were typically obtained on the basis of take-or-pay contracts, fuel suppliers also faced little risk.[10]

Legislative Influence on Entry

Uncertain legislative activity can create obstacles to entry in an industry experimenting with liberalization. Political risks can involve huge uncertainties, such as the potential for outright expropriation or re-nationalization, but may also include more subtle risks such as ever-changing or unpredictable policies on energy issues:

> ... in 1996 the Belgian power company Tractebel stated that it was no longer looking to invest in the UK because of the risks resulting from inconsistencies and uncertainties in the government's policy towards the electricity industry (Daniel 1997, p. 49).

The electricity industry was privatized under a Conservative Government, and while the threat of re-nationalization may have been a perceived possibility at the time of the Labour Government's election in May 1997, it was nonetheless not very likely. Long before the election Labour had claimed that it was concerned about the regulation of the industry, but was not interested in making radical alterations. Nonetheless, two related events demonstrate how the electricity industry is captive to unpredictable politics. The first concerns the way electricity is traded and generators are paid; the second concerns applications for new generation projects.

A fundamental question for restructuring an ESI is how to design trading arrangements that are consistent with competitive markets. This is not a trivial problem, and the choice will affect entry decisions along with incentives for innovation and investment. After privatization and until March 2001, output in England and Wales was traded through a power pool, with dispatched generators all receiving the system marginal price. Complaints over various aspects of the pool, including the ability of major generators to manipulate their bids to increase payments, led to a review of trading arrangements beginning in October 1997. Proposals for new electricity trading arrangements (NETA) resulted from this review, and these were originally scheduled to take effect in November 2000 (see Office of Gas and Electricity Markets 1999). The new rules, which in fact began 27 March 2001, replaced the pool with bilateral contract markets, a balancing mechanism, and pay-your-bid remuneration.

The new trading arrangements will have different consequences for different market players,[11] and one can guess that the 'success' of the new rules will depend on the emergence (or not) of liquid contract markets and price reporters. For many existing generators, the elimination of the pool means that their power purchase agreements will have to be renegotiated since these contracts often referenced the pool price. For consumers, the benefits will depend on the bargaining power of suppliers relative to generators – a bleak situation if the new trading arrangements discourage entry. Unfortunately, the new rules do not purport to mitigate the problem that plagued the old system so badly, namely, the potential to abuse market power.

Another important political manoeuvre in December 1997 was the result of the government's review of energy sources for power generation. This review was initiated under the assumption that distortions in the electricity industry were threatening the diversity and security of long-term energy supplies. The concern was that the rate of entry of CCGT stations and the consequent change in proportion of power derived from gas relative to coal were likely to put stress on the nation's long-term supply of natural gas and lead to an undesirable and premature decline of the coal industry. Thus, during the period of the review the government decided to suspend consents on gas-fired generation schemes. The conclusions of the review were presented in October 1998 and the moratorium was removed only in November 2000.[12]

Together, the new trading arrangements and the short-term moratorium on gas-fired generation have affected market entry not only because gas has been the preferred fuel choice for new projects since privatization, but also because of the uncertainty surrounding the impact of NETA on small generators.

Government's Role in the Privatized ESI

Today, government's investment role in the electricity supply industry of England and Wales is seen mostly in nuclear and renewable generation. Although plans to increase nuclear capacity were dropped in 1995, there is still the large expenditure of decommissioning and managing radioactive wastes, and these activities receive government funding. The Department of Trade and Industry also funds research into nuclear fusion.

Regarding renewable generation, a growing concern is that private companies with strong competitive pressures will not have sufficient incentives to invest in environmentally friendly technology. Like most industrialized countries, the UK faces tight constraints on greenhouse gas emissions from international as well as domestic targets. The UK's obligation to the Kyoto Protocol involves a reduction of greenhouse gas emissions by 12.5 percent relative to 1990 levels by 2010. Domestically, the 1997 Labour Party Manifesto pledged a 20 percent reduction in CO_2 from 1990 levels over the same period. Investment in CCGTs has been mostly a 'commercial' phenomenon but has had the positive side effect of lowering the UK's greenhouse gas emissions. Still, natural gas is a significant contributor to CO_2 emissions, and many technologies with lower CO_2 emissions are unattractive on a cost/kWh basis. Thus, the incentive for investments by private companies in large-scale renewable projects is low. Hydro-intensive countries (e.g., Norway) face a smaller burden from environmental obligations, but only a handful of countries fall into this category.

Most renewable projects in the UK have been funded under the government's New and Renewable Energy Programme. The tariff paid by most customers contains a fossil fuel levy that goes to support the obligation of electricity suppliers (under the non-fossil fuel obligation or NFFO) to purchase some of their energy requirements from nuclear and renewable sources. Thus, suppliers have been willing to contract for this power at non-competitive prices since they are reimbursed for the surplus expenditure through the higher tariffs. The name of the program is a bit misleading, however, because until 1998 the levy's primary use was to fund decommissioning costs in the nuclear industry. The current rate of the levy is 0.3 percent, a significant reduction from its initial rate of 10 percent. Today, the levy no longer subsidizes nuclear generation and is used solely as a support for renewables.

Mitchell (1996) discusses renewable energy and compares spending for projects in the private versus public eras of the ESI. One difference is the type of projects sponsored by the government versus the private sector. In practice, the money spent for renewables under the CEGB was primarily for R&D, and many technologies that received funding were subsequently deemed unpromising, the best such example probably being wave power. According to Mitchell, wave power received 60 percent of the renewables budget in 1978 but only 10 percent in 1991. It was essentially dropped from the budget in subsequent years. The story for geothermal power is similar. The largest number of NFFO projects contracted since privatization, typically small-scale, have been for wind, landfill gas and hydropower. For some technologies such as municipal waste a smaller number of proposals have been contracted, but these are usually higher capacity projects. Table 5.3 in the Appendix shows the capacities, total number, and the average costs of the five NFFO orders. In 1998, 211 NFFO projects were in operation (Department of Trade and Industry 1998a). The fifth NFFO order will run until 2018 (Department of Trade and Industry 1998a, p. 164). Including hydro, renewables accounted for approximately 2 percent of generation in 1997.

It is appropriate to ask whether renewables can survive without subsidies in a competitive market. Once the NFFO is phased out, renewable projects will have to compete on their own merits. Projects commissioned under the last four NFFO orders were submitted on a competitive basis, a procedure initiated with the hope of eventually driving the cost of renewable projects down to the level of conventional generation. While the costs of these projects have fallen over the course of the successive investments, the cost per kWh is too high to make them attractive on their own. The average cost of projects under the third, fourth and fifth NFFO orders were 4.35 p/kWh, 3.46 p/kWh, and 2.71 p/kWh, respectively (Department of Trade and Industry 1998a, p. 164). This compares to approximately 1.6 p/kWh for existing coal plant (not retro-fitted with flu gas desulfurization) and 2 p/kWh for new CCGT stations.[13]

Nevertheless, suppliers campaigning under the green banner have been effective at picking up customers who are willing to pay a premium to foster environmentally friendly technologies. In many ways support for green energy is like a public good that people are willing to pay for even when it is not individually rational to do so. The Environmental Defense Fund in the US reports prices for green options in California. In March 2000, the premium over standard service for most of the companies was between 5 and 22 percent, although several companies were advertising savings.[14]

New Breeds of Market Players

Energy markets and general economic activity are highly interdependent. Throughout most of the twentieth century electricity played a crucial role in enhancing productivity and growth, and this importance continues. Based on forecasts of world GDP and population growth, estimates of the increase in electricity demand tend to be approximately 3 percent a year through 2010. Including replacements, this implies an annual need for new capacity of about 110 GW (Daniel 1997). Demand growth and a changing industry environment hint at an increasing role for IPPs as well as for new and diverse financing options over the next decade.

The monopoly franchises in England and Wales ended June 1999, and so the supply of captive customers no longer exists. A captive consumer base meant lower financial risks, and this was a feature of the industry that aided new entry in the past. Future projects will require different methods of risk sharing. Attractive alternatives may include merchant operations or tolling agreements whereby generators are paid a fee for units of electricity produced.

Merchant plants are typically not supported by long-term contracts and may supply customers directly or have power purchase agreements with, say, power marketers. New project applications for merchant stations have been submitted in England and Wales, and some of these will come on line over the next few years. AES Electric is in the process of completing a project-financed coal station in South Wales that should be commissioned in 2000/01. Likewise, BP Amoco and Arco are the joint owners of a 350 MW CCGT station in Great Yarmouth, England, which is due to be commissioned in 2001.

NETA may affect the commercial viability of merchant operations, but views on this subject are mixed. On the one hand, the fact that many incumbents are facing costly renegotiation of long-term power purchase agreements that are indexed to the pool price should give advantage to generators who are not likewise encumbered. Moreover, because merchant operations are in principle 'efficient, low cost generators that will be constructed on the theory that they will thrive in the wholesale and retail market without the artificial under-pinning of long-term contracts, but on the basis of being truly market competitive',[15] an environment founded on bilateral contracting markets sounds like one in which merchants should thrive. On the other hand, depending on the liquidity of the short-term contracting markets, financing for new merchant operations will be more difficult as there is no longer a guaranteed reference price for which they can sell their output. However, this problem may be mitigated by the emergence of price reporters and market aggregators. There is the additional issue of market distortions that will affect competition and the ease of entry (e.g., proposed CCGT merchant projects by AES Electric, British Energy, and the Southern Company were affected by the gas moratorium).

CONCLUSIONS

A perceived problem of privatization in capital-intensive industries like electricity supply is the lack of incentives for investment. In England and Wales a large investment program took place after the industry was nationalized following WWII. Early problems resulted from rapidly changing technology, a thinly stretched manufacturing industry, and increased orders to remedy previous underestimates in demand growth. Later, expensive dilemmas arose in the development of the nuclear program. With hindsight one can say that much of the investment program of the nationalized industry lacked economic justification and was heavily swayed by the political agenda.

Privatization and liberalization have led most notably to a distinct change in the generation mix on the network. Between 1992 and 1999, the amount of CCGT capacity increased from 3 GW to 18.6 GW while coal declined from 37.4 GW to 23.2 GW. The industry has gained at least some freedom from government intervention, but recent policies such as the moratorium on new gas-fired generation show that the increased freedom is in the guise of a longer leash rather than a severed rope.

The existence for some time of a franchise market for suppliers and the swift expansion of CCGT technology have helped to keep generation capacity at a surplus since privatization. Furthermore, because investment expenditure now comes out of shareholder pockets, government has been more heavy-handed on environmental regulation, and R&D expenditure in this area has improved.

Since June 1999 the franchise market in England and Wales has been abolished. Such liberalization creates new challenges for investment financing, as a captive consumer base no longer exists. In competitive markets without distortions and where long-term contracts are unattractive, one expects more independent generators to turn to risk-minimizing options such as merchant or tolling arrangements. In any case, smaller (modular) generation stations built close to demand are likely to be favored over larger, more expensive stations.

ACKNOWLEDGMENTS

The author wishes to thank Michael Pollitt for useful comments and the Institute for Developing Economies, Japan, for sponsoring research. Support from the ESRC under project R000236828 is gratefully acknowledged.

ENDNOTES

1. The latest government policy in this respect is discussed in White Paper, Department of Trade and Industry (1998b), Cmnd. 4071.
2. The temporary size limitation was caused by the shortage of building materials following WWII.
3. See, for example, Williams (1980), Green and Newbery (1996), and MacKerron (1996).
4. The Conservative Government was not sympathetic to the coal industry in the same way Labour has often been; instead, the government understood the degree to which its buy-British policies left the nation captive to the Coal Board.
5. The last station commissioned under the nuclear program was a pressurized water reactor at Sizewell in Suffolk in 1995.
6. See Tivey (1973) for a broader discussion.
7. The Herbert Report (*Report of the Committee of Inquiry into the Electricity Supply Industry*, Cmnd. 6388, 1956, London: Her Majesty's Stationery Office).
8. PLCs (public limited companies) are characterized by limited liability for the owners, and company shares are publicly traded.
9. British Nuclear Fuel PLC is currently a candidate for privatization.
10. A take-or-pay contract requires the buyer to pay for the fuel irrespective of whether the fuel is used.
11. After less than a month of operation it could be seen that the new rules are not beneficial for renewables whose output may be unpredictable. Bathurst and Strbac (2001) illustrate the losses for a wind farm during the first week of the new electricity trading arrangements.
12. Department of Trade and Industry (1998b), Cmnd. 4071.
13. Department of Trade and Industry (1998b), Cmnd. 4071, p. 7.
14. The Environmental Defense Fund, www.edf.org/programs/Energy/greenpower.
15. 'End-User Benefits from Merchant Plant Development', *Strategic Energy Ltd. Energy Watch Newsletters* (3 January 1998), www.sel.com.

REFERENCES

Bathurst, Graeme and Goran Strbac (2001), 'The value of intermittent renewable sources in the first week of NETA', Tyndall Centre for Climate Change Research Briefing Note No. 2, 3 April 2001.

Chesshire, John (1996), 'UK electricity supply under public ownership', in John Surrey (ed.), *The British Electricity Experiment, Privatization: The Record, the Issues, the Lessons*, London: Earthscan Publications.

Daniel, Martin (1997), *Global Private Power Generation: Risks and Opportunities*, London: Financial Times Energy.

Department of Trade and Industry (1998a), *The Energy Report: Transforming Markets*, vol. 1, London: Her Majesty's Stationery Office.

Department of Trade and Industry (1998b), 'Conclusions of the Review of Energy Sources for Power Generation and Government Response to the Fourth and Fifth Reports of the Trade and Industry Committee', CM 4071, London: Her Majesty's Stationery Office.

Department of Trade and Industry (1999), *Digest of UK Energy Statistics*, London: Her Majesty's Stationery Office.

Finnerty, John D. (1996), *Project Financing: Asset Based Financial Engineering*, New York: John Wiley and Sons.

Green, Richard (1995), 'The cost of nuclear power compared with alternatives to the Magnox Programme', *Oxford Economic Papers*, 47, 513–25.

Green, Richard (1998), 'Electricity deregulation in England and Wales', in Georges Zaccour (ed.), *Deregulation of Electric Utilities*, Boston: Kluwer.

Green, Richard and David Newbery (1996), 'Regulation, public ownership and privatisation of the English electricity industry', in Richard Gilbert and Edward Kahn (eds), *International Comparisons of Electricity Regulation*, Cambridge, UK: Cambridge University Press.

Handbook of Electricity Supply Statistics (1966–1988), London: The Electricity Council.

Henderson, P.D. (1977), 'Two British errors: Their probable size and some possible lessons', *Oxford Economic Papers*, 29, 159–205.

Henney, Alex (1994), *A Study of the Privatisation of the Electricity Supply Industry in England and Wales*, London: EEE Limited.

MacKerron, Gordon (1996), 'Nuclear power under review', in John Surrey (ed.), *The British Electricity Experiment, Privatization: The Record, the Issues, the Lessons*, London: Earthscan Publications.

Mitchell, Catherine (1996), 'Renewable generation – Success story?', in John Surrey (ed.), *The British Electricity Experiment, Privatization: The Record, the Issues, the Lessons*, London: Earthscan Publications.

Monopolies and Mergers Commission (1996), *National Power plc and Southern Electric plc: A Report on the Proposed Merger*, London: Her Majesty's Stationery Office.

National Grid Company, *Seven Year Statement*, Coventry, UK.

Office of Gas and Electricity Markets (1999), *The New Electricity Trading Arrangements*, London: OFGEM.

Surrey, John (ed.) (1996), *The British Electricity Experiment, Privatization: The Record, the Issues, the Lessons*, London: Earthscan Publications.

Thomas, Steve (1996), 'Strategic government and corporate issues', in John Surrey (ed.), *The British Electricity Experiment, Privatization: The Record, the Issues, the Lessons*, London: Earthscan Publications.

Tivey, Leonard (1973), *Nationalization in British Industry*, Suffolk, UK: Chaucer Press.

Treasury (1961), *The Financial and Economic Obligations of the Nationalised Industries*, Cmnd 1337, London: Her Majesty's Stationery Office.

Treasury (1967), *Nationalised Industries: A Review of Economic and Financial Objectives*, Cmnd 3437, London: Her Majesty's Stationery Office.

Williams, Roger (1980), *The Nuclear Power Decisions*, London: Croom Helm.

APPENDIX

Table 5.2 Private generation projects in England and Wales

Power Station	Commission Date	Size (MW)	Cost (£ million)	Ownership	Power purchase*
Barking CCGT	1995	915	650	Scottish and Southern Energy (22.05%) London Electricity (13.475%) Eastern Group (13.475%) Thames Power Ltd (51%)	Long term PPA**
Brigg CCGT	1994	240	100	Yorkshire (75%), IVO (25%)	Long term PPA
Corby CCGT	1994	350	200	East Midlands Electricity (40%) ESB (Ireland) (20%) Hawker Siddeley (40%)	Long term PPA
Derwent CCGT/CHP	1995	214	150	Scottish and Southern Energy (49.5%) Edison Mission Energy (33%) Courtaulds Chemicals (17.5%)	Long term PPA
Fellside Heat and Power (located next to BNFL's Sellafield site)	1995	168	100	Scottish and Southern Energy and British Nuclear Fuels plc.	Long term PPA
Humber Power Bank Power Station CCGT	phase1: 1996 phase2: 1998	750	400	Owned by Humber Power Ltd. Shareholders: IVO Energy, Midlands Electricity, Tomen Corporation, ABB, British Energy, and Elf Aquitaine	Module 1: CfDs with shareholders Module 2: tolling contract with Elf Exploration UK Ltd
MEDWAY CCGT	1996	660	370	Scottish and Southern Energy (37.5%) Seeboard (37.5%) AES (25%)	50/50 to Seeboard and Southern Electric under 15 year contracts for differences
Peterborough CCGT	1994	360	200	Eastern (100%)	Long term PPA (Eastern)

115

Table 5.2 continued

Power Station	Commission Date	Size (MW)	Cost (£ million)	Ownership	Power purchase*
Roosecote (Lakeland Power) CCGT	1991	224	–	Mission Energy (60%) NORWEB (20%) Other (20%)	Offtake contract with Norweb
Rocksavage Power Station CCGT	1998	760	575	Owned by Rocksavage Power Company Ltd	Long term contracts to ICI's Runcorn chemical works and Scottish Hydro-Electric plc.
Seabank Power Station CCGT	1998	755	435	Owned by Seabank Power Ltd, a joint venture between Scottish and Southern Energy (50%) and British Gas (50%)	Long term contract with Scottish and Southern Electricity
South East London Combined Heat and Power (SELCHP) CHP	1993	32	100	A private/public joint venture. Shareholders: Onyx Aurora, Martin Engineering Systems Ltd, London Power Company Ltd (subsidiary of London Electricity), the London Boroughs of Lewisham and Greenwich, Raab Karcher Energy Services Ltd, and the Laing Technology Group Ltd	Long term contract with London Electricity
Teesside CCGT	1993	1875	850	Enron (50%) MEB (19.2%) Northern (15.4%) SWALEC (7.7%) SWEB (7.7%)	Long term PPA

Notes: MEB, Eastern, Southern Electric, Northern Electric, NORWEB, SWEB, SEEBOARD, SWALEC, Yorkshire, East Midlands, London, and MANWEB are the twelve regional electricity companies in England and Wales. IVO is an agent of Imatran Voima Oy (Finland) and Tomen Power Corporation Limited (UK).

*   These contracts are 'pre-NETA.'

** Power Purchase Agreement.

Sources: Electricity Supply Handbook (published annually by Reed Business Information, Surrey, UK); Monopolies and Mergers Commission (1996), Platts at http://www.platts.com, *Power Markets Week Europe,* National Grid Company *Seven Year Statement* (1992 and 1999) and *PowerUK,* issues 56, 67 and 68, published by Financial Times Business Enterprise, London.

Table 5.3   Renewable generation contracted under the NFFO orders

	NFFO-1		NFFO-2		NFFO-3		NFFO-4		NFFO-5	
	Number	MW	Number	MW	Number	MW	Number	MW	Number	MW
Average project cost (p/kWh)					4.35		3.46		2.71	
Hydro	26	11.85	12	10.86	15	14.48	31	13.22	22	13.22
Landfill gas	25	35.5	28	48.45	42	82.07	70	173.68	313.73	
Municipal and industrial waste	4	40.63	10	271.48	20	241.87	16*	241.22	29	485.72*
Other	4	45.48	4	30.15						
Sewage gas	7	6.45	19	26.86						
Wind-large					31	145.92	48	330.36	33	340.16
Wind-small					24	19.71	17	10.33	36	28.68
Wind-total	9	12.21	49	84.43	55	165.63	65	340.69	69	368.84
Energy crops and agriculture & forestry waste-gasification					3	19.06	7	67.34		
Energy crops and agriculture & forestry waste-other					6	103.81	6	6.58		
Total	75	152.12	122	472.33	141	626.92	195	842.73	266	1177.15

*Note:** Includes CHP and fluidized bed combustion.

Source: Department of Trade and Industry, DUKES 1999, and The Energy Report, 1998.

6. Private financing initiatives in India's telecommunications sector

Sunil Mani

India has one of the lowest teledensities, even within the developing world (Table 6.1). Mani (2000) identified the proximate cause of this as very low investment by the state-owned monopoly provider, namely the Department of Telecommunications (DoT).

This picture of India's telecom sector does not adequately portray improvements in the sector since reforms began toward the middle of the 1990s. The number of working lines has increased dramatically (Figure 6.1), and there has been a significant reduction in the waiting list.[1] The figure also shows that the registered demand (though an underestimate of sorts) has increased about 16 percent per annum. This was also a time when India's telecom sector in the country was undergoing major changes with deregulation and the introduction of private-sector participation. I survey these changes in this chapter and present the current structure of the industry. In the first section, I summarize changes in telecom policy since 1994, focusing on the National Telecom Policy of 1994 and the New Telecom Policy of 1999. I then map the structure of the basic telecom and value-added services in the second section and focus on telecom regulation problems in the third section.

CHANGES IN TELECOM POLICY

Changing government policy with respect to the sector is outlined in Figure 6.2. Major deregulation of the sector took place only in the 1990s.

The formal articulation of India's telecom deregulation was announced in the National Telecom Policy of 1994, the first ever policy statement with respect to the telecom sector, although deregulation of the sector had begun in 1984 when the equipment-manufacturing sector was partially deregulated. The subsequent major milestone was the corporatization of the telecom distribution in Delhi and Bombay and the overseas communication wing of the DoT. Corporatization generally involved separating operations (financial accounting)

Table 6.1 Comparison of main features of India's telecom sector with others, 1998

Country	Teledensity (per 1,000 people)		Waiting list		Revenue in $		Cost of calls ($ per 3 minutes)	
	Fixed	Mobile	Number in thousands of lines	Time in years	Per employee	Per line	Local	International (to the US)
China	70	19	812	0.1	197	235	0.01	6.66
India	22	1	2,695.7	1.0	50	284	0.02	5.45
Philippines	37	22	900.2	2.8	132	584	—	4.96
Malaysia	198	9	160	0.4	162	569	0.02	3.82
Thailand	84	32	556.3	1.1	144	322	0.07	3.58

Source: Group on Telecommunications (1999) and World Bank (2000).

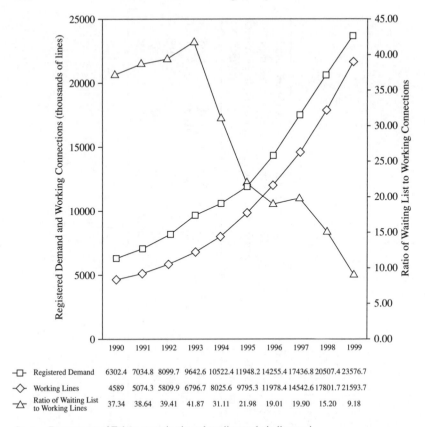

	1990	1991	1992	1993	1994	1995	1996	1997	1998	1999
Registered Demand	6302.4	7034.8	8099.7	9642.6	10522.4	11948.2	14255.4	17436.8	20507.4	23576.7
Working Lines	4589	5074.3	5809.9	6796.7	8025.6	9795.3	11978.4	14542.6	17801.7	21593.7
Ratio of Waiting List to Working Lines	37.34	38.64	39.41	41.87	31.11	21.98	19.01	19.90	15.20	9.18

Source: Department of Telecommunications, http://www.dotindia.com/.

Figure 6.1   Telephone demand, waiting list and working connections, 1990–99

from public-policy implementation. Table 6.2 summarizes the changing government policy with respect to the telecom sector. As can be seen, deregulation of the sector proceeded in small doses and an unstructured manner. For example, it was only in October 2000 that the government decided to corporatize the Department of Telecom Services (DTS) and reduce the monopoly power of this service provider.

The National Telecom Policy of 1994

The basic objective of this first-ever public telecom policy in India was to improve the quality of services to world-class levels. Specific objectives were to ensure the availability of telephone on demand by 1997, to achieve universal service at affordable prices in all rural areas by 1997, and to plan for India's

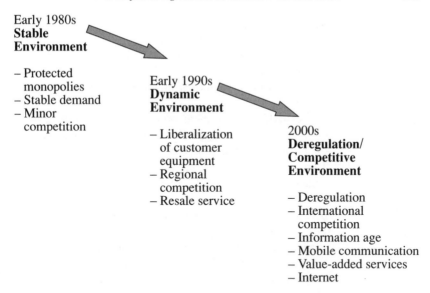

Early 1980s
Stable Environment

– Protected
  monopolies
– Stable demand
– Minor
  competition

Early 1990s
Dynamic Environment

– Liberalization
  of customer
  equipment
– Regional
  competition
– Resale service

2000s
Deregulation/ Competitive Environment

– Deregulation
– International
  competition
– Information age
– Mobile communication
– Value-added services
– Internet

Source: Group on Telecommunications (1999).

Figure 6.2   Deregulation of India's telecommunications sector from the 1980s forward

future as a major manufacturer of telecom equipment and a base for exporting to other countries. In urban areas, a Public Call Office (PCO) was to be provided for every 500 persons by 1997, and all value-added services available internationally were to be introduced in India, preferably by 1996.

Given the huge investment required for achieving the above-mentioned targets (according to the National Telecom Policy, about Rs 23 billion of additional resources are required) and given the precarious financial position of the central government, privatization of both basic and value-added services was considered essential. The actual progress of this policy initiative has been anything but satisfactory. The waiting list in 1999 was 1.98 million lines and only about 44 percent of rural villages had a telephone service. However, the density of PCOs, targeted at 1 per 500 persons, is 1 per 580 persons, on average, in urban areas, and a number of value-added services like cellular mobile telephones, paging, e-mail, voice mail, etc. have been introduced.

New Telecom Policy of 1999

Because the National Telecom Policy of 1994 was more or less a failure in achieving its objectives, as Mani (2000) points out, the government came out

Table 6.2　　Changing telecom policy in India

Time of change	Content of change
1984	Manufacturing of subscriber-premises equipment to private sector.
1985	The erstwhile Department of Posts and Telegraphs was bifurcated, and the Department of Telecommunications was established with a separate board.
1986	Two separate corporations called Maha Nagar Telecom Nigam (MTNL) and Videsh Sanchar Nigam (VSNL) were established to distribute telecom services in Delhi and Bombay and overseas calls, respectively.
1988	The government introduces in-dialing scheme. PABX services only within a building or in adjoining buildings.
1989	Establishment of the Telecom Commission.
1991	Telecom equipment manufacturing opened to private sector. Major international players like Alcatel, AT&T, Ericsson, Fujitsu, and Siemens entered equipment-manufacturing market.
1992	Value-added services sector opened to private competition.
1993	Private networks allowed in industrial areas.
1994	Licenses for radio paging (27 cities) issued.
May 1994	Announcement of the National Telecom Policy.
September 1994	Broad guidelines for private-sector entry into basic services announced.
November 1994	Licenses for cellular mobiles for four metros issued.
December 1994	Tenders floated for bids in cellular mobile services in 19 circles (service areas), excluding the four metros, on a duopoly basis.
January 1995	Tenders floated for second operator in basic services on a circle basis.
July 1995	Cellular tender bid opened.
August 1995	Basic service tender bid opened. The bids caused a lot of controversy; a majority of bids were considered low.
December 1995	Letters of intent are issued to some operators for cellular mobile operations in circles.
January 1996	Rebidding for basic services in 13 circles has poor response. The Telecom Regulatory Authority of India (TRAI) formed by ordinance.
October 1996	Letters of intent are issued for basic services.
November 1998	New policy on Internet Service Providers (ISPs) announced.

Table 6.2 continued

Time of change	Content of change
March 1999	New Telecom Policy announced.
March 2000	Telecom Regulatory Authority of India (Amendment) Bill 2000 was passed by the Parliament.
August 2000	Long distance services opened to private operators.
	ISPs allowed to connect directly to submarine cables that land in India.
	Free right of way to lay fiber-optic cable networks along highways and roads.
October 2000	The cap on foreign equity in telecom services raised from 49 percent to 74 percent.
	No limit on the number of players in cellular services, just as for basic phone services, long distance, and Internet services.
	The cabinet approved a proposal to allow foreign direct investment (FDI) of up to 100 percent in ISPs that do not have satellite or submarine landing stations.
	Reduction in basic customs duties for several types of telecom equipment announced.
	Corporatization of the DTS finally approved and a new company called Bharat Sanchar Nigam was to be formed 1 October with a paid-up capital of Rs 50 billion and authorized capital of Rs 100 billion.

Source: Mohan et al. (1996, p. 101), Government of India (1997–98, p. 129), and Economist Intelligence Unit (2000a).

with another policy in 1999. The primary issues that needed to be resolved are summarized in Table 6.3, with a description of recommended steps to be taken. A major issue was the need to create a truly independent regulatory body by strengthening TRAI. Also important was the need to shift from a fixed to a revenue-sharing licensing regime and the need to reallocate frequencies so that private telecommunications companies have the necessary bandwidth to provide services.

After many fanfares, the new policy was announced in March 1999. Table 6.4 lists the important components of this policy.

The best way to assess the policy outlined in Table 6.4 is to consider it in association with the various issues outlined in Table 6.3. The following three points emerge from this exercise. Regarding the effect on the existing service providers in the private sector, the policy may lead to their exit from the industry, as they

Table 6.3   Issues requiring a new telecom policy

Issue	Recommended steps
Strengthen TRAI	Use the new policy to truly empower TRAI and create a level playing field for new entrants.
New licensing structure	Replace fixed regime with revenue-sharing one.
Effective allocation of spectrum	Migration of current government users to frequency bands outside of the 800–900 MHz and 1800–1900 MHz bands that are required by private-sector operators.
Convergence policy	Telecom, Internet and broadcasting require a cohesive policy spanning all areas of communications.
Increased private-sector investment	Increase foreign ownership in telecom joint ventures during a time when operators are facing a shortage of foreign exchange.
Rural telecom development	Address difficulty faced by many newly licensed private operators in meeting their rural installation targets. Address difficulty DoT is facing in rural development because of insufficient funds.
Liberalization of national local and long distance (NLD) and international long distance (ILD) market	Fix deadline for liberalization.
Change deadline for main line services on demand	Fix a more realistic deadline for providing telephone connections on demand, as the 1994 policy to provide telephones on demand by 1997 has not been achieved

Source: Adapted from Pyramid Research (1999a, p. 3).

will not reap the benefits of the new licensing regime based on revenue sharing. They are still required to pay the high fees of the old licensing regime because government had already included the license fees as receivables for the 1999–2000 budgets. The government anticipated resistance on its ruling and sought a ruling from the attorney general to justify its decision. With no reprieve on the license fee issue and the possibility of new entrants competing on fairer terms, existing operators may be forced to cease operation.

Table 6.4   Highlights of the new telecom policy of March 1999

Issue	Policy initiative
Licensing	New cellular and fixed-line operators will pay a license on a revenue-sharing basis and a one-time entry fee. Existing fixed and cellular licensees will not be affected by the new license fee structure. Cellular mobile service providers will be allowed to provide PCOs and data services. A universal access levy will be imposed as a percentage of the revenue earned by all the operators. This will be used to promote rural telephony. The DoT and MTNL will be awarded cellular licenses and will become the third operator in the circles. Entry of a fourth player may be decided on the recommendations of TRAI.
Powers of TRAI	TRAI will have arbitration powers in settling disputes between the government and service providers. TRAI's recommendation will be sought by the government regarding the number and timing of new licenses to be issued in the future. TRAI will not be the licensing body or policymaker. These functions will continue to fall under the jurisdiction of the Ministry of Communications.
Corporatization of DoT	The DoT will be corporatized by 2001. DoT and MTNL will pay a license fee following corporatization. DoT will be reimbursed the amount equivalent to the license fee as a budgetary subsidy for meeting national and social obligations.
Domestic and international long distance services	Domestic long distance market opened to competition from 1 January 2000. The terms of market liberalization were announced by 15 August 1999 after consultation with TRAI. The existing network of companies such as the Railways, Gas Authority of India Ltd., and the Oil and Natural Gas Commission may be used commercially for long distance data communications from 1 January 2000.
Miscellaneous issues	The Wireless Planning Coordination Committee will be set up as part of the Communications Ministry to review spectrum allocation and management. Cable service providers will be permitted to provide two-way voice and data communication services after obtaining a license for fixed telecom services. The use of Ku-band satellite communications for long distance data transmission will be permitted. Voice-over Internet will not be allowed.

Source: Adapted from Pyramid Research (1999b, p. 15).

Regarding the status of TRAI and telecom regulation, this is not likely to change significantly given that the new policy relegates TRAI to being nothing more than an 'arbitrator of disputes' able to make 'recommendations' only. Under the new policy, licensing and policymaking come under the jurisdiction of the Ministry of Communications. It is therefore unlikely that TRAI will have a say in tariff and interconnect policy matters as stated under the TRAI Act.

The major beneficiary of the new policy is the DoT itself. Although it is required to pay a license fee upon corporatization, the license fee will be returned in the form of a subsidy for fulfilling the obligation to serve less profitable rural areas. Moreover DoT can continue to monopolize the domestic long distance market until 2000 and will also be able to cash in on the cellular market. DoT and MTNL will both be able to capitalize on their already existing backbone networks and thus be in a better position to cross-subsidize and offer lower cellular tariff rates compared to private cellular service providers.

Thus, the new policy has failed to achieve its major objectives. Though the monopoly of the DoT is being reduced, it still retains an unfair advantage over new entrants in both basic and value-added segments. The decision on re-allocating frequencies (so that private telecommunications companies will have the necessary bandwidth to provide services) has been passed on to yet another committee.

STRUCTURE OF THE BASIC AND VALUE-ADDED SEGMENTS

In this section, I analyze the corporatization of MTNL and VSNL, the corporations established to distribute telecom services in Delhi and Bombay and overseas calls, respectively. I also consider the privatization of basic, value-added and Internet services, and look at deregulation of the Internet service segment. The current and future structure of India's telecom sector is also discussed.

Corporatization of MTNL and VSNL

MTNL and VSNL were incorporated as two separate public-sector corporations under the DoT in 1986. The overall financial profitability of both MTNL and VSNL has been increasing in recent years. For instance, VSNL declared dividends to the tune of 80 percent on equity shares in 1998–99, up from 40 percent in 1997–98. It is generally thought that both MTNL and VSNL have upgraded their technology.

The government has so far divested about 46 percent of MTNL's equity. Financial institutions, foreign institutional investors, global depository holders and private individuals hold these shares divested by the government. MTNL has been able to introduce various features like new generation technology switches, valued-added phone plus services, computerized customer service centers, etc. New services such as voice mail and video conferencing have also been introduced. In addition, the entire waiting list for telephones in Mumbai and Delhi has been serviced. Some quantitative evidence of MTNL's better performance since corporatization is presented in Table 6.5.

Table 6.5   Performance of MTNL following corporatization

Indicators	1986	1999
Number of exchanges	46	165
Number of direct exchange lines (DEL)	292,669	1,619,322
Equipped capacity (number of lines)	352,500	1,914,534
Penetration of electronic exchanges (as a percentage of all exchanges)	22.7	100
Revenue per DEL per month (in Rs)	421	1,022.82
Number of public telephones	4,247	39,700
New telephones provided within seven days of registration (as a percentage of such applications)		40.34
Capital expenditure (in Rs million)	2,910 (1988)	9,770

Source: MTNL, http://www.mtnl.net.in/corporateinfo/.

MTNL has effected significant improvements in the area of productivity measured in terms of the number of employees per thousand lines (Figure 6.3). In fact, productivity improvements have almost doubled in both cities where this service provider is operating. However, I lack data to ascertain whether the quality of telecom services offered in Mumbai and Delhi is significantly different from other metros where the service is still provided by the DoT. The number of faults per 100 telephones per month has come down significantly in Mumbai but not in Delhi.

An important point is that DoT has viewed MTNL primarily as an instrument for raising capital from the market to meet its capital expenditure. For instance, MTNL has raised approximately Rs 69 billion from the capital market by issuing bonds; of this, nearly Rs 61 billion has been advanced to the parent department for its investment needs. If the DoT continues to view MTNL as a way of accessing the capital market, this will likely affect MTNL's performance negatively.

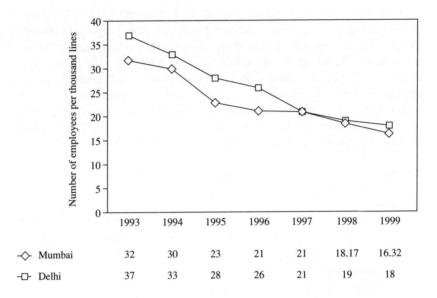

	1993	1994	1995	1996	1997	1998	1999
–◇– Mumbai	32	30	23	21	21	18.17	16.32
–□– Delhi	37	33	28	26	21	19	18

Source: Department of Telecommunications, http://www.dotindia.com/default.htm.

Figure 6.3   Productivity improvements in MTNL, 1993–98

The basic purpose of VSNL is to provide overseas telecom services to domestic subscribers. The firm was supposed to have a virtual monopoly in this area until 2004, but a recent decision by the government ends this monopoly on 1 April 2002. During the year 1991–92 the government divested 15 percent of its paid-up capital in favor of foreign institutional investors and mutual funds. Again, by issuing global depository receipts,[2] the government has reduced its ownership from 82 percent to about 53 percent. Even further divestment of the government's share is expected as part of its general policy on divestiture of public-sector units.

VSNL has played an important role in introducing Internet service and digital leased line service. Digital leased line service makes a dedicated line available to commercial organizations for data transfer. About 250 such circuits are provided. The major beneficiary of this service has been the software industry. An increasing number of Indian software companies now prefer to link up via VSNL lines to their clients abroad, and this has contributed to the significant increases in software exports, from a mere Rs 2.5 billion in 1990–91 to Rs 24.5 billion in 1995–96. This has also contributed to the reduction in migration of software personnel to foreign locations to fulfill their clients' requirements, thus lessening the extent of brain drain.

The revenue from leased lines increased by as much as 31 percent in 1998–99 and stands at about Rs 2.5 billion. But VSNL has charged hefty prices for international calls, given its monopolistic position (see Table 6.1). To illustrate, a one-minute call from India to the US currently costs Rs 61.20 (US $0.94) while a call in the reverse direction costs only Rs 20. This high cost for international calls considerably erodes the competitive advantage India has for many IT-enabled services, such as international call centers, medical transcription services, etc. However, a proposed reduction in international rates should stimulate IT-enabled services.

VSNL has been accused of misusing its monopolistic position in the area of Internet services.[3] Currently, Internet facilities are available in 20 cities. Integrated Services Digital Network has been commissioned in 12 cities. The channel capacity provided is so low that most consumers have to wait a considerable time before they can gain access. VSNL is also accused of lobbying the government to prevent entry by other private service providers. The policy on Internet service providers announced in November 1998 opened the sector to private providers, but VSNL revenues from Internet services skyrocketed by nearly 210 per cent in 1998–99 to about Rs 1.7 billion. Yet, corporatization of MTNL and VSNL has certainly led to improvements in new facilities for their consumers, and further benefits are expected with the opening up of both the NLD and the ILD to increased competition.

Privatization of the Provision of Basic, Value-added and Internet Services

In the area of basic services, controversies have preceded any actual results. Only six companies have signed license agreements with the government to provide basic telecom facilities in the states of Andhra Pradesh, Gujarat, Maharashtra, Madhya Pradesh, Rajasthan and Punjab (Figure 6.4). There are at present eight circles for which no valid bids exist. Consequent to the recent policy of opening up the NLD market, this segment is to undergo a major structural change. The recommendations restrict entry to five players for the first five years.[4] It imposes entry fees, a revenue-sharing formula and prohibits operators from carrying intra-circle calls. The state-owned VSNL is allowed to enter the domestic long distance market, and a one-time entry fee is to be auctioned among the four new players, who will have to match the highest bid. In addition, each player will have to pay a predetermined revenue share. If mergers and acquisitions reduce the number of players to two (DTS and one private player), the government reserves the right to open up the NLD market to unlimited entry before the five-year period ends.

It is too early to assess what impact the entry of these new enterprises will have on the nature and extent of competition in the 'local call markets' of their respective regions. However, a number of points of irritation have cropped up

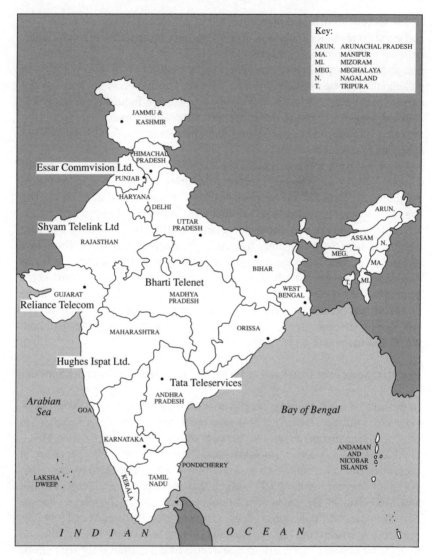

Source: Association of Basic Telecom Operators, http://www.abto.org/.

Figure 6.4   Licensed basic telephone operators and the states covered

between the government and the operators. One concerns the price of the license fees. The six licensees have to pay the DoT close to Rs 300 billion over a period of 15 years. TRAI has recommended a waiver of these fees for a period of four years, but this has yet to be accepted by the government. So the imbroglio continues and shows the attitude of the government in not leveling the playing field.

Another point of irritation concerns the last-mile link, which connects a telephone or Internet subscriber to the telecom or ISP network. The new policy on Internet service allows ISPs to set up last-mile links without payment of a license fee. Basic telephone operators object to this because there is no foolproof method to prevent voice being carried on ISP networks.[5] If ISPs start offering services like voice-over Internet protocol, the operators' revenue could be adversely affected. This issue once again shows the contradictory and piecemeal nature of the reform process in the sector.

In the area of value-added services, a number of these have been franchised to domestically registered companies on a non-exclusive basis (Government of India 1997–98). These include cellular mobile telephone service, radio-paging service, and the like. In addition to the eight licenses issued in November 1994 for cellular mobile telephone services in four metros, 33 licenses have been issued to 13 companies since December 1995 in 18 telecom circles. Of the various value-added services, cellular phones have been growing rapidly, with the number of subscribers increasing from a mere 0.34 million in 1997 to about 1.8 million by 2000. Yet, cellular operators have not been doing well.

The problems of private cellular operators are another instance of weak privatization in the Indian telecommunications market. In 1997, as part of its deregulation move, the central government licensed 22 cellular operators. Although there were more than 1.1 million cellular subscribers by 1999, the industry suffered a loss of Rs 12 billion on a combined turnover of Rs 13 billion in 1998–99 (Economist Intelligence Unit 1999). If license fees and interest payments are taken into account, the total loss is estimated to be Rs 37.9 billion.

After three years of operation, only three operators had achieved break-even. Licenses to operate cellular and fixed-line services in the 18 operating circles were awarded through competitive bidding in 1995 and 1996. Many operators aimed their bids far too high. Many license holders could not secure financing and most have yet to achieve financial closure, primarily because of the high license fees. The four that did achieve closure soon found that they needed additional funds because they had vastly overestimated the subscriber base and the average usage per subscriber.

The new policy of 1999 seeks to correct the problem of unsustainable license fees by shifting to a revenue-sharing regime. New licences are to be awarded on an entry-fee and revenue-sharing basis, which the government has temporarily set at 15 percent. This is far lower than what state-owned operators or the private cellular operators in the major cities pay. The final terms are to be based on the recommendations of TRAI. Existing operators are to be allowed to switch to the revenue-sharing arrangement provided both operators in a particular circle agree to switch and provided all their accumulated dues were paid by 31 January 2000. As of 30 April 1999, these outstanding dues totaled Rs 26 billion. Clearly, both the DoT and the private providers grossly exaggerated the actual size of the market for cellular telecom services. Also, the license fee charged by DoT was too hefty.

Deregulation of Internet Service Segment

Before the new Internet policy announced in November 1998, the provision of Internet service within the country was the sole responsibility of VSNL, the state-owned monopoly. The new policy, which set no limits on the number of ISPs permitted and minimal barriers to entry, was expected to result in competition and spectacular growth of the Internet market and act as the catalyst for convergence. The policy required no license fee for the first ten years of the 15-year license period and allowed ISPs to establish their own domestic transmission links and international gateways and to provide last-mile connectivity to subscribers. Foreign ownership, capped at 49 percent in 1998, can now be 100 percent in some ISPs, according to a recent policy pronouncement.

Many, and especially smaller, companies have entered the industry. By August 1999, the DoT had licensed 132 private ISPs according to some estimates. This marked the end of a three-year monopoly by VSNL, when access charges were high and connect speeds were slow. More competition has already begun to have a positive effect for the end-user and it is expected that Internet-usage in India will rise. For instance, since December 1998, the access cost per hour has decreased by more than 50 percent, and within the space of two years the number of Internet subscribers has exceeded one million. Finally, according to International Data Corporation, the Internet subscriber base will grow at a compound annual rate of 95 percent during 1999–2003 and reach 7.5 million by 2003.

The success of the Internet market is tied directly to the ability of the existing network infrastructure to support demand for the service. A recent set of reform measures requires VSNL to make changes to its existing agreement with Fibre-Optic Link Around the Globe (FLAG), which has a landing station in Mumbai, so that the available bandwidth can be fully utilized. The relatively high charges for Internet services are another barrier to growth. A solution to this problem is to allow for smaller usage options to be paid on a monthly basis. This strategy is unlikely to be adopted by the new ISPs, which are largely start-ups and need operating capital to recoup the high cost of leasing bandwidth by charging for bulk usage. Internet tariffs have shown no tendency to come down despite the liberalization of the market, essentially because of the high cost of leasing infrastructure from VSNL and DoT. TRAI has recommended a major cut in leased line charges as part of its tariff-rebalancing exercise. Unless this happens, it is unlikely that a mere privatization of Internet services will drive down Internet tariffs.

The Current and Future Structure of India's Telecom Segment

The preceding makes clear that the industry is in a state of flux, with changes announced on a daily basis. However, it is possible to map the present and future structure of the industry (Table 6.6) provided various existing policies are implemented and the telecom sector in India starts benefiting from increased competition.

Table 6.6   Current and future structure of India's telecommunications sector

Service	Current structure	Future structure
International voice services	VSNL monopoly	Expected to be open to competition after 1 April 2002
International data services	VSNL monopoly just ended	Unlimited players
Domestic long distance (inter-circle)	DTS monopoly	Unlimited players from 15 August 2000
Basic services	Duopoly in six circles, monopoly in remaining circles (by the DTS)	Multiple players in all circles
Cellular services	Duopoly in all circles	Three to four operators in each circle
Internet	Unlimited players	Unlimited players

Source: Adapted from Economist Intelligence Unit (2000a).

PROBLEMS WITH RESPECT TO TELECOM REGULATION

The rather short history of telecommunications regulation in India can be divided into two phases; the first covering the period 1997–2000, when TRAI was established for the first time, and the second covering the period 2000 onward, when considerable amendments were made to the original TRAI Act. On the whole, TRAI's functioning has been marred by a number of bitter disputes between it and the DoT. I do not attempt to provide a detailed review of TRAI operations since its inception, but rather a quick survey of its place in telecom regulation in India. The purpose is essentially to illustrate the need for a more independent regulator that can effectively oversee the functioning of a gradually deregulated industry. I end the discussion with an analysis of the actual benefits consumers receive from telecom regulation in the form of tariff reductions.

Phase 1: A Muddled Regulator

When TRAI commenced operation 20 February 1997, its primary objectives were to (1) recommend the need and timing of introduction of any new service provider, (2) recommend the terms and conditions of license to a service provider, (3) ensure technical compatibility and effective interconnection between different service providers, (4) regulate arrangements between different service providers to share revenue derived from providing telecommunication services, (5) recommend the revocation of license for non-compliance of terms and conditions of licensing, (6) protect the interests of customers of telecommunication services, (7) settle disputes between service providers, (8) fix rates for providing telecommunication services within and outside India, and (9) monitor the quality of service providers.

Needless to say, the establishment of TRAI was a step in the right direction and the objectives are laudable. One of the more important functions from the point of view of the consumer is to regulate price and quality of service. Given that DoT still has a monopoly in the basic services segment, its activities will now be scrutinized by another public body that is an independent organization.

An examination of the regulatory structure before the amending of the TRAI Act (Figure 6.5) shows that the Telecom Commission, the DoT and TRAI nominally had a framework of checks and balances designed to separate the formulation of policy from the licensing authority, and the regulation of interconnection and tariffs from both. In actuality, this three-part regulatory system was created in an ad hoc fashion to navigate around the operator–regulator, with plenty of gray areas for the various bodies to dispute. The Telecom Commission is responsible for policies affecting technology planning, resource mobilization and R&D issues. The DoT continues to perform both operational and regulatory functions. In addition to being the incumbent local and long distance service provider, the DoT functions as the licensing authority, performs R&D, and provides training functions.

Against this background the TRAI was formed in February 1997 by a judiciary branch decree. TRAI functions as a statutory board with complete autonomy from the Ministry of Communications and the Telecom Commission. This bestows real autonomy on it, at least theoretically. In addition to its role as an arbitrator, the TRAI also makes policy decisions regarding tariff and interconnection issues. However, the functions of TRAI are rather limited, and the new telecom policy of 1999 has sought to widen some of its powers.

The government seeks TRAI's recommendations on the number and timing of new licenses. Further, TRAI has full power to resolve disputes between

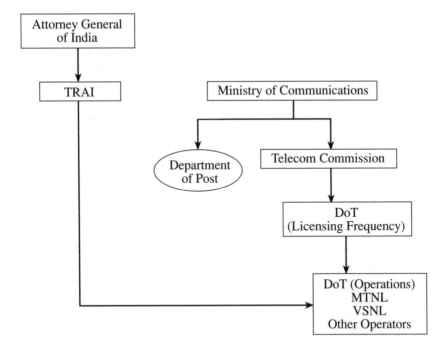

Source: Pyramid Research (1999a).

Figure 6.5   India's telecom regulatory structure in Phase 1 of TRAI

service providers, including the DoT.[6] But the fact that TRAI lacks the power to license new entrants is a major limitation. Instead, the DoT continues to play the role of licenser as well as that of policymaker and service provider, exerting considerable influence on its interactions with its competitors. TRAI's inability to rein in the anti-competitive practices of the DoT is a major weakness of telecom deregulation in India.

In Phase 1, TRAI's functions were poorly defined, and it was viewed as driven by the well-organized and vociferous lobby of private phone service operators. TRAI did little to hide its pronounced contempt for the DoT and MTNL. At the same time it failed to ensure that private operators adhered to their license conditions. Its authority and credibility were undermined by court rulings that exposed its lack of power. Its reputation suffered even more when it allowed the private operators to fight its court battles. In short, it would not be incorrect to state that there was 'regulatory capture' during the initial phase of TRAI operations.

Phase 2: Reinvention of the Regulator

The government finally admitted that the TRAI created in 1997 was not very effective, and the cabinet approved a plan to reinvent the regulator and define its functions more clearly. The government issued an ordinance to replace TRAI with an appellate tribunal with judicial powers and a reconstituted regulator that lacked one of the most important functions of any telecom regulator, namely the power to settle disputes between the various stakeholders. This function has been vested with the newly created Telecom Dispute Settlement and Appellate Tribunal.[7] However, TRAI's role has been strengthened in other areas.

The TRAI can now make recommendations, either suo motu or on a request from the licensor, on (1) the need and timing for introduction of new service providers, (2) terms and conditions of licensing to a service provider, (3) revocation of licenses for non-compliance of terms and conditions, (4) measures to facilitate competition and promote efficiency in the operation of telecommunication services and so promote growth, (5) technological improvements in services, (6) type of equipment to be used by service providers after inspection of equipment used in the network, (7) measures for the development of telecommunication technology and any other matter related to the telecommunication industry in general, and (8) efficient management of the available spectrum.

Although the amendment has further clarified the precise role of the regulator by considerably reducing the gray areas, it has effectively reduced the power of the regulator. TRAI recommendations to the government are binding only with respect to revocation of licenses for non-compliance and efficient use of the spectrum. On the crucial issues of the timing and licensing of new service providers, TRAI's recommendations are not binding. In sum, the TRAI has been reduced to a tariff-setting body empowered only to fix tariffs and interconnection charges and to set norms on quality of service.

In its short existence, the revised TRAI has made two important recommendations that have been implemented by the government. These involve (1) reductions in both the national and international long distance tariffs, discussed next, and (2) opening up the national long distance market to competition, already discussed.

Reforms in Telecom Tariffs

One of the most important and tangible benefits of privatization of telecom services is the potential for tariff reduction. Given the monopolistic position of the DoT, the telecom tariffs in India, especially for NLD and ILD, are among the highest in the world. Taking into account the potential for reducing tariffs, the TRAI passed an order in 1999 now known as the Telecommunication Tariff

Order (TTO) with the objective of rebalancing tariffs for basic services and anticipating an increase in rentals and a reduction in long distance call charges.

The rebalancing was to be implemented in three phases. The first phase, begun May 1999, specified a standard tariff package but allowed service providers to offer alternative packages to the standard one. The standard package contained a decrease in NLD and ILD call charges and an increase in rentals in order to rebalance tariffs and prepare for further opening up of basic services. Most tariff changes were to be achieved during the first two phases, the second scheduled to begin 1 April 2000.

The DoT has responded to this tariff order in a positive way, which has allowed those circles in which it faces competition from private providers to match tariff reductions.[8] However, this option is extended only to subscribers who clear their bills promptly, and it is argued that TTO 1999 is effectively flawed since ordinary subscribers pay higher rental rates (Economist Intelligence Unit, 2000b). This argument assumes that long distance call rates subsidize local call rates. TTO 1999 lowered long distance rates but raised rentals for ordinary subscribers and effectively raised local call rates by reducing the unit call time from five to three minutes. If truly interested in improving telecom access for Indian consumers, TRAI ought to have reduced long distance rates more steeply. The resulting increase in volume would maintain or raise revenues and reduce rentals while keeping the unit call time at five minutes. TRAI also allowed cellular operators to increase their rentals, from Rs 156 to Rs 600, without a compelling reason to do so.

SUMMARY

Deregulation of the telecom sector in India has proceeded in small steps and in an unstructured manner. Teledensity continues to be low and the waiting time for a telephone connection continues to be long except in some of the larger cities. Some value-added services are available, but the service providers are all on the brink of bankruptcy. The DoT continues to behave like a classic monopolist, scornful of any attempts to restrain it. The TRAI has met with some success by setting new tariffs for both cellular and basic services, but several latent issues have surfaced to test its regulatory grip. Although the policy on Internet services sounds attractive, prima facie, there are plenty of hidden catches that hinder a large-scale increase in the number of Internet subscribers. The general state of the new private entrants to the telecom sector is best judged by the amount of dues they owe the DoT in unpaid license fees. The cellular operators owe about Rs 25 billion, followed by basic service operators with about Rs 7,411 million and radio-paging service operators with about Rs 2,290 million. The sector is still in a state of flux, with changes announced almost on a daily basis. All that one can say is that the process of deregulation, though unstructured, is slowly cutting into the monopolistic activities of the DoT.

ACKNOWLEDGMENTS

The author is grateful to Michael Pollitt, Ashok Desai, and R. Nagaraj for comments on an earlier draft. The usual disclaimer holds good.

ENDNOTES

1. Although the relative number of consumers on the waiting list has come down, they remain virtually the same in absolute numbers. The figure for the country as a whole also hides substantial regional variations in access to telecom services.
2. In February 1999, VSNL generated a demand of more than 37 million global depository receipts, approximately $345 million, against the offer of 20 million global depository receipts.
3. VSNL holds nearly 95 percent of the Internet connectivity market in India, but this is bound to be reduced by a significant amount with the progressive entry of new ISPs.
4. The one-time license fee for providing national long distance services fixed by DoT may exceed Rs 5 billion. The regulatory body had earlier recommended a fee of Rs 5 billion in a free-for-all scenario. Of this, Rs 1 billion was non-refundable; the refundable balance would be used as an incentive to ensure timely rollout of the network. The refundable Rs 4 billion was to be deposited as a bank guarantee or in tax-free government bonds. The high entry fee restricts competition to serious players. Of the revenue-sharing part of the license fee, the DoT may accept a figure nearing 15 percent, with 10 percent being government's share and 5 percent for the universal service obligation. Another licensing condition said to be considered by TRAI to discourage non-serious players is a requirement that any consortium that wants to bid for the national long distance license should have a minimum net worth of Rs 2.5 billion.
5. The New Telecom Policy of 1999 prevents voice-over Internet telephony.
6. This is a major achievement since the Delhi High Court ruled in a previous case that the government was the sole licensing authority and the recommendation of the regulator was neither mandatory nor binding on the government. This ruling reduced the role of TRAI to a mere tariff-setting body.
7. The tribunal will adjudicate on disputes between the government and service providers and between service providers and will hear appeals against TRAI orders. It will function as a high court, and its rulings can be challenged only in the Supreme Court. It will be headed by a person not beneath the rank of a chief justice of a high court or a judge of the Supreme Court. The selection of the members of the tribunal will be done in consultation with the Chief Justice of India.
8. These are the DoT networks in Maharashtra, Mumbai, Andhra Pradesh, and Madhya Pradesh. However, the circles are not to engage in price wars with the private providers.

REFERENCES

Economist Intelligence Unit (1999), 'Telecom deregulation in India – Slow and painful', http://wb.eiu.com/search_view.asp?from_page=composite&doc_idE1459509&topic id=IN (accessed 18 September 2001).

Economist Intelligence Unit (2000a), 'India regulations: Telecoms sector updates' (EIU viewswire, 10 October), http://www.viewswire.com/index.asp?layout=display_article&search_text=india+regulations&doc_id=120485 (accessed 18 September 2001).

Economist Intelligence Unit (2000b), 'India regulations: New plans to revamp telecoms sector' (EIU viewswire, 14 February), http://www.viewswire.com/index.asp?layout=display_article&search_text=india+regulations&doc_id=97477 (accessed 18 September 2001).

Government of India (1997–98), *Economic Survey*, New Delhi: Ministry of Finance.

Group on Telecommunications, Prime Minister's Councils (1999), 'Report of the Spectrum Management Committee', http://www.nic.in/got/report/ (accessed 18 September 2001).

Mani, Sunil (2000), 'Deregulation and reforms in India's telecommunications industry', in Mitsuhiro Kagami and Masatsugu Tsuji (eds), *Privatization, Deregulation and Economic Efficiency*, Cheltenham, UK and Brookfield, US: Edward Elgar, 187–205.

Mohan, Rakesh et al. (1996), *The India Infrastructure Report*, New Delhi: National Council of Applied Economic Research.

Pyramid Research (1999a), *Telecoms and Wireless Asia* 7: 1 (January 22).

Pyramid Research (1999b), *Telecoms and Wireless Asia* 7: 4 (April 16).

World Bank (2000), *World Development Indicators 2000 on CD-ROM*, Washington, DC: World Bank Group.

7. Private financing initiatives in India's electricity sector

Sunil Mani

The role played by infrastructure in explaining economic growth differential across countries is now rather well researched.[1] There is a lack of data on the quantity and quality of public infrastructure in developing countries, but measures of telephone networks and electricity capacity have been found to have a significant effect on subsequent growth, although causation runs both ways. Developing countries across the world are currently engaged in various measures to improve and expand their infrastructure sector because, increasingly, foreign direct investments tend to move toward those countries and regions within countries where both the quality and quantity of infrastructure are better.

Infrastructure sectors have traditionally been viewed as natural monopolies, but changes in technology have eroded this status. Infrastructure services were formerly assigned to the public sector because of equity considerations; today, a widespread 'fiscal crisis' of the public sector has made private-financing initiatives the order of the day in most infrastructure sectors.

India too has undertaken a variety of reforms to improve its infrastructure sector. The main component of this reform package has been to encourage private-sector participation. In this chapter, I map general trends in infrastructure investment by the public and private sectors, then survey the current structure of India's electricity industry and analyze the main rationale for privatization. The main policy changes enhancing the role of the private sector in the industry are summarized along with the response to these changes at the overall and state level. I also provide a case study of one of the larger private-sector projects and summarize certain critical issues that impinge on the progress of reforms in the Indian electricity industry.

TRENDS IN INFRASTRUCTURE INVESTMENT

Most of the infrastructure in India is owned by the public sector and retains monopoly status. According to Nagaraj et al. (1999), the public sector's share has been growing continuously and has not shown any significant reductions since the economic reforms of 1991. The public sector's share of GDP was 2.5 times greater in 1994 than in 1960, increasing from 10 to 25 percent. State enterprises are dominant in the mining and power sectors (100 and 90 percent, respectively) as well as in banking and the insurance sectors (more than 80 percent), and the public sector accounts for about 40 percent of economic activity in transportation and telecommunications according to sector data from the National Accounts. The government has identified nine infrastructure sectors where private initiatives are encouraged: electricity, telecommunications, roads, oil and natural gas, coal, mining, civil aviation, ports, and urban infrastructure. Of these, significant private investments have occurred only in the first two sectors. I examine progress in the electricity sector.

THE STRUCTURE OF THE ELECTRICITY SUPPLY INDUSTRY IN INDIA

The total installed capacity in India is about 83,000 MW. Of this, nearly 65 percent is owned and operated by the 19 State Electricity Boards (SEBs) and 29 percent by corporations established and owned by the central government. Prominent among the latter are the National Thermal Power Corporation (NTPC), which uses coal and gas-fired units; the National Hydroelectric Power Corporation; Neyveli Lignite Corporation; and Damodar Valley Corporation, which generates both coal-based and hydroelectric power. NTPC is the largest among these, owning some two-thirds of the total capacity of central undertakings. Nuclear stations account for about 2 percent of the installed generating capacity. Four power-distributing companies own the remaining 4 percent. Power Grid Corporation of India, owned by the central government, provides interstate transmission of power. Clearly, the bulk of India's power-generating and transmissions capacity is still owned by government entities. It is against this background that one has to analyze the private-financing initiatives in India's power sector.

Generation capacity in the government sector has increased in the recent past, yet falls far short of desired consumption at current prices. The gap between quantity demanded and supplied has widened over the last five years and is expected to widen further in the short term. Energy (kWh) deficiency is approximately 11 percent, and peaking shortage is about 18 percent. Despite this shortage, the increase in actual generation has been slow (Figure 7.1). According to the Ministry of Power, the minimum capacity addition needed over the next ten years is more than 83,000 MW, and the investment required to create such a capacity amounts to US$83 billion, at the rate of US$1 million per MW. If one adds the concomitant increase in investments required for transmission and distribution, the total goes up to about US$143 billion. Given the precarious financial position of most SEBs, which is elaborated upon in the last section, the only option would seem to be funding by the private sector, both foreign and domestic.

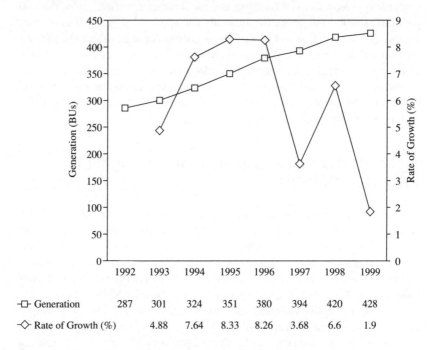

	1992	1993	1994	1995	1996	1997	1998	1999
Generation	287	301	324	351	380	394	420	428
Rate of Growth (%)		4.88	7.64	8.33	8.26	3.68	6.6	1.9

Source: Ministry of Power (http://www.powermin.nic.in/nrg24.htm).

Figure 7.1   Increases in actual generation of electricity

POLICY CHANGES TO ACCOMMODATE PRIVATE-SECTOR PARTICIPATION

To increase private-sector participation in power generation and distribution, both the central and state governments have effected a number of policy changes. The central government has initiated a major change in its power policy since 1991, and the state governments are engaged in restructuring their respective SEBs to pave the way for increased private-sector participation.

At the level of the central government, there have been three major policy changes; namely, changes in the legislation governing electricity supply, establishment of the Central Electricity Regulator, and establishment of specialized financial institutions.

Changes in the Legislation Governing Electricity Supply

It must be stressed that changes in the legislation governing the electricity sector in India have proceeded in a haphazard and unstructured fashion. The first important development was the central government's decision to encourage private investment, both domestic and foreign, in generation. The Electricity Laws (amendment) Ordinance promulgated since January 1997 recognizes transmission as an independent activity and allows private-sector participation by issuing licenses for both interstate and intrastate transmission.

Although distribution of electricity is still the monopoly of the SEBs, with some exceptions, the Electricity Bill 2000 seeks to end this monopoly, as discussed later. The new power policy of the Government of India, also known as the CEA Guidelines, includes the following broad features (Ministry of Power, http://www.powermin.nic.in/nrg5.htm).

The Indian Electricity Act and the Electricity (Supply) Act permit private-sector power generation. The private sector can now set up coal, gas or liquid fuel-based thermal projects, hydroelectric projects, and wind or solar projects of any size. Foreign investors are allowed up to 100 percent ownership of projects, subject to government approval.

Sales made to SEBs are covered by a two-part tariff regime, under which a return of up to 16 percent on the paid-up and subscribed equity is available when a plant functions at the stipulated efficiency levels. This 16 percent is denominated in the currency of the subscribed capital. In addition, an increased rate of return of up to 0.7 percent on equity for every percentage point increase above the normal 68.5 percent plant load factor is allowed for thermal power plants. For hydroelectric plants, the same increased rate of return is allowed beyond the normal 90 percent plant availability factor.

New power projects are eligible for a five-year tax holiday, and duties on the import of equipment for power projects have been reduced considerably. New external commercial borrowing guidelines exempt power projects from a restriction on end use of such funds and provide a fair degree of flexibility in structuring the financing.

One of the most important policy changes since 1991 is the recent approval of the Electricity Bill 2000, which replaces the Indian Electricity Act 1910; the Electricity Supply Act 1948; and the Electricity Regulation Commissions Act 1998. The bill ends the monopoly of the country's 19 SEBs and includes a provision for unbundling SEBs into three separate units for generation, transmission and distribution. The Central Electricity Regulatory Commission (CERC) will issue licenses to private companies for the transmission of power.

Establishment of the Electricity Regulator

Another noteworthy feature of the reform process is the move toward establishing an electricity regulator. An act passed by Parliament in 1999 paved the way for CERC, which will regulate the tariff of generating companies owned or controlled by the central government. It will also regulate interstate transmission, including tariff of the transmission entities, and interstate bulk sale of power. In addition, CERC will aid and advise the central government in formulation of tariff policy. It is still not clear whether the activities of the private-sector power providers, known as independent power providers or IPPs, are to be regulated by CERC.

Several of these policy measures have become contentious, as exemplified by the Enron project.[2] The IPPs are allowed to sell the power to the ultimate consumer through the SEBs only after entering into a power purchase agreement with the boards. It is implicitly assumed in the CEA Guidelines that such agreements will be negotiated one-to-one through the Memorandum of Understanding (MoU) route. The main problem with the CEA Guidelines is that a cost-plus formula provides a guaranteed return without any means of assuring that capacity and operating costs are minimized.

Specialized financial institutions have been established to attract private-sector investment to the infrastructure sector. Apart from the Power Finance Corporation, the Infrastructure Development Finance Company was established in 1997.

RESPONSE TO THE POLICY CHANGES

I analyze the record with respect to privatization at three levels: overall new capacity since the initiation of the reforms, the progress of the original eight fast-track projects, and progress of reforms at the state level.

Although a large number of private-sector projects are in the works, only 20, with a combined installed generating capacity of 4,700 MW, have been commissioned. And about 30 percent of this new capacity has been contributed by existing private-sector providers (Figure 7.2). Much of the increase in actual capacity creation occurred in 1999 when Phase 1 of Enron's project was commissioned. This project alone accounted for nearly two-thirds of the new capacity created in 1999.

The Government of India identified eight projects with a total capacity of 5,700 MW for fast-track approval through the Ministry of Utilities. When the policy was launched, the response from private-sector enterprises, both Indian and foreign, was uncertain since privatization of the Indian power sector was an uncharted area. The financial viability of the SEBs, who would be the main buyers of power from the generating companies, and the international market's previous lack of involvement in targeting India made it necessary for the central government to adopt a flexible approach to attract foreign investment to the sector. Thus, the government opted for direct negotiations, and the so-called fast-track projects were selected to go ahead through the Ministry of Utilities. This approach typically required project developers to enter into an in-principle agreement of understanding to put up a specific power plant. After getting the necessary techno-economic clearances, developers signed the final power purchase agreement.

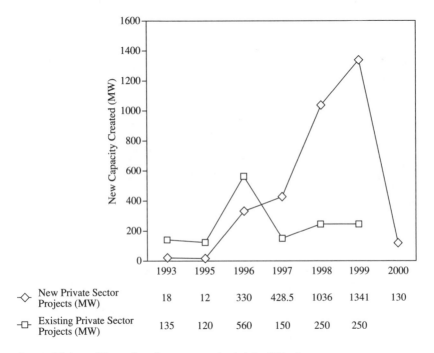

	1993	1995	1996	1997	1998	1999	2000
◇ New Private Sector Projects (MW)	18	12	330	428.5	1036	1341	130
▫ Existing Private Sector Projects (MW)	135	120	560	150	250	250	

Source: Ministry of Power (http://www.powermin.nic.in/nrg24.htm).

Figure 7.2   New capacities (in MW) in the private sector commissioned since 1993

The progress of these so-called fast-track projects has been far from satisfactory. Only three projects, amounting to 20 percent of the total capacity approved, have actually been completed (Table 7.1). The foreign promoter has withdrawn one project, and one of the foreign partners has pulled out from another project. On the whole, progress has been disappointing. Enron's Dabhol project illustrates the difficulties plaguing these fast-track projects.

Table 7.1 Current status of the original eight fast-track electricity projects

Project, capacity (MW), and fuel	Promoters	Location	Status
Dabhol, 740 Phase 1, gas	Enron, Bechtel, GE Capital, MSEB	Dabhol, Maharashtra	Commissioned
Combined-cycle project, 216, gas	GVK Reddy, CMS Energy, ABB	Jegurupadu Andhra Pradesh	Commissioned
Godavari Combined Cycle, 208, gas	Spectrum power	Godavari Andhra Pradesh	Commissioned. Withdrew from counter-guarantee (CG) scheme
Neyveli Lignite Project, 250, lignite	St-CMS Electric, CMS Energy, ABB	Neyveli Tamil Nadu	CG agreement signed in August 1998; has achieved financial closure
Visakhapatnam, 1,040, coal	Hinduja, National Power	Visakhapatnam Andhra Pradesh	CG agreement signed in August 1998. Financial closure pending (seeking escrow cover). Validity of the CG extended to August 2000
Mangalore, 1,013, coal	China Light and Power, Tata Group	Mangalore Andhra Pradesh	Cogentrix withdrew after seven years of development and was replaced by Tata
Bhadravati, 1,082, coal	Ispat, Alsthom Electricite de France (EDF)	Bhadravati Maharashtra	CG agreement signed in August 1998. Fuel supply agreement not signed. EDF has withdrawn
IB Valley Project, 500, coal	AES Transpower	IB Valley, Orissa	Yet to sign CG agreement

Source: Economist Intelligence Unit (2000).

Case Study of Enron's Dabhol Power Company

In June 1992, the Government of Maharashtra signed a memorandum of understanding with Enron, a US-based power company, to build a power station fueled by natural gas in the Ratnagiri coastal district of Maharashtra state. The Dabhol Power Company (DPC) was the first wholly private power project to be approved in India and was a joint venture between three US-based multinational corporations – Enron (with an 80 percent share), General Electric (10 percent) and Bechtel Enterprises, Inc. (10 percent).

In December 1993, a power purchase agreement between the DPC and the Maharashtra State Electricity Board (MSEB) for the purchase of the electricity generated by the project was finalized. The project was approved as a consequence of changes in Indian governmental policy, begun in 1991, relating to foreign investment. Opposition to the policy of economic liberalization and the resulting prospect of globalization of the Indian economy has underpinned many critiques of the project, attracting criticism from various quarters.

Specific criticisms concern (1) the high cost of the power to be purchased by the state government, (2) allegations of corruption surrounding the setting up of the project, and (3) questions about the procedure used for granting official clearance for the project, including the lack of consultation with affected people and inadequate assessment of environmental impact. Land acquisition leading to environmental destruction and displacement of local people introduces the issues of the level and distribution of compensation.

A number of public-interest legal challenges concerning various aspects of the project and its approval have been mounted both in the Maharashtra High Court and the Supreme Court of India. It was in this context that the Bharatiya Janata Party (BJP), in its campaign for the state assembly elections in February 1995, made a commitment to cancel the project. By November 1995, the BJP state government announced that it would renegotiate the project with the DPC. Permission for the project was cancelled but reinstated 16 months later after complete renegotiations of the original contract.

Enron cut its project costs by as much as $350 million and also reduced the electricity rates that it would charge by 22 percent. Further, it sold 30 percent of its stake in DPC at a discount to the MSEB. In return, it got a commitment for raising the installed capacity to 2,450 MW, up from 2,015 MW. The renegotiated project was to be completed in two phases.

Phase 1, with an installed capacity of 826 MW, has a variable fuel capacity but will be fired on naphtha until commencement of Phase 2 (an installed capacity of 1,624 MW). The ownership of Phase 1 is a joint venture comprising: Enron Corporation, 50 percent; MSEB, 30 percent; Bechtel Enterprises Holdings, Inc., 10 percent; and GE Capital Structured Finance Group, 10 percent. Phase 1 was commissioned seven weeks ahead of schedule in May 1999. Its total cost was estimated at $1.2 billion. Construction has begun on the second phase, which will be fired on regasified LNG (liquefied natural gas) delivered from a terminal near the power plant. In this phase Enron owns 80 percent while Bechtel and GE own 10 percent each. MSEB has the option to acquire a 30 percent stake from Enron. The total cost of this phase is placed at $1.9 billion.

The project has achieved financial closure. The total project cost debts accounted for are nearly $1.4 billion. Nearly $1.1 billion of this came from several foreign banks and financial institutions, along with $333 million in local currency from Indian commercial and development banks. Equity accounts for about $0.5 billion. Enron's DPC project is thus the largest private sector project in India's power sector. It also demonstrates the difficulties of electricity privatization in the country.

Progress at the State Level

As noted, electricity generation and distribution in India is the responsibility of both the state and central governments, particularly states. So any discussion of reforms of the electricity sector must explicitly take into account reforms at the level of state government. The main organization responsible for electricity generation and distribution at the state level is the SEB.

Reforms at the state level include allowing new IPPs and restructuring the SEBs to make them more competitive and able to withstand competitive pressures (Table 7.2). The process of establishing an IPP has been considerably simplified for this purpose (Figure 7.3). However, the actual implementation varies considerably across the states, and it can be safely argued that the process has been anything but smooth in most states.

Of 17 states, out of a possible 19 for which such data are available, only three – Orissa and to some extent Andhra Pradesh and Haryana – have effected any actual restructuring. In addition, the states of Karnataka and Uttar Pradesh are in various stages of effecting the necessary legislative changes to reform their respective electricity sectors. No other states have anything much to report by way of concrete action. This shows that reforms at the state level are limited in content and coverage. The major bottleneck has been the lack of political will and strong pressures exerted by large interest groups such as trade unions.

SOME CRITICAL ISSUES

The SEBs are heavily overstaffed, tolerate large-scale pilferage, and set tariffs at subsidized rates. Collectively, they have a dismal financial performance, which has worsened over time (Figure 7.4). As seen earlier (Table 7.2), progress

Table 7.2 Progress of privatization of the electricity sector in three Indian states

State	Legislative changes	Restructuring of the SEB	Appointment of a regulatory commission
Andhra Pradesh	Reform Bill enacted 29 October 1998	SEB unbundled into two entities, generation and transmission, with latter to subsequently be privatized	Electricity Commission established 31 March 1999
Orissa		OHPC, which owns all six hydro projects in state, converted into joint entity with 51% disinvestment for private partners; new distribution arrangement allows GRIDCO to purchase power and sell it in bulk to distribution companies, of which two new ones have been created. Staff cadre transfer and personnel policies have been finalized. Reduction in system losses by 5%. Revenue Improvement Action Program has addressed problems of systems and procedures for energy accounting, billing, collection and customer complaints	Regulatory Commission functional from August 1996; progress made
Haryana	Electricity Reforms Act in force from 14 August 1998	HSEB separated into a power transmission and a generation company, 14 August 1998	Regulatory Commission operational from 17 August 1998

Source: Ministry of Power (http://www.powermin.nic.in/nrg803.htm).

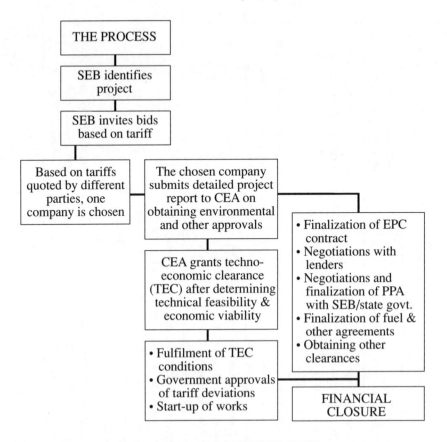

Source: Government of India, http://www.nic.in/india/CHAP2_8.HTM.

Figure 7.3   Establishing an IPP at the state level

toward restructuring and improved performance has been tardy and embroiled in controversies. Given the 'bankrupt' nature of the SEBs, the IPPs had to be offered state guarantees and central counter-guarantees to mitigate the risk that the SEBs might default on payments. Further, the central government required the SEBs to put part of their revenues into escrow accounts earmarked for payments to producers, which led to an indiscriminate offering of escrow cover by a majority of the SEBs. In many cases this far exceeded their revenues.

In Madhya Pradesh, this over-commitment sparked court battles among IPPs. Two other states, Maharashtra and Tamil Nadu, have exhausted their escrow cover. It is now fairly clear that without the escrow cover, institutional lenders are unwilling to finance these projects. The withdrawal of the French company

EDF from one of the fast-track projects (see Table 7.1) is attributed to this lack of adequate escrow cover.

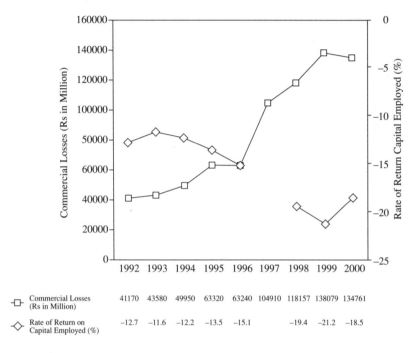

	1992	1993	1994	1995	1996	1997	1998	1999	2000
Commercial Losses (Rs in Million)	41170	43580	49950	63320	63240	104910	118157	138079	134761
Rate of Return on Capital Employed (%)	−12.7	−11.6	−12.2	−13.5	−15.1		−19.4	−21.2	−18.5

Source: Government of India Ministry of Finance, *Economic Survey* (various issues).

Figure 7.4   Commercial losses of SEBs in India, 1992–2000

High Transmission and Distribution Losses

All generation and distribution entities in the public electricity sector in India suffer from high transmission and distribution losses (T&D). This works out on average to about 21 percent of the availability, and it has not shown any tendency to come down during the last ten years or so. (See Figure 7.5.) The high T&D loss is a combined effect of poor maintenance, lack of adequate investments in T&D equipment, and pure and simple theft of power, illegal metering, etc. Theft of power, along with subsidies and technical losses, means that SEBs do not get paid for 45 percent of the power generated, and they have run up uncollected bills of more than US$4.5 billion. If such high T&D losses persist, a mere increase in generation capacity may not really remedy the shortage since the problem is one of transmission and distribution, not capacity. The government has responded by allowing private participation in transmission to induce higher technical and commercial standards. But the SEBs, which together control about 60 percent of transmission and 97 percent of distribution, are blocking this initiative.

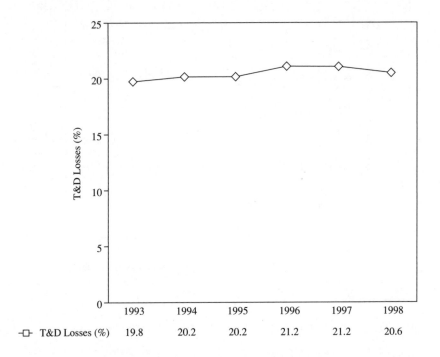

	1993	1994	1995	1996	1997	1998
⊡ T&D Losses (%)	19.8	20.2	20.2	21.2	21.2	20.6

Source: Ministry of Power (http://www.powermin.nic.in/arep10f.htm).

Figure 7.5   Transmission and distribution losses as a percentage of availability

In fact, little in the new policies addresses these huge T&D losses. In response, the central government has been considering a number of options to privatize the transmission segment. A step in this direction is the recently announced policy on 'mega projects',[3] which allows new IPPs to negotiate power purchase agreements with the new power-trading corporations (PTCs). Thus, developers will be able to circumvent the bankrupt and inefficient SEBs by selling their power to a new intermediary, the PTCs. The success of the private initiatives depends on the ability of the SEBs to plug the substantial leakages.

Issues Related to Fuel Supply

A third basic obstacle to privatization has been the supply of fuel to the electricity plants. India has a plentiful supply of water and coal, although of a lower quality, but has hardly any gas and practically no LNG. Even so, all four coal-based projects are stuck (Table 7.1). The two main issues with coal are its supply and transportation, both of which are under the control of inefficient public-sector monopolies that have failed to provide bankable and legally enforceable supply and transportation agreements. New policy changes such as the policy on 'mega projects' have remedied problems to a certain extent by shifting emphasis to locations on the coast or near coal mines, reducing the dependence on the railways.

Clearer guidelines for liquid fuel-based projects have also been announced. This is a significant policy change. In the past, the state-owned Indian Oil Corporation blocked power projects because they could weaken its monopoly over high-cost naphtha. But new policies benefit only projects not yet launched. Projects already under way do not benefit.

SUMMATION

The analysis of private-sector financing initiatives in India's power sector shows that much remains to be done. Only very limited capacity has actually been implemented in the private sector, primarily because of the financial status of the SEBs. Any policy to bring additional private-sector investments without at the same time improving the financial health of the SEBs through restructuring is bound to fail. This survey suggests that the political economy of government intervention in India is one source of poor sector performance to date.

ACKNOWLEDGMENTS

The author is grateful to Michael Pollitt, Ashok Desai, and R. Nagaraj for comments on an earlier draft. The usual disclaimer holds good.

ENDNOTES

1. Easterly and Rebelo (1993) find that the share of public investment in transport and communication is robustly correlated with growth.
2. When economic reforms in India opened up the power sector to foreign private power plants, the Enron Corp. of the US was the first to offer to build a new plant at Dabhol, a coastal town 250 km south of Bombay. In spite of public criticism, the Maharashtra State Electricity Board

signed a power purchase agreement. Subsequently, even though construction had started, a new state government first canceled the deal, then renegotiated a new power purchase agreement. See Parikh (1997) for details.
3. These mega projects include thermal projects with capacity in excess of 1,000 MW and hydropower projects with a minimum 230 MW of capacity under which developers will be pre-qualified through competitive, tariff-based bidding.

REFERENCES

Easterly, W. and S. Rebelo (1993), 'Fiscal policies and economic growth: An empirical investigation', *Journal of Monetary Economics*, 32 (December), 417–58.
Economist Intelligence Unit (2000), 'Another one bites the dust', *Business India Intelligence*, (August), 2–4.
Nagaraj, R., Aristomene Varoudakis, and Marie-Agne Veganzones (1999), *Long-Run Growth Trends and Convergence across Indian States*, Technical Paper No. 131, Paris: OECD Development Centre.
Parikh, K. (1997), 'The Enron story and its lessons', *Journal of International Trade and Economic Development*, 6 (2), 209–30.

PART THREE

US and Emerging Markets: Stakeholders and the Status Quo

8. Public power: Perspectives in electricity restructuring

Salvador A. Martinez

The electric utility industry in the US is undergoing dramatic changes. Among the myriad of issues being debated are many that are unique to public power, which includes electric utilities owned by local, state, and federal governments.[1] This chapter identifies major electricity-restructuring issues facing public power in conjunction with the development of transmission entities to manage and operate the bulk transmission grid.

The main policy initiatives affecting public power[2] and other industry participants in the generation, distribution, and transmission parts of the electricity industry are coming from both the state and federal levels of government. At the state level many legislatures and public utility commissions have implemented or are investigating the implementation of retail choice programs. These programs allow final customers to select their electricity suppliers. Federal initiatives in recent years have seeded the development of independent system operators (ISOs). These are non-profit entities without transmission ownership that manage and operate portions of the bulk transmission grid.

More recently the Federal Energy Regulatory Commission (FERC) has issued Order 2000 on the formation of regional transmission organizations (RTOs), which requires that 'each public utility that owns, operates, or controls facilities for the transmission of electric energy in interstate commerce make certain filings with respect to forming and participating in an RTO.' Public power systems are not required to file under the order since they are not under the FERC's transmission jurisdiction, but the commission's objective is 'for all transmission-owning entities in the Nation, including non-public utilities, to place their transmission facilities under the control of appropriate RTOs in a timely manner.'[3]

In addition, several comprehensive electricity-restructuring proposals have been introduced in the US Congress in the last couple of years, including proposals that give the FERC greater authority in defining the transmission part of the electricity industry. Even though generation markets in the future are likely to be competitive, the transmission and distribution markets collectively known as the 'wires industry' are likely to be regulated at the federal and state levels, respectively. The challenges facing public power in this new wires industry are the focus of this chapter.

After presenting a brief background of restructuring initiatives related to transmission access and electricity network characteristics, I examine perspectives of publicly owned utilities in the context of the debate about whether to have the non-profit ISO entities be responsible for transmission operation without ownership of the wires or allow for-profit Transco entities to both own and operate transmission wires. The availability of non-discriminatory transmission access is a common concern among public power utilities, regardless of the type of transmission model. However, not all representatives in the public power industry agree on the preferred transmission model (including ISOs and Transcos) that should be implemented as RTOs.

I discuss the local, state, and federal regulations relevant to publicly owned utilities, which complicate RTO participation. Numerous local and state requirements originating in charters, constitutions, and case law can affect the participation of public power systems in RTOs. A uniform solution to change the requirements is not immediately apparent, especially as states implement different restructuring legislation laws or regulatory orders. In addition, tax rules directly affect the ability of public power systems to participate in RTOs. For example, the Private Use rules in the Internal Revenue Code place restrictions on non-governmental entities' use of public power facilities financed by tax-exempt bonds.

Finally, I discuss the transmission issues faced by the federally owned utilities, focusing on the Tennessee Valley Authority (TVA) and federal power-marketing administrations in relation to Order 2000. Any attempt to include the TVA in an RTO is precluded by the laws that define its current existence. Transmitting electricity generated inside its service territory to other entities outside its service area is prohibited under the TVA's charter. In addition, several restrictions prevent the power-marketing administrations from joining RTOs, including statutes and congressional appropriations rules. Concluding observations follow a discussion of the future role of public power.

RECENT BACKGROUND

Congressional passage of the Energy Policy Act of 1992 opened the door for more active competition in wholesale electricity markets. It expanded the FERC's authority to order utilities to provide wheeling service for wholesale power transactions. This change gave participants in the wholesale electricity markets the ability to petition the FERC to require the transmitting utilities to provide transmission services even if the request required an enlargement of transmission capacity. Congress reserved some discretion for the states by including a provision that limits the FERC's authority to order transmission access to retail customers. Since public power is not under the FERC's jurisdiction, it was not required to follow these guidelines.

After realizing new concerns in the wholesale power markets, such as complaints from transmission customers about the delays in how transmission service was being provided, the FERC issued Orders 888 and 889 in April 1996 to facilitate wholesale competition. Order 888 requires jurisdictional transmission-owning utilities to use the same transmission tariffs for their own wholesale transactions as for other users of the transmission facilities. Transmission-owning utilities were required to file a pro forma tariff that specified terms and conditions of transmission service to all customers. Order 888 also included principles for the establishment and operation of ISOs as a way to comply with the FERC's non-discriminatory transmission tariff requirements.[4] Order 889 implemented rules requiring transmission providers to give customers timely information on transmission capacity and prices. Again, public power is not required to follow the same guidelines as investor-owned utilities.

As concerns about long-term engineering and economic efficiencies remained, the FERC issued a Notice of Proposed Rulemaking (NOPR) in May 1999 to solicit comments on a possible action to require that utilities make filings regarding participation in or formation of RTOs.[5] As previously noted, Order 2000 implemented the filing requirements of the NOPR. All public utilities in the FERC's jurisdiction that were not currently participating in a regional transmission entity conforming to ISO principles and that own, operate, or control interstate transmission facilities were required to file a proposal with the FERC by 15 October 1999 for an RTO to be operational by 15 December 2001 or provide an explanation of efforts, obstacles, and plans in this regard. The FERC expects 'that such proposals would include the transmission facilities of public utilities as well as the transmission facilities of public power and other non-public utility entities to the extent possible.'[6] Participation of both public power and investor-owned utilities is critically important to resolve engineering and economic inefficiencies.

The operation and management of the transmission grids require a high degree of coordination, given the physical characteristics of electricity. Since electricity cannot be easily stored in large quantities to satisfy current consumption needs, supply and demand need to be matched on a real-time basis throughout the day. Congestion can occur if too much electricity is transported over transmission wires. As a result, utility-generating schedules will need to be altered. Furthermore, moving electricity from point A to point B over long distances requires that voltages be maintained to prevent breakdowns in the transmission system. Even so, some electricity entering at point A will not arrive at point B in an interconnected grid since electricity follows paths of minimum resistance. This loop-flow problem adds to the difficulty of moving power from one location to another. A considerable amount of planning, participation, and cooperation is needed in the organization of RTOs to undertake the grid management and operation historically performed by vertically integrated utilities.

A NEW WIRES INDUSTRY: UNIQUE ISSUES FACING PUBLIC POWER

Publicly owned utilities in the US are a group of more than 2,000 utilities that are owned by local and state governments and that serve customers as non-profit agencies. Municipal utilities represent over 90 percent of the publicly owned utilities. The remaining publicly owned utilities, such as public power districts, irrigation districts, and state authorities, typically serve a larger geographic area than municipal systems and may provide other services for the public, such as water and recreation management. Most of the power sold by publicly owned utilities is purchased from other sources. In 1998, publicly owned utilities accounted for 14 percent of all revenues from sales to final customers.[7] Although there are about eight times as many public power utilities, the investor-owned utilities own about 70 percent of the transmission lines that are 138 kV or higher.[8] Clearly, all publicly owned utilities, whether large state authorities owning substantial amounts of transmission capacity or smaller distribution-only municipal utilities, are affected by the changing structure of the wires industry.

Types of Transmission Organizations

According to Order 2000, for a transmission organization to become an RTO, it must possess, at a minimum, the characteristics of independence, scope and regional configuration, operational authority, and short-term reliability. Further, it must perform eight minimum functions, including tariff administration, congestion management, and expansion. These stipulations are put forth to ensure reliability[9] and efficiently priced transmission service for regional wholesale power markets. Although the FERC does not indicate a preference for any transmission model, both the ISO and Transco satisfy the RTO characteristics and functions.[10]

The ISO model requires transmission owners to yield their facilities to a non-profit entity that operates and controls the system without owning it.[11] Existing ISOs vary in governance, functional responsibilities, and market operations while complying with Order 888 principles. New England ISO, PJM ISO, and

New York ISO are the only independent system operators[12] to operate centralized power markets and as a standard control area.[13] These ISOs evolved from existing power pools and so were created with relative ease. The FERC suggests that these ISOs were formed primarily to comply with an Order 888 requirement to implement a system-wide transmission tariff.[14] Current ISOs could satisfy the FERC's minimum functions and characteristics for RTOs with some modifications.

The ISO model offers several benefits as the appropriate type of RTO model. By separating ownership of transmission assets from generation, ISOs could maintain a high degree of independence in operation while undertaking non-discriminatory market-monitoring activities. This separation may also prevent the concerns about possible market manipulation and anti-competitive behavior that often accompany price spikes in wholesale energy markets. Further, the ISO model may be able to internalize loop flow and other network externalities, especially in regions where ownership of transmission facilities is balkanized by several owners.[15] In addition, ISOs can facilitate power exchanges between smaller, neighboring transmission systems to lower overall transaction costs.

While the ISO model has many proponents, others support the Transco model. Under this model, all transmission facilities within a geographic region, which is usually larger than a single utility service territory, are sold to one company, which then owns and operates them. Ownership of transmission assets provides the direct incentives to price transmission efficiently and internalize network externalities within the control area.[16] The Transco would actively seek to minimize costs and achieve full performance of its assets. Efficient transmission pricing gives the proper signals to market participants in locating new generation capacity. In conjunction with the transmission pricing, price-based transmission congestion management in a Transco gives direct price signals both to the transmission company and to power generation plants. Some ISOs have price-based transmission congestion management, which enables power prices to vary across different points on the transmission system according to congestion. Transcos could use similar types of pricing for congestion management, but the Transco is the residual claimant for all services it provides. Thus, the Transco will likely seek newer technologies or other facility improvements to reduce the accounting costs of all its operations, not just the transaction costs of delivering electricity.

Both the ISO and Transco models have possible drawbacks. In the case of an ISO, it could be difficult to implement operational efficiency since the ISO operates under a governing board of several stakeholders rather than under for-profit objectives. Also, an ISO may be guided toward long-term decisions based

, on the short-term agendas of several groups. This problem could be alleviated with an appropriate incentive scheme for management.

Monitoring may need to be higher for a Transco than an ISO. Given the economies of scale for transmission and network externalities, the Transco would be a natural monopoly, which would probably be subject to regulation. When problems in the transmission system arise, the Transco could determine that investments are needed as solutions under a regulatory regime. Foregoing investigations into other options, such as redispatching generation, may create over-investment in transmission capacity at certain locations. Over-investment not only would create higher transmission prices, but efficient location of generating capacity and distribution lines over the long-run would be distorted.

The American Public Power Association (APPA), a national service organization representing the interests of non-profit, publicly owned utilities in the US, acknowledges some differences among its members regarding RTO formation[17] and suggests the ISO–Gridco hybrid as a possible solution to the ISO–Transco debate. This model allows a single ISO to operate the transmission facilities for a number of transmission companies. The Gridco, owner of the transmission facilities, directly provides transmission capability to the ISO while remaining independent of other market participants. A Gridco would operate like some independent generation company that can contract under a variety of terms. According to the APPA, this model can allow independent operation of the grid and non-discriminatory transmission services while allowing the ISO, Gridcos, and transmission customers to seek performance-based regulation.[18]

A 1998 report by the Large Public Power Council (LPPC)[19] suggests a 'not-for-profit Transco' as a transmission operator:

> The term 'not-for-profit TransCo' is a relatively broad concept that would encompass a variety of organizational and governance structures. Generally speaking, a not-for-profit Transco would look like a conventional ISO except that it could own, lease or contract for transmission assets, and it would be responsible for the planning and operational responsibilities associated with those assets. The not-for-profit TransCo may or may not be in the form of a government entity. Put another way, in terms of organization and governance, the not-for-profit TransCo might look more like a traditional municipal utility or it might look more like a traditional electric cooperative.[20]

The City of Tallahassee, a municipality in Florida that owns both interstate and intrastate transmission, believes for-profit Transcos are the most efficient form of an RTO. The municipal utility emphasizes the importance of combining ownership and operation of transmission facilities in one organization for efficient operation in a Transco. However, the municipal utility suggests that the FERC allow regions flexibility in forming government-owned, non-profit Transcos when public ownership may yield substantial benefits. Furthermore, the municipal utility stresses the importance of allowing public utility commissions to be directly involved with RTO formation.[21]

Another Florida utility, Jacksonville Electric Authority (JEA), the eighth largest municipal utility in the US, also has a significant investment in high voltage facilities and supports the formation of a publicly owned, non-profit Transco to meet the FERC's objectives. The utility is concerned about giving up control of its transmission assets while retaining ownership. Protecting the interests of those consumers who have invested in the development of transmission assets is a vital concern for JEA, which would prefer that a single RTO serve the whole state of Florida since the state has its own reliability council as part of the North American Electric Reliability Council (NERC).[22] With Florida essentially isolated from the rest of the Eastern Interconnection grid, it may be reasonable to have a single RTO for the entire state. [23]

The disagreements among publicly owned utilities on type of RTO present several challenges in RTO formation. Although the FERC is urging RTO formation for all electricity companies, the lack of a formal requirement to become involved creates caution among publicly owned utilities. A publicly owned utility may not even consider joining an RTO if the proposed model type, with associated functions and responsibilities, is not close to the utility's desired model. This could create holes in coverage areas of Transcos, ISOs, or other grid operators. Concerns about market power, congestion, and reliability may easily become accentuated.

Even though Order 2000 states that the FERC is willing to accept a variety of RTO forms and allow flexibility in formation with other guidelines, the amount of participation by publicly owned utilities is not certain. Flexibility in RTO formation across utility companies is a first step in creating open transmission networks, given the heterogeneity across companies and regional peculiarities. Yet, flexibility is not enough since publicly owned utilities incur significant transaction costs in negotiating membership in RTOs because of other tax rules and regulations discussed later. There is no standard regarding the extent to which privately owned utilities must accommodate publicly owned utilities, and the effort required from many smaller publicly owned utilities for membership may be substantial. The benefits of joining an RTO may not exceed the costs from the publicly owned utility's perspective.

One guideline in Order 2000 is a FERC decision to allow limited active ownership in RTOs. In the five-year RTO transition period, market participants may hold up to 5 percent of an RTO's voting securities. Likewise, a class of market participants may hold up to 15 percent of an RTO's voting securities. Active ownership permits participation in the operating and investment decisions of the RTO. The APPA would prefer no active ownership so that transmission operation can be separated from market participation. To help achieve the FERC's requirement of independence, Order 2000 requires RTOs that allow active ownership by a market participant to employ some type of independent auditing to keep a check on decision-making control through voting interests.

Local, State, and Federal Rules

Several local, state, and federal rules may prohibit public power utilities from participating in RTOs. In comments submitted to the FERC, the LPPC explicitly identifies examples of legal requirements affecting members' participation in the RTO ownership of facilities, ability to sell or lease transmission facilities, and authority to transfer operation of facilities by contract. As an example of a constitutional constraint that would prevent participation in an RTO, Public Utility District No. 1 of Chelan County in the state of Washington is bound by the Washington Constitution (art. VIII, § 7), which stipulates that:

> No county, city, town, or other municipal corporation shall give any money or property, or loan its money or credit to or in aid of any individual, association, company or corporation, or become directly or indirectly the owner of any stock in or bonds of any association, company, or corporation.[24]

The Chelan utility is also subject to public meetings and public disclosure laws. Ratepayers could be prevented from having full information if its facilities were transferred to a non-public RTO.[25]

The constitutional restrictions vary among the LPPC members regarding authority to sell or lease transmission facilities. Colorado Springs Utilities is subject to a law that 'authorizes a city to sell and dispose of electric light works or other public utilities, subject to voter approval' (Colo. Rev. Stat. § 31–5–15–713(1)). The JEA charter requires city council approval for a transfer of more than 10 percent of the total utility system by sale, lease, or other exchange (Section 21.04(p)).[26] In summation, all public power utilities – large and small alike – have bond covenant restrictions that affect their ability to sell or lease public power transmission facilities.

Many of the same regulations that restrict the sale or lease of public transmission facilities restrict the ability of public power systems to transfer operation of transmission to other entities. As a specific case, the Lower Colorado River Authority is restricted by bond covenants that require its board of directors to retain rate-making authority even with the transfer of operation. Transmission facilities transferred to an RTO would be under multiple layers of oversight responsibility.[27]

The ability of public power entities to issue tax-exempt bonds to finance capital investments is restricted under the US Internal Revenue Code, Section

141. These 'private-use' restrictions limit the amount of power sales by publicly financed facilities. The rules were designed to prevent private parties from benefiting from low-cost, tax-exempt financing. Too much 'private use' of facilities owned by publicly owned utilities results in increased financing; bond-holders lose their tax-exempt status for investments and utilities have to redeem some of the bonds.

The LPPC notes that private use could result when the RTO is a non-governmental entity that controls and operates the transmission facilities of a municipal utility. And even if the RTO were a government entity, further investigation would be required under private-use rules since an investor-owned utility may be obtaining transmission service. The bonds of public power utilities that violate the private-use rules become taxable, and the IRS could collect unpaid taxes or penalize the issuer. By taking actions to make the bonds taxable if private use were violated, many public power utilities would violate local bond covenants.

The temporary private-use rules were extended in January 2001 to 2004. Clarifications, which are subject to further modification, now essentially allow publicly owned utilities to surrender transmission facilities to an RTO without violating private-use regulations. Legislation to clarify private-use rules on a permanent basis that would encourage competition in the electricity industry and give publicly owned utilities the opportunity to open their transmission systems was introduced in the 106th Congress. This was not passed, but similar legislation known as the Electric Power Industry Tax Modernization Act has been introduced in the 107th Congress.

Just as privately owned utilities invested large amounts in transmission lines under regulation from state public utility commissions, the publicly owned utilities made similar investments under a given set of financing rules. In conjunction with uncertainties in restructuring, the temporary rules put forth by the IRS make it difficult for publicly owned utilities to develop long-term strategies in a constantly changing electricity industry. Permanent changes to the IRS code are needed. Not penalizing public power systems for past investments and allowing an adequate transition period to eliminate tax-exempt financing are two important elements in drafting permanent private-use rules.

Challenges Facing Federally Owned Utilities

To this point, I have focused on publicly owned utilities – municipals, public power districts, state authorities, irrigation districts, and other state organizations. I now consider federally owned utilities in connection with RTO formation. This group is comprised of five wholesale power producers (the US Army Corps of Engineers, US Bureau of Indian Affairs, US Bureau of Reclamation, and the Tennessee Valley Authority) and power-marketing administrations (Bonneville Power Administration, Southeastern Power Administration, Southwestern Power Administration, and Western Power Administration). I look primarily at transmission issues affecting the Tennessee Valley Authority (TVA) and Bonneville Power Administration (BPA).[28]

TVA, the largest electric utility in the US with a service area covering almost all of Tennessee and parts of Kentucky, Georgia, Virginia, North Carolina, Mississippi, and Alabama, is a government corporation created by the TVA Act of 1933 to provide navigational control, flood control, agricultural development, and other services. The TVA was soon providing electricity for the Tennessee region in conjunction with its other responsibilities. TVA's 17,000 miles of transmission lines provide full power requirements to 159 retail distributors, all municipal or cooperative utilities in its territory. Nearly all distributors purchase the power under wholesale contracts and are not allowed to acquire power from other non-TVA sources. A three-member board of directors (appointed by the US President and confirmed by the Senate) sets power rates. In addition, TVA sells directly to 67 large industrial and federal customers.[29]

The TVA Act of 1933 was amended in 1959 to preclude transmission provision outside the TVA service area, except for 14 surrounding utilities with which the TVA was already doing business. Outside utilities are limited in being able to sell wholesale inside TVA's territory because of the existing all-requirements contracts with distributors inside its service territory. In addition, TVA is exempt from the FERC's authority to order transmission services under Sections 210, 211, and 212 of the Federal Power Act if the transmission service is for power consumed inside its service territory. These 'anti-cherry picking' provisions were enacted under the Energy Policy Act of 1992 to protect the TVA from competition by erecting the so-called 'TVA fence.' As a result, the inability of TVA to participate in any RTO is at the core of its creation and current existence.

The TVA's existing long-term contracts present obstacles to participation in RTOs. For example, Memphis Light, Gas and Water (MLGW) division, a municipal utility with transmission and distribution ownership as TVA's largest customer and accounting for close to 11 percent of TVA's power sales, has a contract with TVA that requires ten years' written notice to terminate. MLGW and its customers would receive financial penalties in the remaining years of the contract once a notice of termination is given. The municipal utility would not be able to receive alternative power supplies unless (1) the anti-cherry picking provision is repealed, (2) suppliers are given access to customers inside the TVA service territory, or (3) competitors can connect MLGW's system to another supplier.[30]

BPA markets wholesale power and transmission services, operating more than 15,000 miles of transmission facilities in Oregon, Washington, Idaho,

Western Montana, Nevada, Utah, Wyoming, and parts of Northern California. Its power comes from 29 federal dams, a non-federal nuclear plant, and other renewable-source power plants. The BPA gives preference to public utilities in selling low-cost hydropower and sells only excess power outside of the Pacific Northwest.

Reliance on hydroelectric power in the Northwest deserves attention as a factor influencing possible BPA participation in an RTO. The Seattle City Light Department, the seventh largest publicly owned electric utility in terms of customers served, notes the following:

> With hydroelectric power as the dominant resource in the region, unit commitments are made according to objectives that are very different from systems consisting of thermal power plants. As with existing institutions, any prospective organization must continue to recognize special characteristics of hydroelectric generation such as fishery needs, public benefits, and hydraulic relationships – mostly imposed by FERC licenses.... With the lowest cost electricity in the nation, and an already thriving wholesale market with little price volatility, Northwest consumers have less to gain from restructuring the transmission system than do other regions being considered by the Commission under this proposed rule. Assuming that an RTO is projected to result in additional transmission costs, Northwest consumers will be less willing to incur these costs when compared to consumers in regions where power costs are high and wholesale prices are extremely volatile.[31]

Bringing federally owned utilities under the same regulatory jurisdiction that governs privately owned utilities is a first step in integrating them in the new wires industry. The federal power producers and power-marketing administrations set their own transmission and generation rates while remaining exempt from Orders 888 and 2000. About a third of the bulk interstate transmission grid is not covered by FERC's 'open access' rules, a portion that includes more than 45,000 miles of transmission wires owned by the federally owned utilities.

Long-distance transmission of power for wholesale exchanges may become more difficult unless regional areas are integrated into larger transmission areas. Reliability and congestion concerns increase when power is imported and exported between smaller regions with different structures for grid management and operation. Although not required by law, the transmission-owning power-marketing administrations have filed 'open access' transmission tariffs with FERC. Also, the Department of Energy has ordered them to make appropriate participation filings in regard to Order 2000. These voluntary actions by the power-marketing administrations and the Department of Energy are important steps toward bringing federally owned utilities into the new wires industry, but the future remains uncertain.

The challenges facing the federally owned utilities are daunting, but the BPA has been working with neighboring utilities and other stakeholders to design an RTO that is compatible with the needs of the Northwest and meets the FERC requirements. The Bonneville Transmission Operating Agreement, a preliminary rule of conduct created in the RTO development process, ensures that the BPA would not violate any of its obligations under existing statutes and regulations. For example, should conditions in the RTO region require unplanned dispatching of hydroelectric facilities owned by BPA, existing fish- and non-power-related operations will not be violated. To comply with federal law, the agreement would even prevent the RTO from adding charges to BPA's revenue requirement that could result in a profit on federal assets. The parties submitting a general framework for an RTO have developed a set of principles, established an RTO Collaborative Process Plan, and put forth responsibilities for future work.

CONCLUSION

Public power entities are now searching for redefined roles in the new wires industry. Given the complexity of federal, state, and local regulations in ongoing electricity restructuring and with a large number of municipals participating in distribution only, some suggest the role for municipal utilities will be in retail aggregation, where the utility combines the load for the city with residential and small commercial loads and seeks purchases on the wholesale market.[32] John Kelly of the APPA argues that more opportunities for public power should exist, such as providing meter reading and billing services, since the utilities 'collectively and individually have been a major factor in the gradual evolution toward a more competitive industry.'[33]

Differences in states' restructuring laws combined with existing regulations present various options for publicly owned utilities. Some states allow publicly owned utilities to either 'opt in' or 'opt out' in offering retail competition. In conjunction with this choice, states are requiring publicly owned utilities to allow competitors to sell in their service territory if the publicly owned utilities decide to sell outside of their own territories.

It is likely that publicly owned utilities will continue to own and operate a significant amount of distribution lines in the future because this is a default role for public power in that many of the existing distribution systems serve rural areas of the US. Municipal utilities could also invest in renewable generation to offer residents a green alternative where such opportunities are limited. Like so many of the decisions to be made, the benefits from this option, aside from environmental and consumer benefits, depend on state retail competition plans and the nature of the wholesale market.

Finally, uncertainty about the performance of state-level restructuring initiatives could result in the creation of new municipal utilities. Reliability concerns coupled with high electricity prices may push communities served by investor-owned utilities to create their own electric utility. But the newly created municipal utility would still need to address the new federal and state initiatives.

Integrating the federally owned utilities in the new wires industry is not a trivial process. In transferring authority to an RTO, power-marketing administrations must ensure that their obligations are not compromised as the RTO takes control of federally owned hydroelectric generators. The public services made possible through the federally owned utilities have significant value to society in addition to the electricity produced. Finding the right balance in maintaining public benefits while making electricity available for long-distance transmission is definitely a challenging task. Other large countries with complex national, regional, and local systems (Brazil, Russia, India) face similar issues as they try to restructure and reform their electricity sectors. Policymakers in emerging and developed markets can learn lessons from one another as they attempt to create institutional arrangements that support greater competition where there is a mix of government and private ownership.

The effort to identify win–win options for public power, investor-owned utilities, and consumers will define the evolving wires industry. The participation of both publicly owned and federally owned utilities is important to ensure reliability and maximum efficiency in wholesale electricity markets. Successful initiatives will bridge the gap in regulatory treatment between public power and the investor-owned utilities and will allow flexibility for firm heterogeneity and regional differences. Public power should not be penalized for past decisions, but should be provided with incentives and options to become part of the new wires industry as RTO members.

ACKNOWLEDGMENTS

Comments on a previous version of this chapter from Sanford Berg, Barry Moline, Karen Palmer, David Sappington, Paul Sotkiewicz, Bob Trapp, and Amy Zubaly are gratefully acknowledged. The statements made here do not necessarily reflect the views of sponsors of the Public Utility Research Center.

ENDNOTES

1. An overview of the electricity industry can be found in Warkentin (1998). A primer from Resources for the Future that explains the restructuring process is Brennan et al. (1996). A shorter treatment is Joskow (1997).
2. See Schap (1986) and Kwoka (1996) for comprehensive examinations of public power.

3. See Federal Energy Regulatory Commission, Regional Transmission Organizations, Order No. 2000, December 1999: 1–4.
4. See Federal Energy Regulatory Commission, Promoting Wholesale Competition Through Open Access Non-discriminatory Transmission Service by Public Utilities, Order No. 888, April 1996: 279–87.
5. See Federal Energy Regulatory Commission, Regional Transmission Organizations, Notice of Proposed Rulemaking: Docket No. RM99–2–000, May 1999.
6. Order 2000: 7.
7. Energy Information Administration, 'Electric Sales and Revenue 1998', US Department of Energy, Washington, DC, October 1999: 14.
8. Michael Kurtz, 'Testimony on Behalf of the American Public Power Association before the House Commerce Committee', Subcommittee on Energy Power, Hearing on Market Power, 6 May 1999: 3.
9. The tremendous growth in the volume of trading in the wholesale electricity market has raised concerns about the reliability of the bulk transmission systems. A report from the North American Electricity Reliability Council ('Reliability Assessment 1998–2007', September 1998: 6–7) suggests numerous near- and long-term concerns for the bulk transmission grids. Several of these relate to the movement toward competitive electricity markets.
10. Order 2000: 5–6.
11. See 'The Changing Structure of the Electric Power Industry: Selected Issues, 1998' (Washington, DC: Energy Information Administration: 29–50) for a detailed description of ISO proposals. Legal implications can be found in Angle and Cannon (1998).
12. The other two ISOs in operation are the California ISO, created by state legislation as part of California's electricity restructuring experience, and ERCOT ISO, created by the Public Utility Commission of Texas.
13. A control area is comprised of one or more electrical systems; a control center matches the power output of generators within the system, given transmission constraints, and energy purchased outside the system with the current load of the system. A recent discussion of ISOs and spot markets can be found in Larry E. Ruff's 'Competitive Electricity Markets: Why They Are Working and How to Improve Them' (*NERA*, 12 May 1999).
14. Order 2000: 23.
15. Comments of Professor Paul Joskow in Response to the Notice of Proposed Rulemaking: Regional Transmission Organizations, 16 August 1999: 20.
16. Lenard (1998).
17. APPA's response to the NOPR states, 'Frankly, APPA's membership is divided on the issue of public power participation in RTOs. Most systems – both transmission-dependent and transmission-owning utilities – believe FERC lacks the legal authority to require our participation on a legal basis. Most members also believe FERC lacks an appreciation of the very real barriers to public power participation and the changes needed to eliminate these barriers. Most members also believe that RTOs are inevitable and that public power's participation will be valuable to our customers and to the nation' (Comments of the American Public Power Association in Response to the Notice of Proposed Rulemaking: Regional Transmission Organizations, 23 August 1999: 12).
18. Ibid.: 25.
19. The LPPC is an organization of twenty-one of the largest locally owned and controlled power systems in the US, with members owning 10 percent of the nation's interconnected transmission network.
20. 'Uncrossing the Wires: Transmission in a Restructured Market', LPPC, December 1998: 12.
21. Comments of the City of Tallahassee, Florida, in Response to the Notice of Proposed Rulemaking: Regional Transmission Organizations, 17 August 1999: 7.
22. NERC has operated as a non-profit organization working to ensure reliability of the North American bulk power system. Its members are comprised of ten regional councils, each containing different types of participants in the electric power industry, including investor- and publicly owned utilities. It is working toward reorganization as the North American Electric Reliability Organization to implement enforceable compliance with reliability standards.

23. Comments of JEA in Response to the Notice of Proposed Rulemaking: Regional Transmission Organizations, 13 August 1999.
24. Comments of the Large Public Power Council in Response to the Notice of Proposed Rulemaking: Regional Transmission Organizations, 20 August 1999: Appendix A.
25. Comments of Public Utility District No. 1 of Chelan County, Washington in Response to the Notice of Proposed Rulemaking: Regional Transmission Organizations 7.
26. Large Public Power Council, supra 23.
27. Large Public Power Council, supra 23.
28. The Alaska Power Administration Asset Sale and Termination Act of 1995 authorized and directed the Department of Energy to sell the Alaska Power Administration, consisting of Eklutna and Snettisham hydropower facilities. The Eklutna Project, near Palmer, AK, was transferred to non-federal ownership in October 1997, while the Snettisham Project, near Juneau, was sold in August 1998 for a price close to $82 million.
29. See 'Report of the Tennessee Valley Electric System Advisory Committee', 31 March 1998, for an in-depth discussion of TVA issues in the national restructuring process.
30. Initial Comments of Memphis Light, Gas and Water Division in Reponse to the Notice of Proposed Rulemaking: Regional Transmission Organizations, 23 August 1999: 9
31. Comments of Seattle City Light Department in Response to the Notice of Proposed Rulemaking: Regional Transmission Organizations, 20 August 1999: 14.
32. See Vince et al. (1997), Schuler (1996), and O'Donnell (1995).
33. Kelly (1999).

REFERENCES

Angle, Stephen and George Cannon Jr. (1998), 'Independent transmission companies: The for-profit alternative in competitive electric markets', *Energy Law Journal*, 19, 229–79.

Brennan, Tim J., Karen L. Palmer, Raymond J. Kopp, Alan J. Krupnick, Vito Stagliano, and Dallas Burtraw (1996), *A Shock to the System: Restructuring America's Electricity Industry*, Washington, DC: Resources for the Future.

Joskow, Paul (1997), 'Restructuring, competition, and regulatory reform in the US electricity sector', *Journal of Economic Perspectives*, 11, 119–38.

Kelly, John (1999), 'The future role of distribution utilities: A dissenting view', *Electricity Journal*, 22–9.

Kwoka Jr., John E. (1996), *Power Structure: Ownership, Integration, and Competition in the US Electricity Industry*, Boston: Kluwer.

Lenard, Thomas (1998), 'Getting the Transcos right', *Electricity Journal*, 47–52.

O'Donnell, Kevin W. (1995), 'Aggregating municipal loads: The future is today', *Public Utilities Fortnightly*, 26–8.

Schap, David (1986), *Municipal Ownership in the Electric Utility Industry*, New York: Praeger.

Schuler Jr., Joseph F. (1996), 'Retail aggregation: A guaranteed right for small customers?', *Public Utilities Fortnightly*, 29–31.

Vince, Clint, Sherry Quirk, and Cathy Fogel (1997), 'The future of public power and electric cooperative systems', *Electricity Journal*, 40–46.

Warkentin, Denise (1998), *Electric Power Industry in Nontechnical Language*, Tulsa, OK: Penn Well.

9. Domestic and international environmental issues in restructuring electric industries

John Tschirhart

Government intervention in the electric industry is an old story. Throughout the world, electric companies have been monopolies either privately owned and regulated or publicly owned. Under either ownership form, the purpose of government actions has been to protect consumers by ensuring adequate supplies of power produced at low costs and sold at affordable prices. Regulation has also protected private firms from competitive entry to ensure adequate returns on investments. Today, regulated monopolies are being abandoned in favor of letting competitive market forces in a restructured industry ensure adequate supplies, low costs and affordable prices. At the same time, public ownership is being replaced by privatization in many countries.

Generally, in a competitive industry, a good is sold in the marketplace and market forces balance consumer benefits against industry production costs to yield optimum quantities of the good. This ideal outcome is more complicated in the electric power industry. While electricity is central to living standards in developed and developing countries, its production has side effects that negatively impact the quality of life.[1] These side effects or externalities, mostly in the form of air emissions, typically fall outside the marketplace. The damages from emissions are true costs to society, yet historically they were not included along with production costs in the market for electricity; therefore, market forces delivered neither an optimum amount of electricity nor an optimum amount of emissions. Thus, on the one hand, government intervention into electric markets is becoming less necessary because of industry restructuring; on the other hand, it is becoming more necessary because generation emissions affect human health and natural ecosystems in all countries.

During a century of industrialization, governments rarely intervened to address externalities. With a relatively small population, two billion in the 1930s, the earth's ability to absorb pollution appeared limitless. By the late 1960s, with population approaching four billion, the earth's limits were apparent and governments became more active. Now, in a new millennium and with more than six billion people, governments are recognizing the need for international cooperation to reduce emissions, toxic wastes, ocean dumping, desertification, rain forest destruction and a host of other environmental ills.

In the electric industry, government intervention for the purposes of moving toward an optimum level of emissions can be placed into two broad categories, one that affects the supply side and one that affects the demand side of the electricity market. On the supply side, the goal of intervention is to internalize the externalities, which will have the effect of either reducing the supply of electricity via increasing the cost of generation or, for a given supply, reducing emissions by using cleaner technologies. On the demand side, the goal of intervention is to reduce the demand for electricity while maintaining the benefits that flowed from the original demand.

In this chaper I discuss both supply- and demand-side interventions that address domestic and global externalities. I briefly review the damages caused by generation emissions, then consider the supply side of the market and the tools available for addressing domestic damages from emissions. A look at the problems of global damages from the so-called greenhouse gases is followed by consideration of the demand side of the market and regulatory efforts to encourage energy conservation. Finally, I present implications for developing countries and a brief final word.

ENVIRONMENTAL DAMAGES FROM GENERATION EMISSIONS

The electric power industry worldwide is a very visible and concentrated source of pollutants, and it will continue to be near the center of many environmental programs. The types of pollutants and their effects traceable to fossil fuel use are as follows.[2]

- NO_x – Nitrogen oxide contributes to groundlevel ozone, which decreases visibility and causes human health problems such as asthma and other respiratory illnesses. It also damages crops, forests and other plant life. In the US, electric generation contributes about a third of total NO_x emissions.
- SO_2 – Sulfur dioxide mixes with other chemicals in the atmosphere to reduce visibility and create acid rain, which damages human health and private property and leads to the acidification of lakes and streams. In the US, electric generation contributes more than two-thirds of total SO_2 emissions.

- Particulates – When fossil fuels are burned, dust, soot and other solid matter are sent into the atmosphere. These particulates reduce visibility and have been traced to human mortality. Power generation contributes about a third of the total particulates in the US.
- Heavy metals – Coal and oil contain heavy metals that are released in the atmosphere during combustion. These end up in soil and water and can be toxic to humans and wildlife. About a quarter of the mercury emissions in the US are from power generation.
- Greenhouse gases (GHGs) – These include carbon dioxide (CO_2), methane, NO_x and chlorofluorocarbons. GHGs reflect long-wave radiation that otherwise would escape into space back into the earth's atmosphere. Although the meteorology and geophysics behind this greenhouse effect are complicated, the weight of scientific evidence is leaning toward the notion that human-made GHGs are accumulating sufficiently to warm the climate. CO_2 is the major GHG, and power generation contributes about a third of the CO_2 in the US from human sources.

The generation of electricity impacts the environment in many ways besides air emissions. Fossil-fuel mining scars landscapes and damages rivers, streams and groundwater. Power plant operation can also contribute to local groundwater problems and heat up water temperatures in lake and river water used for cooling. However, these types of non-air emission damages will not be addressed here.

REDUCING DOMESTIC ENVIRONMENTAL DAMAGES FROM GENERATION EMISSIONS

What is the potential benefit from restructuring the electric industry? Presumably, relying more on competition among firms and less on regulatory oversight will increase efficiency by decreasing the costs of production.[3] If competition works, then consumers will benefit because the lower costs will be passed along to them in the form of lower electric rates. This is good news for consumers' standard of living, but can be bad news for their qualities of life if the lower prices and concomitant greater demands lead to more emissions. To ensure that the latter does not occur, it is important to incorporate into the price of electricity the environmental costs of generation. If this is done correctly, then the future might be one in which the industry is restructured but prices do not fall, even though competition is successful, because the cost of emissions damage is included in the price. In this case, restructuring may not improve living standards as traditionally measured but will improve quality of life.

Because rising prices are unpopular, restructuring offers an opportunity to maintain prices while protecting the environment. Whether this will occur depends on the policies governments adopt.

Reducing air pollution in general can be thought of as a two-step process: determine the optimum level of pollution and then determine how the reductions to achieve the optimum are allocated across polluters. Understandably, some people abhor the notion of 'optimum' pollution as anything more than zero, but we live in a world of difficult choices. Given current technology, zero pollution would mean shutting down industry.

The first step comprises most of the controversy. Should benefit/cost analysis be used to determine the optimum? Should risks to human health be the driving criterion? How do we factor in the value of healthy ecosystems? In short, what are the air pollution damages and what are the costs of cleaning it up? Answers vary by interest groups because this first step is the one that determines the ultimate level of air pollution.

In practice, in the US, measurement methods are still too crude for finding an optimum, so after all groups have had their say, a target pollution level is chosen, usually on the basis of human health. When the target is lower than current pollution, reductions are required. Which polluters should reduce their emissions and by how much is addressed in step two.

Reductions should be assigned across polluters efficiently, which means minimizing cost of cleanup, given the target level. Because the cost of reducing emissions varies considerably across polluters, efficiency calls for polluters for whom reducing is expensive to reduce less than polluters for whom reducing is cheap. Unfortunately, governments do not have the information to distinguish between expensive and cheap polluters, so the traditional approach, labeled 'command and control', has called for all polluters to reduce by the same percentage. This is inefficient, and the costs above the efficient solution can be very large.

Effluent charges and tradable permits are alternatives to command and control. The former requires emitters to pay a charge for each unit of emissions pumped into the atmosphere, and ideally the charge reflects the cost of the emissions' damages. Using the permit approach, the government issues permits to polluters, and each permit allows the polluter some stated level of emissions. The sum of all permits equals the target pollution level. Who gets how many permits is usually based on historical emissions, and the permit holders can buy permits from and sell permits to one another. (In the SO_2 permit program in the US, non-industry groups such as the American Lung Society may hold and retire permits.) The polluters for whom it is expensive to clean up will buy permits and clean less, while polluters for whom it is cheap to clean up will sell permits and clean more. Efficiency is achieved because the least-cost means of reaching the target pollution level is realized. The government does not need to identify those for whom cleaning up is expensive or cheap because the newly created permit market does it automatically.

There are some difficulties with permit systems. The permit market may be difficult to set up and maintain, especially if there are few firms or if their costs of reduction are similar. If the agency charges a fee for the initial allocation of permits, the system will be politically unpopular. The method of allocating the permits could be controversial, and if total costs are a more important consideration than total emissions, a permit system is less desirable than a charge system, since the agency does not know the eventual price of permits in the market.[4]

If environmental damages are internalized by a charge or permit system, they are included in the costs of generation and in electricity prices. Inclusion in generation cost is desirable in that it gives emitters an incentive to develop cleaner technologies or invest in conservation to lower either their charges or permit costs, or to increase their permit revenues. Inclusion in electricity prices is desirable in that consumers have an incentive to conserve and at the same time be more willing to switch to new technologies. Solar and wind power, for example, are more likely to penetrate the supply side of electric markets when prices for fossil-fueled generation are economically correct.

Tietenberg (1995) offers a number of reasons why tradable permits would be desirable in developing countries. First, the opportunity cost of capital is high in developing countries; thus any investments made in cleaner technologies ought to take advantage of the cost-minimizing properties of permit systems. Second, the incentive effects with permits will help to stimulate progress in designing new and better pollution-control technologies. Third, tradable permits and fees for excess pollution can raise revenue in countries where more government revenues are needed.

Regarding the third reason, there is the possibility of a 'double dividend.' That is, if revenues raised from taxing 'bads' such as pollution are used to displace taxes on 'goods' such as income, the economy benefits twice. However, whether the double dividend is really attainable has been the subject of considerable debate. As Parry and Bento (2000, p. 67) state:

> These debates arose in response to the so-called double dividend hypothesis, that is, the claim that environmental taxes could simultaneously improve the environment and reduce the economic costs of the tax system. The latter effect seemed plausible, if the revenues from taxes on carbon emissions, gasoline, traffic congestion, household garbage, fish catches, chemical fertilizers, and so on were used to reduce the rates of pre-existing taxes that distort labor and capital markets.

Studies by Bovenberg and Goulder (1996), Goulder (1995) and others suggest that the double dividend does not exist because the environmental taxes can exacerbate the distortions being caused by taxes on capital and labor, thus adding to an inefficient tax system. In contrast to these studies, Parry and Bento (2000) find that the double dividend is real if one accounts for the fact that some goods such as housing and medical care receive favorable tax treatment. Labor taxes distort the relative prices of consumption goods as well as wages, and displacing some labor taxes with environmental taxes can reduce the distortions when one accounts for the favored consumption goods.

There is concern that developing countries may not be able to achieve adequate organization and monitoring capabilities to operate a permit system. But a tradable permit system probably requires little additional infrastructure beyond what developing countries are investing in price and entry regulation of their utilities. According to Tietenberg (1995, p. 29), 'Most emissions monitoring is based on a system of self-reporting. Although self-reporting systems immediately raise concerns about possible abuse, in practice they work remarkably well, particularly when complemented by an effective system of criminal penalties for falsification.'

GLOBAL IMPACTS OF GHGs AND THE KYOTO PROTOCOL

Greenhouse gases that trap long-wave radiation include CO_2, methane, NO_x and chlorofluorocarbons, although CO_2 is the main concern from the burning of fossil fuel by the electric industry. The atmospheric concentration of CO_2 is about 0.04 percent. There were 280 parts per million of CO_2 in the air during pre-industrial days; today the parts per million has risen to 350. This increase is not disputed, nor is the fact that it is largely attributable to human activity. What is in dispute is how much the earth's climate will change from this increase in CO_2. Even more controversial is what should be done about it.[5]

Typical predictions call for a warming of the earth's atmosphere by several degrees. Because humans have adapted to climates all over the world, physically adapting to a change of a few degrees will not be problematic. However, many plants and animals are less tolerant, and habitat ranges could change significantly even with small temperature changes. Placing a value on these changes is difficult because the benefits from most plants and animals fall outside the marketplace.

The loss of land if the sea level rises according to predictions could have a potentially enormous impact. The sea has risen 8–12 cm over the last 80 years, and some estimates call for a 44-cm increase over the next century. The US Environmental Protection Agency (EPA) has estimated $100 billion in capital costs would be needed to protect coasts should this rise occur (EPA 1989). When aggregated over the world, the costs are not large, but disaggregation is important here because a rising sea will not affect countries uniformly. Indeed, some low-lying island countries could be submerged.[6]

Weather changes will impact industries to varying degrees. The most severely affected will be agriculture and resource extraction industries such as logging and fishing. Construction, water transportations, recreation and the energy industries will be moderately affected, the latter because of an increased demand for cooling and decreased demand for heating. Only minor impacts are expected in industries such as mining, manufacturing, finance, and so on (Nordhaus 1991).

Because the effects of global warming are so uncertain, the benefits of avoiding it are uncertain as well. Moreover, most benefits fall well into the future. Quick action means the costs begin now and fall on current generations, which makes the costs easier to estimate than the benefits.

In spite of the uncertainties and uneven distribution of costs and benefits, representatives of 160 countries met in Kyoto, Japan, in December 1997 to map out a course of action at the Third Conference of the Parties to the United Nations Framework Convention on Climate Change. Countries agreeing to the Kyoto Protocol to reduce GHGs were to sign on between March 1998 and March 1999. The US was the sixtieth country to sign, although the US Senate has still not ratified the treaty and there is strong domestic opposition to ratification. In March 2001, President George W. Bush announced that the US would withdraw from the Kyoto Protocol because it was 'fatally flawed.' Nevertheless, delegates from 178 countries met in Bonn, Germany, in July 2001 to set emissions requirements for developed countries. Japan was reluctant to join the agreements without US participation but accepted the requirements before the meetings ended, with the understanding that negotiations on enforcement would be postponed.

Shogren (1999) characterizes the Kyoto Protocol as 'broad and deep': deep in the sense that the proposed cuts in carbon emissions by developed countries are substantial in some instances, broad in the sense that developing countries, which have no obligations under the protocol, are encouraged to join once convinced it is in their best interest to do so. In Article 3, the protocol calls for legally binding targets on 39 of the most developed countries for an aggregate 5.2 percent reduction from 1990 levels of GHG emissions by 2008–12. The cuts vary across countries.

A major feature of the protocol, Article 17, allows for emissions trading across countries. GHGs are excellent candidates for a tradable permit system. Regardless of where in the world the gases are emitted, they are believed to contribute uniformly to climate change. In economic jargon, the benefits of reducing GHGs are a pure public good that would be underprovided in a market system without government intervention.

The system envisioned would allow permits, or units of national emissions quotas, to be traded across countries as other homogeneous commodities might be traded. At the end of 5-year commitment periods, there is a check to make sure the permits held by a country cover its actual emissions. Trading centers would operate as stock exchanges and could be located around the world so trades could be made 24 hours a day.

Monitoring emissions is critical if countries are to have confidence and agree to participate. Rather than monitor emissions directly, an alternative is to monitor fossil-fuel use, then multiply the amount of each fuel used by its carbon content. A country's fossil-fuel use will equal its production plus its imports minus its exports. Because an exporter has an incentive not to under-report and an importer has an incentive not to over-report, there is a check on traded quantities of fuel. Tracking inventory changes within countries will be more problematic.

Under the Kyoto Protocol, only Annex B countries (those that have committed to emissions limits and have ratified the protocol) can participate in trading. The maximum number of traders would be 36 plus the European Union. The United States would have 35 percent and Russia 18 percent of the assigned GHGs by 2008–12. In spite of these large participants, the expectation is that the trading will be competitive (Bohm and Carlen 1999).

Whether developing countries will join a trading system is speculative. They would need to be issued sufficient permits to be fully compensated for the first five-year period. According to Bohm and Carlen (1999), nine of 17 developing countries asked whether they would join said they would. Having more countries enter trading is advantageous to all countries. As new countries enter, there would be new, lower cost-abatement opportunities, which lowers the price of permits and the cost of emission limits for Annex B countries. The joining countries benefit from having a commodity to sell to increase their export earnings. All countries benefit from greater levels of the public good, viz., diminished costs of climate change.

Participating countries must decide how they will allocate their allotted permits domestically. A popular approach will probably be to use the international tradable permits in a domestic tradable permits system (Tschirhart and Wen 1999). Thus, a country accepts its permits and either gives them away or auctions them off to domestic emitters. The domestic firms then hold or trade the permits as they would permits for other pollutants such as SO_2. If the domestic firms are allowed to trade the permits in the international market, this would mean many more traders in the market, which would ease the fears of market dominance in the international market by the US, the largest emitting country.

CONSERVATION

Integrated resource planning became a widespread practice for electric utilities in the US during the 1980s. Kahn (1992) depicted it as one of the two major industry developments in the decade, the other being the advent of competition. Integrated resource planning pertains to minimizing the cost of electric energy needs, where cost includes not only the usual production cost associated with whatever technologies are adopted, but also the cost of externalities and conservation.

Conservation practices are also referred to as demand-side management (DSM). DSM encourages consumers to cut back on their use of electricity through conservation, thereby reducing the need to construct and operate new generation facilities, and DSM is often considered a resource in the same way that new generation facilities are.

Public utility commissions (PUCs) have been active in promoting DSM. Twenty-one states were providing some sort of incentive for DSM to utilities at the start of 1993 when IRT Environmental, Inc. (http://solstice.crest.org/efficiency/irt/) reported that hundreds of utilities were running thousands of DSM programs in North America.[7] Although a wide variety of programs were employed, most relied on incentive instruments since PUCs confronted a tradeoff in making DSM attractive to utilities on the one hand and consumers on the other hand.

A utility's disincentive to participate in DSM was rooted in traditional rate-of-return regulation and the utility's role as a supplier of electricity only. A utility was unlikely to promote programs that reduced demand for its core product. During the period after a regulatory hearing, the utility's price of electricity was fixed at a level that typically exceeded the marginal operating cost of production. A successful conservation program reduced sales of electricity, thereby reducing the utility's profit. Because the utility's profit rose and fell with sales and because conservation dampens sales, the utility had a strong disincentive to participate in DSM.

Utilities have since repositioned themselves as multiproduct suppliers, with electricity at the core of related electric services, but regulators responded to utilities' initial disincentive to promote conservation with a variety of programs that can be characterized by their use of the following three instruments: a direct charge for conservation, a promotional or marketing plan, and a transfer scheme. The first instrument allowed the utility to charge consumers for conservation. This represented a significant shift in emphasis because the utility entered the business of selling conservation in addition to electricity. Depending on the cost of supplying conservation and the price charged, a utility could increase profit through conservation sales. In practice, the conservation price was usually set by PUCs and could be as low as zero. Therefore, whether the price instrument was effective in removing the utility's disincentive to sell conservation depended on the specific DSM program.

The second instrument was the marketing plan. PUCs were very explicit in dictating what the utility must do to promote conservation. A plan might include advertising, energy audits, education and measurement of savings. Marketing plans were thought to be important because of the possible market failures that discouraged consumers from investing in cost-effective conservation. Lack of knowledge, lack of access to credit and the tenant/landlord relationship were cited as sources for possible market failures.

The third instrument was a transfer scheme. The term 'transfer' is used broadly here to represent any scheme wherein the utility raised revenue from some source other than the price charged for conservation. The utility stood to lose profit if its electricity sales decreased, if it sold conservation below cost, or if it expended resources on a marketing plan. To ensure that the utility was able to maintain the rate of return set at the most recent hearing, a transfer would be necessary.

Transfers took a variety of forms. Some regulators permitted a surcharge on the price of electricity while others used a flat, per-customer charge to recover the cost of conservation. Direct government transfers, while popular in the economics literature on incentive schemes, are rare in the US. Another form of transfer was decoupling, wherein the utility's revenue was decoupled from actual sales. The revenue received by the utility was fixed at its expected level in the absence of any conservation. With the revenue fixed, the reduction in electricity sales attributable to conservation did not reduce the utility's profit. California has used a form of decoupling, the Electric Rate Adjustment Mechanism, and Maine, New York and Washington have used other forms of decoupling.

One might expect that because conservation efforts were ongoing for more than a decade, PUCs would have honed in on the optimum combination of the three instruments. Instead, across the US, regulators continued to use varying combinations of these three instruments. This suggests that the optimum combination may vary across regulatory jurisdictions with the parameters that characterize the jurisdictions.

DSM practices encouraged by PUCs in 1996 produced 61,800 gigawatt-hours of savings (a 2 percent saving) and a 29,900 gigawatt-hours decrease in peak demand at the zenith of traditional DSM (Energy Information Administration 2000, p. 75). However, today the situation has changed. The electric industry is undergoing significant restructuring, and conservation has taken a back seat to questions about competitive generation markets, alternative forms of regulation, supplier of last resort, and so on. DSM expenditures by utilities declined steadily in the 1990s as the electric industry moved to more competition. This has happened in spite of the President's Climate Change Action Plan of 1993 that stipulated energy efficiency as the most cost-effective way to reduce CO_2 emissions (Meyers and Hu 1999).

Some initiatives in the US encourage continued conservation. Sixteen states, including California and New York, have established public benefit charges to be levied on electric distribution companies. The revenues are used to fund energy efficiency, renewable energy, research and development and low-income assistance (Eto et al. 1998). A similar charge has been proposed at the national level as well in the Comprehensive Electricity Competition Plan (Department of Energy, March 1998). According to Meyers and Hu (1999), the states see it as a tradeoff: they exercise less regulatory oversight in the generation and transmission stages of vertically integrated firms while collecting the benefits fee on distribution.[8]

California's ongoing 'energy crisis' that resulted in brown and black outs has brought conservation and the search for new supplies to the forefront in the US. Interest groups and the public have pointed their fingers in many directions when arguing about what caused the crisis. Was the deregulation of generation poorly designed and too quickly implemented? Was it the drought conditions in the Pacific Northwest that prevented that region from exporting hydropower? Was it lifting price controls on wholesale rates while the retail rates remained regulated, which resulted in large utility losses? Did environmental groups prevent the construction of new power plants in the state? Whatever the cause, the future of the electricity industry in California may be a sign for the structure of the industry elsewhere.

With respect to the supply side, what seems certain is that the mix of generation will gradually change from heavy reliance on coal to heavy reliance on natural gas. New technologies allow relatively small gas-fired plants to be competitive with large coal units. Relying on natural gas will greatly reduce SO_2 and NO_x emissions, although carbon emissions will remain a problem. With respect to conservation, one very promising possibility is real-time pricing wherein consumers can respond instantly to price changes. If environmental damages are built into those prices, then the incentives for consumers to conserve may be more effective at promoting conservation than traditional DSM programs.

DEVELOPING COUNTRIES

As developing countries increase their productivity and enjoy higher living standards, the energy and communications industries will be key sectors. Therefore, devising sound regulatory policies is an important component in devising sound economic policies in general. However, 'national and international economic policy has usually ignored the environment' (Arrow et al. 1995, p. 520). The demonstrations at the 1999 World Trade Organization meetings in Seattle illustrate the depth of concern among some groups that international agreements do not take into account environmental and natural resource issues.

One justification for ignoring environmental problems when promoting economic growth is the professed relationship between growth and environmental quality. As a country's per capita income rises, there is a deterioration of the environment up to a point, followed by improvements. The explanation seems obvious: for people in grinding poverty, environmental amenities are luxury goods. These people must attend to the basics, including where their next meal will come from. Only when they achieve a more comfortable standard of living can they begin to devote resources to protecting the environment. This inverted U phenomenon has been shown to apply to sanitation, water supplies and SO_2, NO_x and CO (Grossman and Krueger 1993). However, to conjecture that the inverted U applies to environmental quality more generally is misleading. Raising living standards is neither sufficient to promote environmental quality in general, nor sustainable if the earth's natural resource base, which makes possible the improved living standards, is sufficiently depleted (Arrow et al. 1995). In other words, while the inverted U may apply narrowly, it says nothing about accumulations of stocks of waste such as CO_2, depletion of natural resource stocks, or how the gains in one country may result from the exportation of pollution to another country.

The concern that economic growth and environmental preservation may be at odds with one another has spawned a vast literature on sustainability, a concept that is universally accepted, perhaps because nobody knows what it is. Different groups paint their own picture of what it is. The most quoted definition is from the Bruntland Commission. Sustainable development '... meets the needs of the present generation without compromising the ability of future generations to meet their own needs' (World Commission on Environmental and Development 1997, p. 43).

Of course, as we embark on this new millennium, the needs of present generations are not being met in many developing countries. Understandably, these countries want a better standard of living, with affordable food, shelter and clothing, not to mention the good life enjoyed by many people in the developed countries. To achieve this goal requires greater productivity, which in turn requires more energy use. The largest countries, China and India, are typical. Their current energy consumption is small per capita, and they want to increase this usage, largely through burning more coal. China, for example, is the second largest emitter of GHGs after the US, but its per capita emissions are one-seventh that of the US. If China alone among the developing countries consumed as much energy per capita as the US, using current technologies, then the world's emissions would more than double what they are today. Yet to ask developing countries to follow a different energy path than the ones pioneered by developed countries promotes such responses as 'What they [developed nations] are doing is luxury emissions, what we are doing is survival emissions' (Huber and Douglass 1998).

The problem is that the traditional models of economic growth pursued by developed countries may be inappropriate for developing countries because the economic activity needed to eradicate poverty may also eradicate ecosystems and deplete the natural resources needed to sustain the activity. According to Tietenberg (1998), the former director of the World Commission on Environment and Development, Jim McNeill, put it this way, 'If current forms of development were employed, a five- to ten-fold increase in economic activity would be required over the next fifty years to meet the needs and aspirations of a population twice the size of today's 5.2 billion, as well as to begin to reduce mass poverty.' And Tietenberg (1998, p. 404) states:

> Whether increases of this magnitude could be accomplished while still respecting the atmosphere and ecological systems on which all economic activity ultimately depends is not at all obvious. Increased energy consumption to support new industry would add GHGs. Increased refrigeration would add more of the gases depleting the stratospheric ozone level. The industrialized nations have freely used the very large capacity of the atmosphere to absorb these gases. Little absorptive capacity is left. Most observers seem to believe that in order to meet the challenge, we need to take an activist stance by controlling population, severely reducing emissions of these gases in the industrialized world, and discovering new forms of development that are sustainable.

If the carrying capacity of the planet cannot be sustained with the business-as-usual approach to economic development spread over all countries, what is the alternative? Certainly emphasizing human capital in developing countries is important both for productivity increases and quality of life. At the same time, environmental policies should be integrated with general economic and regulatory policies at the outset, and not relegated to a side street to be run out only after significant and even irreversible environmental damage has been done.

For the electric industries, the first challenge is to get the prices right. The price of power should reflect the true social cost (production cost plus environmental damage cost) of delivering the power to consumers, and this can be accomplished best through either charges for emissions or tradable permits as outlined earlier. To be sure, internalizing externalities would lead to higher prices, which is seemingly a cruel prescription in countries where prices are already beyond the reach of many citizens. But making electricity affordable at the expense of environmental degradation is also a cruel prescription because the burden of such degradation often falls disproportionately on the poor. If greater electricity penetration is a social goal, then aiding the poor through low-income electricity subsidies made available through taxes on a more efficient electric sector is a better remedy.[9]

In addition, consumers should take advantage of conservation that is cost-effective, and the best incentive to get consumers to conserve is higher energy prices, which will follow if the price of power reflects the true social costs. Finally, all countries should participate in CO_2 trading so that all countries can take advantage of the lowest cost methods for reducing emissions.

This latter strategy does not appear to hold enough direct benefit for many developing countries to obtain their participation, but there may be ways to provide incentives. For example, consider that the Annex B countries will be trading CO_2 permits among themselves. After some time, the price of these permits can be expected to settle at some stable level that reflects the opportunities for low cost abatement in these countries. If the developing countries do not join in, there will be more emissions and climate change than is desirable worldwide, which harms all countries, and some of the lower cost-abatement opportunities in the developing countries will not be utilized. However, if developing countries do participate, the Annex B countries would benefit by the lower permit prices that would follow as lower cost-abatement techniques are used. Consider, therefore, the following proposal, which would provide incentives to developing countries to join the Kyoto initiative: following entry of the developing countries into the permit system, the Annex B countries commit to transferring all of the benefit from lower permit prices to the developing countries with the stipulation that this transfer be used for investment in renewable energy. The result would be that the developed countries would be financially no worse off than when the developing countries did not participate, developing countries would have permits to trade and subsidies available to invest in non-polluting renewable energy, and all countries would be better off because overall there would be fewer emissions and a more rapid move away from fossil fuels.

FINAL WORD

As developing countries encourage private participation in their utility industries and developed countries restructure their utility industries, the former are in a position to adopt regulatory policies and incentives mechanisms based on the new models that the latter are discovering. In other words, developing countries do not have to follow the same path as developed countries did with traditional regulatory models; instead, developing countries can jump directly to the new forms of regulation that developed countries are moving toward.

The same strategy can be followed with environmental issues. Developing countries need not pursue the same path the developed countries followed for years, one of largely ignoring environmental problems; instead, they can pursue sound environmental policies similar to those that are finally finding their way into the agendas of developed countries. All countries will enjoy the resulting benefits.

ACKNOWLEDGMENTS

I thank Sanford Berg, Patricia Mason, an anonymous referee, and participants in the Institute for Developing Economies workshop at Makuhari Messe, Chiba-shin, Japan, in January 2000 for their comments, although I am solely responsible for any errors.

ENDNOTES

1. Here, standard of living is equated to the amount of manufactured goods people consume, a measure roughly reflected in Gross Domestic Product. Quality of life is equated to a broader measure, one that includes standard of living in addition to environmental amenities such as clean air and water, healthy ecosystems, and many other services provided by nature. (See, for example, Daly 1997.)
2. For more detail on damages, see Rosen et al. (1995), from which most of this section is taken.
3. In spite of the potential benefits, White (1996) finds that the real impetus for restructuring in the US was regional price differences.
4. For a good, detailed description of charges and permits, see Tietenberg (1998).
5. See Solow (1991) for a synopsis of the global warming problem.
6. In a panel discussion at the American Economic Association's January 2000 meeting in Boston, leading economists in the field of climate change addressed what has been learned in the past ten years about the impacts of GHGs. There was disagreement about the level of action that should be taken now. Some argued that current aggregate economic damage estimates do not justify substantial action now, while others questioned this view because the economic damages are so unevenly distributed across countries; e.g., some countries will likely experience little change, but others may be inundated with rising seas. Both sides agreed that the potential for unknown catastrophe may justify action now.
7. However, DSM has been controversial. One controversial aspect is the effectiveness of DSM, with estimates showing a wide range. For divergent views and measures, see Fickett et al. (1990) and Joskow and Marron (1992). Critics argue that investment in conservation is better left to the marketplace unless there is compelling evidence of market failure, in which case DSM programs should address the failure directly instead of promoting broad-based DSM programs that are often misguided and ineffective. See, for example, Hirst (1989), Kahn (1992), or Costello (1992). Wirl (1995) emphasizes that DSM is risky under price caps because of strategic behavior and inefficient under rate-of-return regulation because of over-investment incentives.
8. In the UK, a tariff containing a 'fossil fuel levy' is used by electric suppliers to support the use of renewable energy sources. (See McDaniel, Chapter 5, this volume.)
9. Noll (2000) makes this argument in the context of the telecommunications industry in developing countries.

REFERENCES

Arrow, K., B. Bolin, R. Costanza, P. Dasgupta, C. Folke, C.S. Holling, B. Jansson, S. Levin, K. Maeler, C. Perrings, and D. Pimentel (1995), 'Economic growth, carrying capacity and the environment', *Science*, 268 (April), 520–21.

Bohm, P. and B. Carlen (1999), 'Emission quota trade among the few: Laboratory evidence of joint implementation among committed countries', *Resource and Energy Economics*, 21, 43–66.

Bovenberg, A.L. and L.H. Goulder (1996), 'Optimal environmental taxation in the presence of other taxes: General equilibrium analysis,' *American Economic Review*, 86, 985–1000.

Costello, Kenneth W. (1992), 'Comments on "demand-side management: Reflections of an irreverent regulator" by Myron Katz', *Resources and Energy Economics*, 14, 205–14.

Daly, Grethchen (1997), *Nature's Services*, Washington, DC: Island Press.

Energy Information Administration (2000), *Electric Power Annual 1999*, vol. 2, Washington, DC: US Department of Energy.

EPA (1989), *The Potential Effects of Global Climate Change on the United States: Report to Congress by the U.S. Environmental Protection Agency*, EPA-230–05–89–050.

Eto, J., C. Goldman, and S. Nadel (1998), *Ratepayer-Funded Energy-Efficiency Programs in a Restructured Electricity Industry: Issues and Options for Regulators and Legislators*, http://www.aceee.org/pubs/u982.htm [accessed 26 September 2001].

Fickett, Arnold P., Clark W. Gellings, and Amory B. Lovins (1990), 'Efficient use of electricity', *Scientific American*, 263, 64–74.

Goulder, L.H. (1995), 'Effects of carbon taxes in an economy with prior tax distortion: An intertemporal general equilibrium analysis', *Journal of Environmental Economics and Management*, 29, 271–97.

Grossman, G.M. and A.B. Krueger (1993), 'Environmental impacts of a North American Free Trade Agreement', in P. Garber (ed.), *The US Mexico Free Trade Agreement*, Cambridge, MA: MIT Press.

Hirst, Eric (1989), 'The great demand-side bidding debate rages on', *Electricity Journal*, 2, 41–3.

Huber, S. and C. Douglass (1998), *Two Perspectives on Global Climate Change: A Briefing Book*, St. Louis, MO: Center for the Study of American Business, Washington University.

Joskow, Paul L. and Donald B. Marron (1992), 'What does a megawatt really cost?: Evidence from utility conservation programs', *Energy Journal*, 14, 41–73.

Kahn, Alfred E. (1992), 'Least cost planning generally and DSM in particular', *Resources and Energy*, 14, 177–85.

Meyers, Edward M. and Grace M. Hu (1999), 'Demand-side carbon reduction strategies in an era of electric industry competition', *Electricity Journal* (Jan/Feb), 72–81.

Noll, Roger G. (2000), 'Telecommunications reform in developing countries', in Ann O. Krueger (ed.), *Economic Policy Reform: The Second Stage*, Chicago: University of Chicago Press.

Nordhaus, William D. (1991), 'Economic approaches to greenhouse warming', in R. Dornbush and M.M. Poterba (eds), *Global Warming: Economic Policy Responses*, Cambridge, MA: MIT Press.

Parry, Ian W.H. and Antonio M. Bento (2000), 'Tax deductions, environmental policy, and the "double dividend" hypothesis', *Journal of Environmental Economics and Management*, 39 (Jan), 67–96.

Rosen, Richard, Tim Woolf, Bill Dougherty, Bruce Biewald, and Stephen Bernow (1995), *Promoting Environmental Quality in a Restructured Electric Industry*, prepared for NARUC by Tellus Institute, Boston, MA.

Shogren, Jason (1999), *The Benefits and Costs of the Kyoto Protocol*, Washington, DC: AEI Press.

Solow, Andrew R. (1991), 'Is there a global warming problem?', in R. Dornbush and M.M. Poterba (eds), *Global Warming: Economic Policy Responses*, Cambridge, MA: MIT Press.

Tietenberg, Tom (1995), 'Design lessons from existing air pollution control systems: The United States', in S. Hanna and M. Munasinghe (eds), *Property Rights in a Social and Ecological Context*, Beijuer International Institute of Ecological Economics and the World Bank.

Tietenberg, Tom (1998), *Environmental Economics and Policy*, 2nd edn, New York: Addison-Wesley.

Tschirhart, John and Shiow-Ying Wen (1999), 'Tradable allowances in a restructuring electric industry', *Journal of Environmental Economics and Management*, 38, 195–214.

White, Mathew (1996), 'Power struggles: Explaining deregulatory reforms in electricity markets', *Brookings Papers on Economic Activity: Microeconomics*, Washington, DC: Brookings Institution, 201–50.

Wirl, Franz (1995), 'Impact of regulation on demand side conservation programs', *Journal of Regulatory Economics*, 7, 43–62.

World Commission on Environment and Development (1997), *Our Common Future*, Oxford, UK: Oxford University Press.

10. Infrastructure management: Applications to Latin America

Sanford V. Berg and Maria Luisa Corton

Water systems are key components of a nation's infrastructure, whether they are owned privately or by the government. In either situation, utility managers have far more information about operations than oversight agencies. The way government policymakers address information asymmetries has a significant impact on sector performance. We examine the issue of infrastructure management by considering the risks facing a set of private investors deciding whether to invest in or operate an existing utility system. Although the examples in this chapter are drawn from Peru and other parts of Latin America, they apply to any emerging market. The fundamental point is that information and incentives are central to problems facing various stakeholder groups.

Information is limited because past accounting and engineering systems are often not designed to promote cost minimization. Furthermore, the future is a great unknown. Executives evaluating a project lack information on utility operations and seek to reduce risk by ensuring that the rules of the game will not be changed unilaterally. Investors considering whether to fund the project discount the expected net cash flows at a rate commensurate with the perceived risk. They will structure the firm to take advantage of the best ways to process and act on information, reducing transactions costs. In particular, bondholders will not want managers to take on projects that threaten to reduce bond ratings, although equity investors may want managers to 'go for broke' if the firm is near bankruptcy. Information and incentive issues permeate the organizational design factors affecting the firm.

Regulators face a parallel set of problems. Once a firm gains some operating experience, a new information asymmetry arises. Whether a firm is government-owned or privately owned, the managers know more about the opportunities for cost containment and demand patterns than do sector regulators. This situation leads to regulatory procedures and policies that attempt to reduce the information disparities between corporate managers and those implementing public policy. In the case of municipal utilities, oversight by a national agency is further complicated by local political objectives.

INFORMATION ISSUES FOR POTENTIAL INVESTORS

The key determinant of value is the expected future cash flow, including (as a negative) additional outlays that may be required as part of the bundle of rights and obligations being acquired. Two factors significantly affect the estimates: the adequacy of existing operating data, including demand forecasts and input price changes, and the projected stability of the rules under which the firm will operate in the future. The first provides a baseline and needs to reflect reality *today*. Reality *tomorrow* depends on commercial and technological developments. Commercial uncertainties like demand growth and the availability of substitutes can be addressed by modular planning and keeping customers satisfied. Technological uncertainty requires managers to monitor engineering developments so they can adapt to changes in a timely manner.

Regulatory rules represent an equally important determinant of projected cash flows. For example, investors need to know system expansion requirements and the likelihood of changes in environmental standards. Similarly, if customers cannot be cut off because of non-payment or if returns are capped at excessively low levels, managers can do very little to improve performance. When the returns are inadequate for capital attraction, investments will not be forthcoming to improve quality or expand customer penetration.

The decision to acquire a company that is being privatized will be conditioned on how well risks can be identified, quantified, and mitigated by private investors. The sharing of the risks between each party should follow the guiding principle that whoever can control the risk best should assume it and should receive adequate compensation for doing so.

Let us consider the main problems experienced by water utility companies in developing countries, which generally have been associated with poor performance and low productivity.[1] Risks associated with each problem will be identified, to illustrate the challenge facing outside investors.

Technical and Operational Problems

These problems involve inefficient operational practices, inadequate maintenance, high unaccounted-for water losses (40–50 percent of the total), limited service expansion, and inadequate water quality procedures. How can an outside decision-maker evaluate the technical and operational risks associated with these problems? Unless a government-owned firm has an outstanding reputation for keeping adequate records, there will be insufficient knowledge about the state of installations and the need for replacement, rehabilitation and expansion. And a system's operational performance may also be questionable. How old are pipes and pumping devices? Have maintenance procedures been adequate in the past? What is the percentage of water not accounted for? Is the source of loss from leakage or theft (commercial loss)? What procedures are used to guarantee water quality? What is the level of operating costs? What possibilities exist for system expansion? Are water sources adequate? This litany of questions illustrates the range of uncertainties presented by the acquisition of a water utility.

Commercial and Financial Concerns

These concerns cover a range of potential problems. For example, the system may be unmetered, which creates distortions in consumer charges. Also, the amount of water produced may be estimated instead of being based on actual measurement. There may be no reliable consumption data because of poor consumer records. Billing and collection practices may be inefficient, and laws may prohibit cutting off service for non-payment of bills. If revenues are insufficient, there will be inadequate funds to expand service and protect water quality from contamination.

Tariff policies need to reflect the true economic cost of future water supplies. Tariff structures with large cross-subsidies create additional distortions: excessive consumption and waste. Further, low prices may not help low-income groups but primarily benefit a privileged few.

An outsider considering investment will be concerned that cost recovery cannot occur when there is great uncertainty regarding particular aspects of operations. The baseline is always current procedures and capabilities, so organizational changes will be required if these are inadequate. New administrative procedures are likely to be disruptive and will require internal education and buy-in by current employees. For example, what are the mechanisms for responding to customer complaints? Sometimes it is easier to start from scratch than to try to graft new systems onto old procedures. Similarly, historical records are required for making forecasts. How has demand evolved over time? Are the seasonal and hourly patterns predictable?

In the area of financial risks, currency valuation and convertibility raise issues. Mechanisms for hedging risks will be a high priority for external investors. They need to be fully aware of current government rules regarding remittances by foreign companies as well as likely developments in this area.

Human Capital and Personnel Issues

Excess staff is a typical problem, along with political appointment of staff and intervention in hiring and firing. Another problem is inability to attract managerial talent and qualified technical staff because of a lack of adequate incentives. There may be frequent turnover of high-level staff and low productivity and lack of discipline in the labor force. Investors will want to know the current turnover of staff at various levels of responsibility and whether job descriptions are accurate and flexible. Also, were current managers politically appointed?

Due diligence by a potential buyer will involve an investigation into the way contractual disputes will be resolved and other issues. It is important to know whether a union contract is in place and, if so, when it will expire. Also relevant is whether pension fund contributions have been kept up, as is the managerial compensation scheme.

Regulatory Governance and Incentives Issues

Financial markets view the regulatory regime as a major determinant of how risky the cash flows are likely to be. Subsequently, potential investors seek a number of features in the environment to insulate decisions from day-to-day politics while ensuring the long-run sustainability of the regime itself.[2] Regulatory *governance* refers to the procedures used by the agency to conduct its activities, and *incentives* are the result of particular policies adopted. Both are important, but the first provides a foundation for the latter.

Recently, Australia's Utility Regulators Forum prepared a discussion paper of 'Best Practice Utility Regulation' as part of a program to promote the exchange of ideas regarding regulatory activities. The following best practice principles were identified: (1) communication of information to stakeholders on a timely and accessible basis, (2) consultation with stakeholders and their participation in meetings, (3) consistency both across market participants and over time, (4) predictability reflected in a reputation that facilitates planning by suppliers and customers, (5) flexibility, including use of appropriate instruments in response to changing conditions, (6) autonomy and independence from undue political influence, (7) effectiveness and efficiency, with cost-effectiveness emphasized in data collection and policies, (8) accountability, apparent in clearly defined processes and rationales for decisions and with appeals of decisions possible, and (9) transparency or openness of the process.

These principles are then embodied in best practice processes, as problems are identified and addressed in a systematic manner.[3] The third component emphasized in the discussion paper relates to best practice organization: the role, resources, and structure of the agency. The staff's expertise in making decisions and the clarity of responsibilities within and among government entities are important aspects of this third component.

Of course, policies also affect the risk to be faced by investors. Price cap regimes result in slightly higher costs of capital than rate-of-return (cost-of-service) regulation. Caps place more of the commercial risk on firms. Although cost-containment programs can result in higher returns, downside risks are also present. In practice, price caps have tended to reflect the net present value of future outlays and revenues, so the two regimes tend to be similar in practice.

Environmental Issues Requiring Attention

Related to the sector regulatory institutions are the environmental regulations and associated rules for reducing ecological impacts. For example, if sewerage coverage is much lower than water coverage, has this produced contamination of shallow groundwater aquifers? Is there currently a discharge of large quantities of untreated sewage into rivers or lakes in the proximity of population centers? What regulations are likely to be applied in the future? Are existing facilities grandfathered into a system that accepts lower standards or are investments in upgrades going to be required?

Clearly, these issues are important from the standpoint of estimating future cash flows, and they illustrate how political risk comes into play. By changing the rules of the game, the government can effectively expropriate assets. Potential investors are concerned about the predictability of policy decisions made by the executive and legislative branches. Political stability and a commitment to keeping promises are essential for an emerging market to attract needed capital.

In response to the risk elements, firms have a number of alternative strategies for limiting exposure. The World Bank has described the strengths and limitations of these alternative arrangements,[4] which range from simple and lower risks to the most complex and higher risks. These begin with service contracts, which permit firms to provide assistance by performing specific tasks. Management contracts allow firms to operate and maintain a government-owned business, while a lease arrangement goes further and allows receipt of the income stream from operation. A concession is like a lease, except that it includes investment responsibilities. A build–operate–transfer scheme is similar to a concession but is used for greenfield (new capacity) projects such as a water or wastewater treatment plant. Joint ownership involves partial divestiture by government.

With full divestiture, the government is concerned solely with the task of regulating the provision of monopoly services. At the other end of the spectrum, returns may be limited, but risk exposure is also limited. These simpler forms of private participation do give firms experience in working within a country. They can be viewed as mechanisms through which government, suppliers, and consumers become familiar with the realities of the political and commercial environment. Phasing in private participation represents one strategy for acquiring managerial skills and attracting investment capital.

ORGANIZATIONAL RESPONSES TO OPPORTUNITIES AND REGULATIONS

Figure 10.1 in the Appendix depicts a relatively comprehensive set of relationships affecting international risk perceptions. Not all the important links and feedbacks are shown but, as the arrows indicate, institutions, especially as they affect regulatory governance, influence external attitudes toward a nation's investment climate. Historical experience in a particular nation provides signals regarding likely future treatment of capital. Political stability is certainly a relevant factor here. A commitment good only until the next election (or revolt) causes investors not to give much weight to potential future cash flows.

General macroeconomic conditions and factor markets also matter. If the input markets do not provide the capital, labor, entrepreneurship, and natural resources, then local production will be problematic. In the case of water utilities, local natural monopolies are likely, so the market structure is relatively simple compared with, say, telecommunications. Similarly, the behavior of the utility can be monitored and should yield good performance with appropriate regulatory incentives.[5]

One way firms adapt to the information and control issues that arise in the context of international operations is to select an organizational form that facilitates the attainment of available economies of scale and scope. Each organization type has unique strengths and limitations, and the type preferred and chosen will also depend on the company objectives (long-term or short-term). Holding companies, shared services, and fully integrated operations represent types of organizations within a continuum of options.

In holding companies, each subsidiary is an independent company. This is the best option for a company that wants to maintain each region's culture for its subsidiaries (local or national) and that seeks cash flows from its financial portfolio as its business driver. However, the level of control at each subsidiary is low. Usually, there is not much involvement in local operations since the central leadership will be unfamiliar with local conditions. Directives from headquarters will emphasize priorities and project analysis. Reports from subsidiaries will address these issues and provide information on past and expected performance.

Shared services feature central consolidation of the overhead functions common to the subsidiaries. The business driver may vary from attaining economies of scale to becoming more operationally efficient in common functions to preparing for future mergers or acquisitions. In any case, obtaining a high level of shared services takes careful planning, good coordination, hard work, and detailed follow-up.

Fully integrated operations represent a full integration of all operations, not just those associated with overheads. When a number of similar businesses, such as electricity-generating units, are owned, this option facilitates sharing of expertise, processes and systems across like operations. However, if the extent of common operations is not high, the gains will be low. Partial ownership would also eliminate this organizational option, and international activities will not be fully integrated into the parent company.

Public policy affects the choice of what organization to select. Regulatory limitations in foreign countries can force a firm to adopt one of the described types. Antitrust laws can also limit a firm's selection of organization type.

The importance of cost containment in a profit-maximizing firm is clear, and motivation of management is a key factor in overcoming the barriers to implementing a cost-containment system. The pressure for efficient production and appropriate investment must come from institutions that replicate the kinds of pressures placed on firms by competition. At the initial phase of a regulatory regime's life cycle, the agency has to recruit staff, establish internal procedures, obtain information from firms, and develop rules that facilitate the transition to a new governance system. While cost containment is important, investment in new capacity, outlays on maintenance, improved quality of service, and rate rebalancing represent competing areas for regulatory attention.

In the case of public ownership, price floors can be useful in ensuring the financial sustainability of a water utility. Mayors or regional managers might have only a short time horizon when making decisions. Capacity additions and system expansions for new connections and quality improvements require investments over longer time periods. So if prices are set excessively low (or disconnection for non-payment not utilized) performance is likely to deteriorate.

It is important to distinguish how alternative approaches to capacity valuation can affect 'revenue requirements.' Historical or book data do not necessarily reflect economic reality in terms of reproduction costs. Proxy cost models are subject to manipulation of inputs and model parameters to obtain the results desired by particular stakeholders. Similarly, forecasted values also involve errors. Depending on the regulatory regime and ownership type, these valuation methods may over- or underestimate future capacity needs. For example, privately owned systems might seek to increase cash flows by overestimating investment plans. In contrast, public systems have an incentive to underestimate needs if that means prices can remain relatively low. This is a politically popular stance if voters do not recognize the link between price and service quality and expanded connections.

APPLICATION TO PERUVIAN WATER UTILITIES

The economic and political issues facing water utilities are complex and embedded in local institutional settings. To make some concrete points about the mutual dependence between regulators and managers, we draw upon the situation in Peru. Like other nations in Latin America, Peru is in the process of decentralization, deregulation, and privatization of the infrastructure industry. In general, Latin American countries are facing serious difficulties in the area of water infrastructure. Poor performance, inadequate system maintenance, high levels of unaccounted-for water, excess staff, low rates of metering, and low water quality are the main problems to be solved by companies and governments.

The water and sanitation sector in Peru has undergone several changes in parallel with its political system. From being highly centralized, the water sector has moved since 1990 to a decentralized system under the responsibility of municipalities. In 1992, the government created the regulatory agency Superintendencia Nacional de Servicios de Saneamiento (SUNASS) to regulate water and sanitation services either under the municipalities or under a private regime. SUNASS has the responsibility for establishing fair rates to ensure that the entities providing services are economically efficient.

An important problem currently facing SUNASS is some utilities' serious financial difficulties. At issue is how SUNASS might determine the causes of these financial difficulties. Are the companies efficient? Are the typically low rates responsible for these difficulties? What factor or factors make a difference regarding the sustainability of a company?

A recent study by Solo (1998) from the World Bank asserts that where groundwater is available and extending pipelines is costly, bulk water supply systems generally bring water from private wells to secondary vendors. Such vendors account for more than 30 percent of supply in Honduras, Guatemala City and Lima, Peru. Under these circumstances, it is hard for general citizens to evaluate quality. In addition, the high percentage of water not accounted for (above 35 percent) has multiple explanations. It is possible that poor maintenance results in leakage and lost water. It is also possible that water is taken in low-income neighborhoods without payment.

Under government provision of water services, price becomes a salient political issue. Public companies suffer from a variety of managerial problems. One of them, the principal–agent problem, can make managers deviate from cost minimization to benefit their own situation, rather than provide good performance for customers. Political factors can interfere with cost control programs and network expansion programs. It could be that the objective of government managers is not to minimize costs, for a given mix of quantity and quality, but to maximize mayoral votes in the next election. A low price seems to be a stable equilibrium aligned with this objective.

Another possibility is that the prices facing consumers are not that low. As Solo found in her study, small-scale entrepreneurs (vendors who provide bulk water to citizens) are able to offer competitive prices compared to the connections costs and service provided by water utilities (with service available only a few hours per day). In fact, as Solo mentions, in Argentina, Aguas Argentinas had to review and renegotiate its concession under pressure from low-income families who refused to hook up because of the high rates.

All in all, the lack of appropriate comparative data about quality, price, quantity, and service coverage has made it hard for customers to exert pressure on the water companies. Such pressure could act as an incentive for managers to become concerned with company performance. In late 1999, SUNASS published comparative statistics that represent the first step toward educating citizens and informing political leaders about the relative performance of 45 municipal utilities.

What kinds of lessons might be drawn from these comparisons? If a firm is operating on the production frontier, for a given level of resources, managers could achieve either a large number of connections (to a system that provided service, say, only six hours per day) or provide very high-quality service to a small number of customers. Increased connections require resources that imply reduced quality, holding total resources constant. The key point is that utility managers must make choices reflecting the overriding objectives of water users (and policymakers). If a firm is operating far *inside* the frontier, it is wasting resources and citizens are not receiving the services they could be obtaining, given the resources that local citizens (and external funding agencies) are providing to municipal water suppliers.

Furthermore, the production frontier could be expanded by the acquisition of additional resources from customers, taxpayers, or financial markets. Thus, additional capacity investments or expansion of operating resources can enhance performance. If managers lack incentives for cost containment or are not using best practice production technologies, their water systems will not be operating on the frontier. Benchmarking data provide some yardstick comparisons for determining how near to the frontier various firms are, when density and other relevant cost-drivers are taken into account.

The basic principles of opportunity costs and customer valuations shed light on a number of operating issues. For example, there are also trade-offs between different types of quality, such as absence of organic material versus number of hours per day that water pressure is adequate to provide service. Again, for a given amount of resources, say $100,000, a cost-minimizing firm could be anywhere on the 'quality frontier.' On the basis of the SUNASS benchmarking, it is clear that many municipally owned water systems are operating inside the quality frontier, and thus inside the overall production frontier.

It is likely that cost minimization is less important to managers than objectives like maximizing mayoral votes in the next election. A low price coupled with poor quality seems to be a stable equilibrium, mainly because average citizens find it hard to evaluate quality. Those benefiting from the system via political patronage know very well how they gain from the present arrangements. The question is how to inform all the affected parties of the relative inefficiency of current arrangements. A recent study by Tamayo et al. (1999) documents the lack of incentives for good performance.

Benchmarking enables comparisons to be made, so citizens can be made aware of the poor management of their systems. Whether there really are significant opportunities and incentives for private investment in water in Peru is still an open question. Certainly the need for additional capacity and improved operating procedures is real, but the willingness to pay is not great because of low incomes, lack of best practice comparisons, and lack of awareness regarding the true costs of 'dirty' water.

Another activity of regulators involves reviewing developments in other countries. The experiences of Chile, Argentina, Venezuela, Colombia, and Brazil illustrate how Peru's problems are not unique. Chile's use of proxy cost models represents one approach to price setting, although when firms deviate from investment plans, the agency lacks the power to sanction firms. Argentina has huge privatization concessions, but each contract sets the norms, which leaves the regulator with only limited responsibilities. In Venezuela, the oil crisis has precipitated change. National funding has been dramatically reduced, but no regulatory framework exists. Like Peru, Colombia has a decentralized production system, with municipal mayors having significant power and discretion. However, 30 percent of the service is now privatized, which should soon yield evidence regarding the relative performance of firms.

Managers and investors look at regulatory procedures and policies when considering new investments or cost-containment activity. Without appropriate incentives, managers are unlikely to achieve cost savings that exceed minimal amounts. Utilities could be allowed high returns as an incentive; however, this regulatory strategy may not be politically acceptable. A part of 'above-normal' returns could be returned to customers, but such schemes dampen incentives for managers' further cost containment. Incentives can also be incorporated into price trajectories. For example, a firm that is relatively efficient, based on a benchmarking study or a proxy cost model, might be required to reduce prices only a little over the next year since it is already utilizing best practice in its production process. A relatively inefficient firm might be forced to lower price substantially since there are significant opportunities for cost containment that are untapped at present.

What is the best way to evaluate government agencies responsible for water supply? One can argue that the best indicator is the actual performance of the water utilities. Excellent staff, technically sophisticated studies, and planning documents mean nothing if these are not translated into improvements in sector performance. If the law is ambiguous or does not give appropriate tools to agencies responsible for the oversight of the water sector, then it should be revised by targeting the sources of current inefficiencies. In particular, SUNASS seems to lack regulatory instruments that could provide incentives for good performance, although benchmarking offers some promise. One issue that warrants attention is how to promote the consolidation of small water systems, which are generally inefficient. Another issue is how to promote cooperation among the various government agencies currently influencing municipal water utilities, and how to reduce duplication and identify gaps in sector responsibility.

To summarize, cost containment creates value by freeing up resources that can be applied to other valued activities, including movement toward the production frontier from 'inside' the frontier. Innovations and additional investments can further expand the frontier, providing more services to citizens. Thus, benefit–cost analysis is a key tool for policymakers in this sector. If firms are not minimizing cost, communities (taxpayers) and multilateral lending agencies can just watch their resources being wasted. Documented inefficiencies are bound to affect willingness to support future investments in the water sector.

Rules constrain decision-makers only when enforcement mechanisms exist. Any kind of regulation or government intervention creates incentives. However, if an agency cannot reward excellent performance, it can be argued that it regulates nothing since it has little power to influence the behavior of utilities. At present, SUNASS can collect 'master plans' and announce quality standards, but this has little impact if municipal managers face no consequences for poor performance. When the political authorities fail to give an agency the tools necessary to effectively regulate, then politicians and associated government bureaucracies are basically choosing *not* to regulate.

CONCLUSIONS

Saleth and Dinar (1999, p. ix) have provided the first comprehensive evaluation of the performance implications of different institutional features of the water sector. 'The results show that sector performance is linked more to the performance of water law and water policy than to water administration.' Their empirical analysis of sector performance (measured in terms of physical, financial, economic, and equity dimensions) draws upon 43 water sector experts from 11 nations. They find that the following institutional features are most important: 'integrated legal treatment of water sources, the existence of an independent body for water pricing, the balance in functional specialization, the legal scope for private participation, and the seriousness of the budget constraint.' These results reinforce the points identified here regarding the importance of the regulatory framework and supporting legal structures.

Comparative analysis and publication of performance indicators represent one mechanism for influencing firm efficiency. However, the instrument is not a robust one because the impacts on managers are relatively indirect. What is the lesson for policymakers interested in promoting efficiency and access to safe, reliable water? For government-owned municipal utilities, the cost of capital is either the opportunity cost of internally generated funds or the cost to external funding agencies. Presumably the former is very high, given the limited taxing authority and low incomes of affected parties. The latter is not low because water investments compete with education and other programs with high social payoffs.

Under capital rationing, the 'announced cost of capital' could be low, involving subsidies or accounting fictions, but the true cost of capital should reflect the value of funds in other productive activities. Multilateral and national funding agencies should recognize the need to integrate their priorities into well-designed incentive schemes for the entire water sector. In the past, government capital has been made available without appropriate incentives for cost containment or quality improvement. Managers have wasted valuable funds (according to benchmarking data) without negative consequences. In addition, multilateral and national agencies wishing to support investments in water could leverage their activities by linking funds to performance indices prepared by appropriate agencies, such as SUNASS. This strategy could also promote the combination or coordination of current entities, thus enhancing the accounting, engineering, and business capabilities of existing utilities. Private participation in the provision of water services is one way to introduce new pressures for cost containment and efficient resource utilization.

In many nations, the status quo appears to be unacceptable in terms of the lack of significant improvements in water sector performance. However, some groups must be benefiting from existing arrangements or they would have been altered already. The net gains from movements toward the efficiency frontier should enable the special concerns of narrow interests to be addressed. Creating value means that win–win options can be identified so no stakeholder is disproportionately harmed. However, change benefiting the vast majority of the citizenry should not be held hostage to narrow interests. The situation calls for continuing education and sharing of experiences among agencies facing similar problems.

In conclusion, the greatest enemy of a 'good policy' is the pursuit of a 'perfect policy.' Regulators should focus on the basics before attempting refinements! For example, delays by an agency can create expectations that deadlines need not be met by entities that are supposed to be complying with rules. The resulting pattern involves delay, non-compliance, and lack of sanctions. Such a situation damages the oversight agency's credibility. Ultimately, potential investors in and managers of infrastructure will adapt to such delays in ways that raise costs and waste resources. The water infrastructure sector is far too important to let that happen. Benchmarking represents one way to provide valid comparisons across utilities, creating pressure for cost containment. However, the regulatory agency must also be a model of administrative fairness and effectiveness if it is to provide credibility to those who might supply capital and managerial techniques to water utilities.

ENDNOTES

1. See, for example, Savedoff and Spiller (1999).
2. King and Pitchford (1998) provide an overview of privatization issues. See also Berg (2001).
3. Stern and Holder (1999) use a similar framework for appraising regulatory systems. They emphasize three principles that relate to institutional design (the formal elements of regulation): clarity of roles and objectives, autonomy, and accountability. They also identify three areas related to regulatory processes (informal accountability): participation, transparency, and predictability. These six criteria are used to rate agencies in six Asian nations.
4. *Toolkits for Private Participation in Water and Sanitation*, The World Bank, Washington, DC, 1997.
5. For a more complete discussion of these determinants of performance, see Berg (1997).

REFERENCES

Berg, Sanford (1997), 'Priorities in market reform: Regulatory structures and performance', *Pacific and Asian Journal of Energy* 7 (Dec.), 89–101.

Berg, Sanford (2001), 'Infrastructure regulation: Risk, return, and performance', *Global Utilities*, 1, 3–10.

King, Stephen and Roban Pitchford (1998), 'Privatisation in Australia: Understanding the incentives in public and private firms', *Australian Economic Review*, 31, 313–28.

Saleth, R. Maria and Ariel Dinar (1999), *Evaluating Water Institutions and Water Sector Performance*, World Bank Technical Paper No. 447, Washington, DC: World Bank.

Savedoff, William and Pablo Spiller, (eds) (1999), *Spilled Water: Institutional Commitment in the Provision of Water Services*, Washington, DC: Inter-American Development Bank.

Solo, Tova Maria (1998), 'Competition in water and sanitation – The role of small-scale entrepreneurs', *World Bank Viewpoint*, December, note 165.

Stern, Jon and Stuart Holder (1999), 'Regulatory governance: Criteria for assessing the performance of regulatory systems – An application to infrastructure industries in the developing countries of Asia', *Utilities Policy*, 8, 33–50.

Tamayo, Gonzalo, Roxana Barrantes, Elena Conterno, and Alberto Bustamante (1999), 'Reform efforts and low-level equilibrium in the Peruvian water sector', in William Savedoff and Pablo Spiller (eds), *Spilled Water: Institutional Commitment in the Provision of Water Services*, Washington, DC: Inter-American Development Bank.

APPENDIX

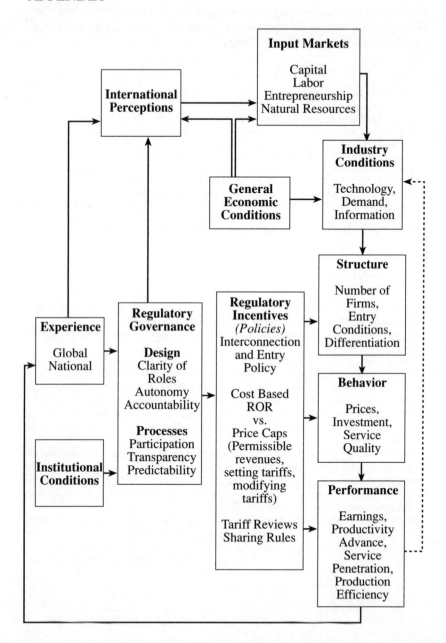

Figure 10.1   Regulatory governance, incentives, and performance

11. Institutions and telecommunications performance in Africa: Stability, governance, and incentives

Sanford V. Berg and Jacqueline Hamilton

Africa's telecommunications industry has been undergoing major reforms since the 1980s, especially in the past few years. In accordance with recommendations of the World Bank and the World Trade Organization (WTO), many countries are in the process of instituting sector reforms. These include the privatization of basic telecommunications service, the creation of separate (and ideally) autonomous regulatory institutions, as well as the introduction of competition in selected services.

Sector performance is the result of a combination of factors: regulatory governance and incentives, competition, ownership, and political stability. Some African nations are beginning to put into place institutions and policies that will promote improved performance in telecommunications. This chapter examines the effect of relevant demographic, economic, political, and institutional factors on telecommunications investment (main lines per 100 inhabitants). Recent studies have focused on the influence of political and institutional factors on telecommunications performance (Henisz 1998, Henisz and Zelner 2001). This study extends earlier work by examining the situation in Africa and identifying patterns of investment activity.

During the 1985–94 period, the growth rate of main lines in those countries that experienced political stability was twice the rate in unstable countries. Certainly, growth in GDP per capita was also important over this period, but the institutional endowment of a nation is a significant determinant of that as well. Because investors are aware of the potential for governments to behave opportunistically by altering the rules of the game, to take advantage of those who have made fixed investments, they require credible assurances against expropriation of property, destruction of property (resulting from civil or political strife), and bureaucratic hold-ups that negatively affect profitability. Managers of government-owned firms face similar issues when they make decisions regarding operations and investments. Their incentives are weak for making tough cost-containment decisions and for utilizing limited funds for long-term investments.

This study uses data on 24 African countries to provide a critical assessment of the state of basic telecom infrastructure in Africa within an economic and institutional framework. Telecom development in Africa is among the worst in the developing world (Kerf and Smith 1996). Sector performance has been weak because of antiquated facilities, financial constraints related to government subsidies, and inefficient operations. Africa has potential as an immense and fertile market for telecom investment despite its low per capita incomes. With a reformed regulatory framework and a reduction in institutional and political risk, improvement in sector performance is feasible within the next decade.

THE STATE OF TELECOMMUNICATIONS IN AFRICA

African nations are currently in the process of modernizing and privatizing their telecommunications sectors, which for the most part lag behind the rest of the world. Despite recent technological change and economic growth, access to telecommunications in Africa is still limited. As in most developing regions, telephones lines are concentrated in the cities, with only limited access for rural areas. The poor quality of infrastructure compared to other developing countries means that the scope for telecommunications development in Africa is immense. Currently, the sector is predominantly state-owned, but some governments have embarked on reform programs, most of which involve two elements: gradual commercialization by separating operational management from government ministries and the transfer of responsibility for regulation away from government ministries to independent agencies. Privatization options being considered include public offers for sale to financial institutions, sale to private investors and employees, private sale to strategic investors, or divestiture and management contracts with foreign operators. Often privatization ventures are with operators with whom the countries have some historical connection. South Africa and Mauritius have led the way by issuing white papers outlining their liberalization processes.

The change occurring in the region is often obscured by factors such as political constraints, which limit a government's desire or ability to make policy commitments that would promote sector development (Mustapha 1997). Analysts argue that special attention must be given to establishing stable and independent regulatory agencies that promote credibility for investors, legitimacy for consumers, and result in more efficient sector performance (Kerf and Smith 1996). The creation of suitable regulatory systems is important because the success of the restructuring process will depend heavily on the credibility and consistency of reform. Figure 11.1 compares access to main telephone lines in Africa with that in Latin America and the Caribbean. We analyze access within Africa in more detail in a subsequent section.

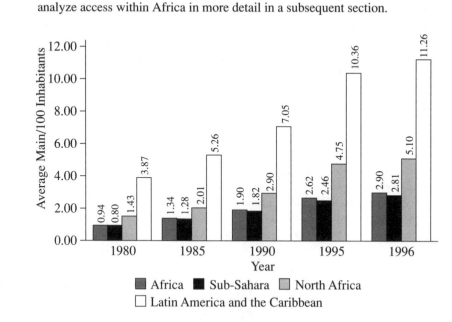

Source: World Development Indicators, World Bank CD-ROM, 1999.

Figure 11.1   Telephone access in developing regions

Many countries in Africa are now concerned with telecom infrastructure for the same reasons that they limited foreign and private ownership in the past. Telecom investment is strategic and can contribute to a country's economic development (Madden and Savage 1998). Most African countries, however, still require a substantial increase in investment in telecom infrastructure to even catch up with other developing regions. As Figure 11.1 shows, basic telephone service in Africa is way below the level in Latin America and the Caribbean. Even northern Africa, which has been doing significantly better than the rest of the continent, lags behind other developing regions.

Growth in the number of telephone lines in Africa has been moderate for the most part, but the growth in teledensity has been slow, mainly because of rapid increases in population in some countries. It is difficult for network development to match high population growth unless incomes are also rising. Madden and Savage (1998) found some evidence that growth precedes investment in transitional economies of Central and Eastern Europe. Figure 11.2 shows that, apart from the 1985–90 period, per capita GDP has been declining in the region as a whole (Collier and Gunning 1999), despite the fact that GDP per capita has been growing in some African countries at a higher rate than in other developing countries. Although GDP per capita in Latin American and Caribbean countries has not been growing at a phenomenal rate, growth there has been far more consistent than in Africa. In Africa, even when GDP growth is positive, the growth in population is 1.3–2 times that in Latin America and the Caribbean. During the periods when Latin America and the Caribbean had higher per capita GDP growth, it was as much as 6.3 times that of Africa. The data, however, indicate that the growth in population does not provide a complete explanation for the sluggishness of economies in Africa. Collier and Gunning (1999) and Sachs and Warner (1999) have provided possible explanations, including the degree of Africa's openness to trade and geographical factors such as climate and the landlocked location of many countries. The rankings given in Table 11.1 show differences between regions in Africa in terms of per capita GDP and teledensity.

Throughout the 1980s and 1990s, access to main telephone lines in North Africa was almost twice that of sub-Saharan Africa, on average. However, the

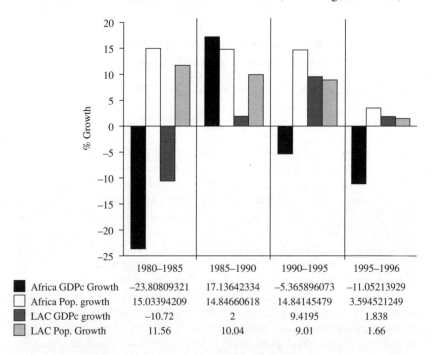

	1980–1985	1985–1990	1990–1995	1995–1996
■ Africa GDPc Growth	−23.80809321	17.13642334	−5.365896073	−11.05213929
□ Africa Pop. growth	15.03394209	14.84660618	14.84145479	3.594521249
■ LAC GDPc growth	−10.72	2	9.4195	1.838
▨ LAC Pop. Growth	11.56	10.04	9.01	1.66

Source: World Development Indicators, World Bank CD-ROM, 1999.

Figure 11.2   GDPC growth in developing regions

sub-Sahara has been catching up with the north in terms of teledensity growth. Between 1990 and 1996, teledensity in the sub-Sahara grew by about 10 percent, which is more than in North Africa. In the early stages of cellular competition, sub-Saharan Africa outperformed North Africa in the number of subscriptions received. This is significant only insofar as the sub-Saharan countries were some of the first in Africa to introduce this service. Per capita subscription is much higher in North Africa. In terms of public policy, the initial apparent reluctance in North Africa to introduce competition parallels an initial reluctance to allow private participation.

Table 11.1   Regional ranking

Region	Per capita GDP	Teledensity	Cellular subscriptions
North Africa	1	1	Fewer than in sub-Sahara
Sub-Sahara	2	2	More but less per capita
Arabic-speaking	1	1	2
English-speaking	3	3	1
French-speaking	2	2	3

Former French colonies tend to have lower access to both cellular and main telephone service. Although the regional ranking in Table 11.1 suggests a positive correlation between per capita GDP and telecom performance, former French colonies perform worse than English-speaking nations in all categories despite higher per capita income. Some researchers have suggested a link between the laws of the land and governance. La Porta et al. (1999) found an inferior quality of government in countries with a French or socialist background and laws. If the quality of government is taken to mean the degree of democracy, this may be one explanation for French-speaking nations' relatively poor performance. However, in a more comprehensive study, Hamilton (2001b) showed that, after controlling for other institutional and economic factors, French-speaking nations perform significantly better than English-speaking nations.

PUBLIC VS. PRIVATE OWNERSHIP

It is no longer a foregone conclusion that government must operate telecommunications in order to meet national objectives. Many socialized entities have not performed well. The extent of investment required in developing countries is usually too large and expensive for the government to manage on its own. This is one reason infrastructure (telecommunications) development in Africa has been slow and sometimes nonexistent. There is evidence of successful telecommunications privatization in many developing nations, including those in Latin America and the Caribbean (Gutierrez and Berg 2000). Once privatization is accomplished, modernization and system expansion can increase the efficiency and availability of the service. As Table 11.2 indicates, the telecommunications sector in Africa is still largely state-owned. However, following world trends as well as demands by international lending agencies, including the World Bank, some African countries are in the process of reforming the sector. Joint ventures are a typical first step employed by African countries to change the market structure of the sector. The extent to which governments commit to privatization and sector development depends on economic and political considerations, as well as the risk environment of the country.

The approach of most African nations then has been to comply with the World Bank's advice to open up their markets, but they are doing so only tentatively. The lack of government commitment to privatization is impeding the speed of sector development. In the last two or three years, however, more and more governments are turning to the private sector for investment in and proper development of the telecom infrastructure, which is now recognized as a necessity if a country is to participate effectively in the global economy.

Table 11.2   Ownership of telecommunications in Africa

100% State-owned	Privatized by 1998	Amount and year privatized	Commitment to privatize
Algeria	Cote d'Ivoire	51%, 1997	Botswana
Botswana	Gabon	39%	Congo
Cameroon	Ghana	30%, 1996	Egypt
Congo	Madagascar	34%, 1995	Kenya
Egypt	South Africa	30%, 1997	Morocco
Kenya	Tanzania		Uganda
Malawi			Zambia
Mali			Zimbabwe
Morocco			
Niger			
Nigeria			
Rwanda			
Sierra Leone			
Togo			
Tunisia			
Uganda			
Zambia			
Zimbabwe			

The increased commitment to private investment shown in Table 11.2 is an indication that African countries have come to accept that there are benefits from privatization. Some of these include increased services and quality of service, as well as improved access at lower cost and the availability of additional capital and management skills. Countries that have recently privatized or are currently involved in privatization efforts include Cote d'Ivoire, Kenya, Tanzania, Uganda, Zambia, and Zimbabwe. These countries expect increased private-sector participation to result in rapid telecom network expansion and improved quality of service. Competition is also promoted along with the establishment of the required regulatory agency. To foster competition, many African countries issue licenses for cellular service.

Countries in Africa began to privatize their telecommunications industry as early as 1976–77 when Chad and Djibouti sold part of their operations to international companies. No further privatization took place until 1989, when Guinea-Bissau and Sao Tomé each privatized by 51 percent. Although the public sector still has majority control of the industry, by 1998 18 countries had either sold portions of their telecom operations to local or international investors or had seen a fusion of partly private international operators with the state-owned operator. It would be interesting to compare telecom performance in these countries before and after privatization.

BASIC ECONOMIC CONDITIONS: NATURAL MONOPOLIES VS. POTENTIALLY COMPETITIVE MARKETS

The view that the telecommunications sector is a natural monopoly has been challenged, just as government ownership and operation is no longer presumed necessary for strong sectoral performance. For example, technological change enables the use of radio spectrum instead of fixed wireline systems. One important and noticeable trend in Africa is the emergence of widespread cellular networks, shown in Table 11.3. Experience in developed telecom markets indicates that competition brings with it substantial benefits for the consumer since it provides strong incentives for incumbent operators to increase efficiency, reduce prices, and provide new services like call waiting and an answering service. A number of countries in Africa currently sustain multiple (at least two) cellular telephone operators, regardless of per capita GDP and access to main lines. With multiple operators, some degree of competition is certain, not only among cellular providers but also between incumbent firms and cellular providers.

Prior to 1990, cellular subscriptions were, on average, virtually nonexistent in Africa. Noticeable change began in 1990–91, with dramatic increases throughout the rest of the decade. Again, sub-Saharan Africa lags behind the

Table 11.3 Cellular networks in Africa (1998)

Country	Startup	Subscriptions	Subscription date	Operator	Coverage
Algeria	12/89	15,000	12/97	Algerian PTT	
Angola	2/94	7,052	12/97	Angola Telecom	Luanda then nationwide
Benin	1995	4,295	12/97	OPT	
Botswana	6/98			Macom: Portugal Telecom, Masiyiwa, DECI Vista: FCR (51%), others (49%)	
Burundi	9/93	600	12/97	Telecel Burundi: ONATAL (40%), Telecel International (57%), others (3%)	
Burkina Faso	12/96	1,503	12/97	Onatel	
Cameroon	1994	2,200	9/96	Dirtel	
Central Africa Republic	1996	800	6/97	TELCEL-CAR: Telecel International (90%)	Bangui
Congo	Sep-95	1,500	7/97	Crytel: Nexus (70%), ONPT (30%)	
Cote d'Ivoire	1996	3000	12/96	Comstar: International Wireless	
	1996	13,000	12/97	Loteny Telecom	
	10/96	6,000	10/97	Societe Ivoirienne de Mobile (SIM): FCR (70%), Comafrique (30%)	
Djibouti	1996	110	12/96	OPT	
Egypt	5/87	7,224	12/97	Arab Rep. Of Egypt Nat'l Telecom Org.	Cairo, Luxur, Alexandria, Aswan
Ethiopia	07/98			Ethiopia Telecom Auth.	
Eq. Guinea	10/96	61	12/97	GETESA	
Gabon	1987	9,500	12/97	OPT	
Gambia, The	1992	3,096	13/97	Gamtel	

Country	Date	Subscribers	Date	Operator	Location
Ghana	1/95	2,000	12/96	CelTel: Ghanians (95%), AT&T (5%)	Nationwide
	6/96	400	12/96	Sancom: Investcom	
	5/92	10,004	12/96	Mobitel: Millicom Ghana (80%), others (20%)	
Guinea	1996			Francis Walker Ghana Ltd.	
	6/93	1,100	12/97	Telecel Guinee: Telecel International (90%), Guinean partners (10%)	
	1993			Spacetel Guinee: Investcom	
	9/97			Sotelgui	
Kenya	3/93	5,345	6/97	Kenya Post and Telecom	
Libya	3/97	4,500	7/97	ORBIT	
Lesotho	4/96	1,262	03/97	Vodacom* Lesotho: Lesotho Telecom (40%), Vodacom South Africa (20%), others (40%)	
Madagascar	05/97			Sacel Madagascar S.A.	All
	08/94	4,000	12/97	Telecel Madagascar: Telecel International (100%)	
	12/97			Madacom	
Malawi	12/95	2,910	12/96	Telekom Network Ltd.: Telekom Malaysia (70%), Malawi P&T (30%)	
Mali	9/96	2,842	12/97	Sotelma	
Mauritius	5/89	23,000	10/97	Emtel: Millicom (50%), C. Jeewanjee Co. (50%)	
	10/96	5,563	12/96	Cellplus: Mauritius Telecom	
Mauritius	6/89	12,000	6/96	Emtel/Currimjee Milicom	Jeewanjee
	1/96	1,000	12/96	Cell Plus Mobile Commis	
Morocco	5/87	74,442	12/97	ONPT	Rabat, Casablanca
Mozambique	1989	35,000	12/96	Office National des Postes et Telecom	Main cities and roads
	9/97	3,000	12/97	Empressa Nacional de Mozambique (TDM) (74%), DeTeCon (Germany) (26%)	('97)-maputo, Matola, 'Maputo Corridor'

Table 11.3   continued

Country	Startup	Subscriptions	Subscription date	Operator	Coverage
Namibia	4/95	12,500	9/97	Mobile Telecommunications Co. Ltd.: Namibia Telecom (51%), Telia (26%), Swedfund (23%)	Windhoek/Rehobeth area
Nigeria	1995			EMIS Nigeria	Lagos
	1993	15,000	12/97	Mobile Telecom Services	
	1995	20,000	12/97	Int'l Wireless Inc./Comstat	Lagos, Abuja
Reunion	9/95			SRR (SFR 100%)	
Rwanda	7/98			Rwanda Cell	
Senegal	1994	6,942	12/97	SONATELL	Nationwide
	4/92	500	mid-95	SONATELL	83 km radius of Dakar
Seychelles	1995	1,149	3/97	Cable and Wireless	Nationwide
South Africa	5/86	10,000	6/95	Vodacom	Nationwide
	6/1/94	1.1m	9/98	Vodacom	Nationwide
	6/1/94	470,000	9/98	Mobile Telecommunications Networks: Multichoice (25%), Cable & Wireless (25%), Transtel, Naftel, FABCOS, Costau (50%)	
	3/94	553,000	7/97	Vodacom: Telekom South Africa (50%), Vodafone (UK) (35%), Rembrandt Finansiele Beleggings Beperk (15%)	Nationwide, 80% population at 1995
Sudan	01/97	3,800	12/97	Mobitel: Sudatel (40%)	Khartoum, Pot Sudan
Swaziland	7/98			MTN	Nationwide
Tanzania	1996	6,200	10/97	Tritel: TRI (Malaysia) (60%), VIPEM (Tanzania) (40%)	Dar es Salaam, other cities
	1998			Zanzibar Telecom	Zanzibar

	9/94	14,000	12/97	MIC: Tanzania Ltd. (25%), Millicom (51%), Ult. Telecom (14%), Reserve (10%)	Dar es Salaam, other cities
Togo	9/97	2,995	12/97	Togo Telecom	
Tunisia	4/85	5,539	12/96	Tunisie Telecom	60% territory at mid 1995
Uganda	5/95	5,000	12/97	Colverem Celtel Ltd.: Vodafone (UK) (37%), msi (42%), ifc (10.5%), cdc (10.5%) MTN and Partner	Kampala, Entebbe, Jinja
DR Congo	7/98 / 1991	8,900	12/97	Telecel Zaire: Telecel International (90%), SAIT (10%)	Kinshasa
	1994			Trans Global Telecom	
Zambia	1986	11,500	12/96	Telecel-Zaire	Lusaka only
	1995	2,721	3/97	Zamtel	Lukasa
	16/97	800	12/97	Telcel-Zambia: Telcel International (70%) Zamtel and Partner	
Zimbabwe	Unknown			Telcel Zimbabwe (PVT) Ltd.	Harare and Bulawayo
	3/97	11,300	6/97	NetOne: PTC	Harare and Bulawayo
	9/96			Econet	
	1998			T.S. Maisiyiwa Holdingd/Econet	Local
North Africa	3/97	106,705			
Sub-Saharan Africa		22,5050			
South Africa		1,023,000			
AFRICA		1,354,755			

Source: African Cellular Systems, Common Market for Eastern and Southern Africa (COMESA), September 1998; African Telecommunication Indicators (ITU 1998).

213

north, although exceptions are Mauritius, Reunion, and Seychelles – all small islands in the Indian Ocean with relatively high access. Some small coastal countries, such as Djibouti, also have access comparable to the average rate on the continent. By 1996, Eritrea had relatively low access, but was doing better than Ethiopia. Size effects may explain this, since the necessary investment outlays are smaller in small countries and thus involve less sunk cost. However, this argument suggests that economies of density outweigh economies of scale. Note that Djibouti and Eritrea, although not islands, are situated along the coast. It would be interesting to explore the role of geography to see whether location along the coast or access to ports provides some positive incentive to invest in telecommunications infrastructure.

The trend toward cellular service can be viewed as an indication of the degree to which competition is beginning to pervade the telecommunications market in the region. It represents the level of government commitment to sector reform. Both foreign and private-sector participation are becoming commonplace. Ghana, for example, is just one of the many countries that have recently opened their doors to competition. CellTel Ghana enjoys nationwide coverage, as does Anglo Telecom. Likewise Vodacom is well established in southern Africa. In South Africa, cellular service has successfully introduced competition in the sector. Most countries now have access to cellular service, at least in the major cities. The use of cellular service not only indicates the development of a competitive sector, but substitutes for direct exchange lines where penetration (teledensity) is low. For example, Uganda has one of the lowest levels of penetration of telephone lines in Africa, but enjoys nationwide coverage in cellular service provided by Anglo Telecom.

One has to be cautious, however, in using the increase in cellular networks across Africa as an indication of the growth in private-sector participation and competition. In some regions with cellular ventures, the telecommunications sector is still state-owned or a monopoly. Angola, Mozambique, and Zambia are examples. In Botswana and Lesotho, the sectors are still 100 percent state-owned despite the opening up of the market to competition in 1996. In addition, new monopolies may be created after the introduction of cellular service. TELECEL-Zaire mobile operator, for instance, operates its own system and is a virtual monopoly. In addition, the existence of cellular operators is not a perfect measure of competition since cellular service is often available only to the wealthy, who represent a small portion of African economies. However, present limitations on cellular service as a strong competitive force because of cost will become less notable as time passes.

Uganda and Cote d'Ivoire are examples of countries with per capita income below $1,000 and with at least two cellular operators. Cellular operators can be potential threats to incumbent firms, since they can increase penetration at relatively low cost per additional subscriber. The threat of competition may be enough to give the incumbent the initiative to improve service. The potential threat is enough to provide the impetus for telecom growth (Hamilton 2001a).

THE PACE OF CHANGE

Africa is currently one of the most troubled areas in the world. It faces many problems with diseases, environmental decline, poverty, and internal conflicts. Often these conflicts are politically motivated. Political conflicts throughout the 1980s and 1990s created instability and are at least partially responsible for the relatively slow development in telecom infrastructure in the region. Bennett and Green (1972), Balkan (1992), Green and Korth (1974), Svensson (1998), and Levis (1979) are among studies that examine how political instability disrupts investment and retards growth. The data in Table 11.4 indicate that during the 1985–94 period, those countries that experienced political instability had, on average, nearly two times less growth in main lines than those that were stable. Despite this, countries that experienced political instability throughout the entire sample period managed to secure at least moderate growth in telecommunications. Growth was, on average, 27 percent. Countries that experienced political disturbance in the 1980s but none in the 1990s did worse than those that were unstable throughout the period, on average. This may seem counterintuitive, but might be explained by investors' being better informed regarding risk as the 1990s approached and therefore more willing to enter even politically unstable markets. In addition, countries like Zimbabwe were reluctant to allow foreign participation in the telecom market, which explains in part the stagnation of telecom infrastructure in that country. South Africa's network development far exceeds that of any of the countries whose political instability persisted into the 1990s. In South Africa, access grew from 7.6 to 9 main lines per 100 inhabitants. In countries with continuing instability, access remained below 1 per 100 individuals.

Countries that experienced political stability only in the earlier years did better than those that experienced stability only in the later years. On average, teledensity in the former grew by 43 percent, perhaps because investors are compelled to stay once investment takes place and large sunk costs are incurred. Stability throughout the 1980s encouraged investments; as a result, instability in the 1990s had a smaller impact on telecom growth. Countries that remained stable throughout the period of study do better than any other group. Teledensity rose by 70 percent on average for countries in this category, although some did not do as well as others. Growth in Botswana and Morocco indicates that politically stable countries would probably have experienced even higher growth except for other political conditions. Property rights are less likely to be restricted, thus encouraging investments, if governments are stable (Clague et al. 1996).

Table 11.4   Growth of main telephone lines and political stability in countries

Time periods and stability	Politically stable, 1984–89		Politically unstable, 1984–89	
Politically stable, 1990–94	Botswana	1.40	Togo	0.56
	Cote d'Ivoire	0.20	Gabon	0.69
	Niger	0.09	Mali	0.49
	Tanzania	0.16	Tunisia	0.59
	Morocco	1.64	Madagascar	0.20
			Rwanda	0.60
			Sierra Leone	–0.03
			Zambia	0.18
			Egypt	0.76
			Congo	0.29
	Average	0.70		0.43
Politically unstable, 1990–94	South Africa	0.187	Algeria	0.408
	Zimbabwe	–0.003	Cameroon	0.359
	Uganda	–0.030	Kenya	0.314
	Average	0.16		0.270

Figures 11.3 and 11.4 summarize the institutional conditions in Africa during the period 1980–94, and their relation to the development of basic telecommunications.

As can be seen, the political environment and institutional framework at a point in time appear not to matter in terms of investment in telecommunications. There is little or no apparent relation between democracy and telephone access in any given year. Countries with high levels of democracy had very low access and vice versa.

This haphazard pattern may be explained by the fact that democracy in Africa does not necessarily guarantee the political and civic rights that most western countries would expect (Haan and Siermann 1995). Many African countries are democratic solely in the sense that political pluralism exists on paper. In reality, citizens in some of these countries are allowed only very narrow political participation. Some 'democratically' chosen governments manage to maintain their positions by political coercion and corruption. The 1990s witnessed a growth in the number of multi-party systems, but many elections were rife with corruption. For example, analysts have concluded that the elite manipulated elections in Ghana and Kenya. Despite weak democratic systems, the trend in

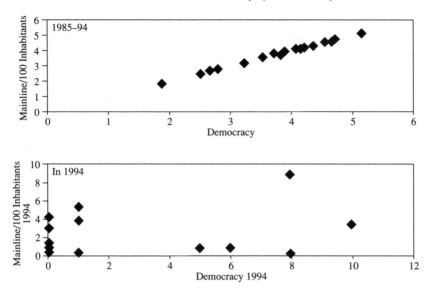

Source: 1995 Polity III (Jaggers and Gurr 1995), IRIS-3 file of international country-risk data, 1982–97.

Figure 11.3   Political institutions and main line access, 1985–94 and in 1994

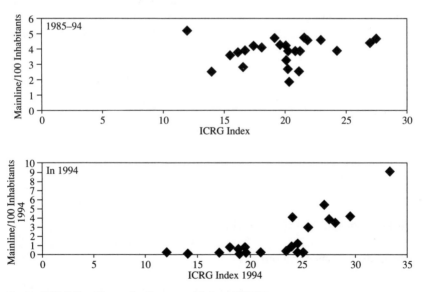

Source: IRIS-3 file of international country-risk data, 1982–97.

Figure 11.4   Institutional factors and main line access, 1985–94 and in 1994

the 1990s has been toward political pluralism and a more active role for citizens. It is this movement toward more accountable systems of government that explains the much clearer relation between main line access and democracy.

Institutional factors in Figure 11.4 indicate more of a pattern in 1994, but the trend is a lot more pronounced when measured over 1985–94. Throughout the period of this study, many countries in Africa have been undergoing some form of political adjustment. Some countries like Uganda and South Africa have experienced a more organized and smooth transition, while change in other countries has been chaotic. Even though some countries still experience political repression, many have made strides in improving their political environment.

Good government has been shown to contribute to the economic development of European countries (Knack and Keefer 1995). Likewise, Bergara et al. (1998) have shown that political conditions influence the level of electricity investments. The data utilized here show that political conditions and government do in fact have some correlation over time with telecom development. Investors' expectations play a major role in their decisions to invest. Current conditions are therefore important only insofar as they contribute to a picture over time. Telecom investors are more interested in the long view, especially given the nature of their investments. Potential investors are more willing to invest in countries with a stable institutional history and more democratic systems of governance. Investments will occur so long as those in power have sufficient incentive to take the legal actions necessary for the protection of property rights. A democratic system allowing for participation by stakeholders promotes legitimacy and can result in greater policy stability. The trend in African institutions over the period studied conforms to theory and empirical evidence from other countries.

The large external debt of some countries also slows development. In addition, there are often conflicts between political and economic motivations, leading to indecision and delay. Public uncertainty increases perceived risk, raising the cost of capital and limiting private investment. Instability in certain countries is another factor. In Rwanda, for instance, civil war decimated the telecommunications sector. High risk provides a disincentive to potential private investors and managers of government firms (since high performance is beyond their control).

SOME POLICY IMPLICATIONS

Regulatory Considerations

The success of telecommunications development in Africa, as elsewhere, depends on the willingness and ability of governments to provide regulatory and legislative environments that promote development of telecommunications infrastructure and service offerings. Most African leaders realize the importance of regulatory reform, and countries that have not yet undertaken reforms are planning to do so in the near future. Politicians are becoming aware that shifting the burden of infrastructure management and investment to private firms can be beneficial, in terms of increased efficiency in this sector and also with respect to the possibility of securing additional private investments in other economic sectors of the economy. Table 11.5 is a summary of some recent legislative and regulatory developments in Africa, and Table 11.6 gives information on foreign ownership and market access in some African countries.

Autonomy of Regulatory Agencies

Many regulatory agencies in Africa are still connected to a government ministry and have no real autonomy or power because the ministry often maintains the authority to appoint members and issue directives. Policy must move toward greater autonomy of the agencies if private investors are to be attracted. Independence of the regulator is required to ensure that short-term political objectives or pressure do not influence policies. This will be challenging for countries where politics have so much influence on everyday life. Because infrastructure development is so important, governments are reluctant to relinquish control. Zimbabwe, for example, although committing to some degree of privatization, distrusts foreign operators and has not committed to allowing them. However, governments need not give up control; they need only to subject private entities to strict regulation of prices and service quality. Discretion has to be strict and specific enough to maintain agreed quality, but broad enough not to discourage efficient and effective participation. Investors are aware of the potential for governments to interfere and therefore require sound and credible guarantees against the expropriation or destruction of property during civil or political strife, and against bureaucratic hold-ups that negatively affect profitability.

Incentive Structure and Goals

As more countries privatize their operations, regulators need to implement incentive schemes that will guarantee increased service quality as well as higher penetration levels (Berg and Foreman 1996). If this is not done, the move to allow private participation will be a failure. One way to ensure efficiency is to encourage competition. Therefore, the next step for countries in the privatization process is to start thinking about how best to encourage competition and how much competition should be allowed. Competition is not always feasible, but the economic consensus is that competition in services such as cellular telephony improves infrastructure development. Countries planning to privatize should have clear goals and policies to attract potential entrants.

Table 11.5   Legislative and regulatory developments in Africa

Country	Year	Development
Ghana (accelerated development program)	1996	–Authorization of two national network operators: Ghana Telecom and a new independent operator. –Privatization of Ghana Telecom through sale of strategic stake combined with measures to broaden share ownership in Ghana. –Removal of restrictions on private network construction. –Creation of a single regulatory agency (NCA) to regulate communications, including wire, cable radio, TV, satellite.
Botswana	Dec. 1995	–Telecom policy paper outlining planned sector liberalization and competition.
	July 1996	–BTC (amendment) bill and telecom bill became law in September. It defined sector development for the future. –End BTC monopoly over telecom services. –Allow BTC to enter joint ventures or partnership with the private sector but stopped short of mandating the privatization of the national operator. Still 100% state-owned. –Independent regulatory body established (the Botswana Telecommunications Authority – BTA) to oversee and regulate the sector. Duties include tariff setting and access licensing.
Lesotho	April 1996	–Lesotho Telecom Corp (LTC) has monopoly and is not subject to independent regulation. –Sector reform considered, including the establishment of a new independent regulatory body. –Planned competition in the supply of customer premise equipment and the issuance for VSAT, paging and radio trunk network.
Namibia	1992	–Namibia Communications Commission established as a quasi-independent regulatory body.
Mozambique	1992	Telecom law established: –Telecommunications of Mozambique as an independent company. –National Telecommunications Institute of Mozambique (INCM) as an independent regulatory body. Responsibilities include licensing and interpretation of sector policy.
Zambia	1994	–Telecommunications legislation created new regulatory body (ZCA) to oversee the sector.
Zimbabwe	Currently	–No independent regulatory body. Tariff setting, licensing, etc. is made by the PTC.
Swaziland	Currently	–No regulatory body; PTC operates under a 1994 performance contract with the government.

Table 11.5   continued

Country	Year	Development
Tanzania	1994	–Tanzania Communications Commission established to regulate the provision of telecommunications in Tanzania. Responsibilities include licensing, approval of tariffs and the promotion of competition.
Tunisia	10 April 1995	–Law creating National Office of Telecommunications. It changed the entity from an administrative structure to a public enterprise with industrial and commercial orientation.
Mauritius	1988	–Telecom Act – establishment of independent regulatory body, Telecommunications Authority (TA), as sector regulator. –Mauritius Telecom Services Ltd. established as a state-owned company to provide domestic service.
	15 Feb. 1997	–Accepted a commitment to open the telecom sector to competition and to end the monopoly and exclusive rights by 2004.
	1997–98	–Plan to create a new legislative body and to establish a new Mauritius Telecommunications Authority.
South Africa	1991	–Transferred the running of telecommunications service from Department of Post and Telecommunications to a public company – Telkom South Africa Ltd.
	March 1996	White Paper on the telecommunications sector: –Outlined a structured six-year process in the liberalization of sub-sector markets. No limit was set on the period of exclusivity or continued monopoly for Telkom, the sole provider of local access, pay phones, national long distance and international services in South Africa.
	15 Nov. 1996	–Telecommunications Act provided a framework within which the sector will be liberalized. It includes the creation of a regulatory body, separate from the national operator and the Ministry of Post and Telecommunications Board.

Sources: Ministry of Telecommunications and Information Technology, Republic of Mauritius White Paper on the Telecommunications Sector. Ministry of Transport and Communications, Telecommunications Policy for an Accelerated Programme 1994–2000 (Ghana). *Africa Communications* (magazine), Privatization in Africa: Country Privatization Efforts, 1997. Telecommunications Policy in South Africa. South Africa Non-profit Internet Provider (SANGONET), South African White Paper on Telecommunications. The Southern Africa Regional Telecommunications Restructuring (RTR) Program. Luhanga, M.L., Telecommunications in Tanzania. Dierks, Klaus, Namibia's Telecommunications – Link to Africa. The National Communications Authority Act, 1996, Republic of Ghana.

Table 11.6 Regulatory principles, foreign ownership and market access (1998)

Country	Regulatory principles[1]	Maximum foreign ownership allowed	Commitent to market access
Cote d'Ivoire	Adopted entirely	100%	Monopoly for voice telephone over fixed network infrastructure and telex services for seven years. In 2005, full competition for all services. Open access for all other services, including data transmission services and satellite services, links, capacity and earth stations.
Ghana	Adopted entirely	No limitation, but local participation required	Commitment to duopoly operators for the provision of local, domestic and international long distance services and private leased circuit services for an exclusive five-year period. Commitment to competition in services, including telex, telegraph, facsimile, Internet, fixed satellite (excluding voice), teleconferencing, trunked radio and telecommunications equipment sales and rentals, and mobile services. Commitment to allow global satellite services to be supplied through arrangements with licensed public operators.
Mauritius	In the future	100%	Existing de facto monopoly and exclusive rights in all basic telecom services to be eliminated by 2004. Commitment to competition in paging, private mobile radio services and mobile satellite-based services.
Morocco	Partial adoption	Foreign equity participation may be limited (level as yet unspecified)	Telephone service over fixed infrastructure, telex and ISDN are reserved to a monopoly until 2001. Open market access for packet switched data transmission and frame relay. Licenses for various types of mobile services will be issued by means of public tenders.
Senegal	Adopted entirely	100%	Commitment to terminating monopoly between 2003 and 2006 in local domestic and international voice telephony, data transmission, telex, facsimile, private leased circuit services and fixed satellite services. In 2003, the government will consider whether to allow additional operators. Three operators are allowed to provide cellular mobile services, including mobile data, from 1998.

South Africa	Adopted entirely	30%	Commitment to end monopoly supply and introduce a second supplier by the end of 2003 in public switched, facilities-based services including voice, data, transmission, telex, facsimile, private leased circuits and satellite-based services. Commitment to review the feasibility of allowing additional suppliers of public switched services by the end of 2003. Cellular mobile services are provided on a duopoly basis with an additional license to be granted within two years. No limitations on the number of suppliers of paging, personal radio communication, and trunked radio systems. Liberalization of resale services between 2000 and 2003.
Tunisia	49% from 2002, foreign participation in the capital of Tunisia. Telecom will be allowed up to 10%		Competition in telex and packet switched data transmission from 1999, in mobile telephone, frame relay, paging and teleconferencing from 2000, and in local telephone services from 2003. Extend telephone coverage in certain areas as a condition for liberalization of basic telecommunication services in rural areas; to supply emergency telecommunication services, to contribute to the national formation and research in the telecommunication sector.

Source: African Telecommunication Indicators (ITU, 1998).

Since Africa's markets are relatively small because of low per capita incomes, the markets may not be particularly attractive to investors seeking big profits. Telecom access in Africa is mostly confined to urban areas because many people cannot afford telephones. The immediate aim of public policy in privatization should be to achieve universal shared access to telephones in Africa, rather than universal individual access. This 'reasonable' access can be achieved through the provision of public telephones by private investors, who should supply achievable targets. Ghana, South Africa, Kenya, and Malawi have adopted variations of this policy.

To take advantage of the positive effects of competition, regulators must guarantee appropriate interconnection agreements between competitors and the incumbent firm. Both parties must be clear on matters such as points of interconnection, cost responsibilities, and pricing.

Country Risk and Transparency

The telecommunications industry is changing in Africa much more rapidly than it did in developed countries. As a result, governments are expected to adjust rules as changes occur. Development in African tends to leapfrog in the sense that, even with very low penetration of basic telephony, Internet and cellular usage is commonplace. The development process was more sequential in other countries. There has to be discretionary public policy to deal with rapidly changing conditions. This type of discretion can easily be used for political gains or to satisfy the individual interests of regulators (see Kerf and Smith 1996). In this instance, more specific rules are required. Possible misuse of authority can be curtailed by increasing the accountability of the policymakers.

Political conflicts resulting in disruption of service or discouragement of investment have been more of a problem in Africa than in other developing regions. Regulators will have to develop approaches that reduce the perceived risk of investing in Africa for private investors. Governments may enter into partnerships with the private entity, such as joint ventures where the government shares risks. When governments maintain a share of the profits, they will be more committed to creating an environment that will promote political stability. Obtaining stakeholders among private, local individuals may also encourage public interest. When private individuals are claimants to some of the profits, they have a vested interest in maintaining stability and freedom from political turmoil.

While telecom development in Africa has been slow, there are indications that improvements are likely. Even though only a few countries have privatized so far, many more are preparing to do so. Governments fully appreciate the importance of participation in an environment where economies are increasingly more global and more dependent on information technology. They are therefore more willing to encourage potential entrants. The potential gain to investors from tapping into this market, which is large despite low income levels, is substantial. Regulatory and institutional reforms are necessary to indicate the intentions of governments and to encourage both foreign and local investments.

ENDNOTE

1. The WTO has an agreement with the eight countries listed in Table 11.6. The countries have agreed to progressively liberalize their telecommunications market, and some have also agreed to adopt the regulatory principles proposed by the WTO. These principles allow for transparent regulation, including the establishment of an independent regulatory body.

REFERENCES

Balkan, E. (1992), 'Political instability, country risk, and probability of default', *Applied Economics*, 24, 999–1008.

Bennett, P.D. and R. Green (1972), 'Political instability as a determinant of direct foreign investment in marketing', *Journal of Marketing Research*, 19 (May), 182–6.

Berg, Sanford and R. Dean Foreman (1996), 'Incentive regulation and telco performance: A primer', *Telecommunications Policy*, 20 (9), 641–52.

Bergara, M., W. Henisz, and P.T. Spiller (1998), 'Political institutions and electric utility investments: A cross-nation analysis', *California Management Review*, 40 (2), 18–35.

Clague, Christopher, P. Keefer, S. Knack, and M. Olson (1996), 'Property and contract rights in autocracies and democracies', *Journal of Economic Growth*, 1, 243–76.

Collier, Paul and Jan W. Gunning (1999), 'Why has Africa grown slowly?', *Journal of Economic Perspectives*, 13 (3), 3–22.

Green, R. and C. Korth (1974), 'Political instability and the foreign investor', *California Management Review*, 17 (1), 23–31.

Gutierrez, L. and S. Berg (2000), 'Telecommunications liberalization and deregulation: Lessons from Latin America', *Telecommunications Policy*, 24 (10), 865–84.

Haan, J. and C. Siermann (1995), 'New evidence on the relationship between democracy and economic growth', *Public Choice*, 86, 175–98.

Hamilton, Jacqueline (2001a), 'Are main lines and mobile phones complements or substitutes? Evidence from Africa', working paper, Public Utility Research Center, University of Florida, Gainesville.

Hamilton, Jacqueline (2001b), 'Institutions, political regime, and access to telecommunications infrastructure in Africa', working paper, Public Utility Research Center, University of Florida, Gainesville.

Henisz, W. (1998), *The Institutional Environment for International Investment: Safeguarding Against State Sector Opportunism and Opportunistic Use of the State*, Chap. 3, unpublished Ph.D. dissertation, University of California, Berkeley.

Henisz, W. and B.A. Zelner (2001), 'The institutional environment for telecommunications investment', *Journal of Economics and Management Strategy*, 11, 123–45.

IRIS-3 file of international country-risk data, 1982–97, compiled by Stephen Knack, Iris Center, University of Maryland, College Park.

ITU (1998), *African Telecommunications Indicators*, Geneva: International Telecommunication Union.

Jaggers, Keith and Robert Gurr (1995), *Polity III: Regime Change and Political Authority, 1800–1994*, 2nd ICPSR version (computer file), Ann Arbor Inter-university Consortium for Political and Social Research, University of Michigan.

Kerf, M. and W. Smith (1996), *Privatizing Africa's Infrastructure: Promise and Challenge*, Washington, DC: World Bank Group.

Knack, Stephen and P. Keefer (1995), 'Institutions and economic performance: Cross-country tests using alternative measures', *Economics and Politics*, 7, 207–27.

La Porta, Rafael, F. Lopez-de-Silanes, A. Shleifer, and R. Vishny (1999), 'The quality of government', *Journal of Law, Economics and Organization*, 15 (1), 222–82.

Levis, M. (1979), 'Does political instability in developing countries affect foreign investment flow? An empirical examination', *Management International Review*, 19, 59–68.

Madden, Gary and Scott Savage (1998), 'CEE telecommunications investment and economic growth', *Information Economics and Policy*, 10, 173–95.

Mustapha, M. (1997), *Telecommunications Policies for Sub-Saharan Africa*, Washington, DC: World Bank Group.

Sachs, Jeffrey and Andrew M. Warner (1999), 'Slow sources of growth in African Economies', *Journal of African Economies*, 6 (3), 335–76.

Svensson, Jakob (1998), 'Investment, property rights and political instability: Theory and evidence', *European Economic Review*, 42, 1317–41.

Conclusion

Sanford V. Berg, Michael G. Pollitt, and Masatsugu Tsuji

This book has discussed private initiatives in the provision of public services and infrastructure in developed as well as developing countries. Boundaries between the public and private sector are not defined a priori, but rather attention is given to historical background, stage of economic development, and the economic systems of each country. With innovations in technology, finance, and management, as well as the globalization of the world economy, the private sector is expected to expand its role in most developed countries. Even developing countries are experiencing the same trend. However, changes in the mix of economic activity also raise significant political and social problems. Issues warranting further attention include incentive problems in public–private partnerships, mechanism design for governance and cost containment, measures supporting private participation, and frameworks for addressing emerging environmental/congestion issues.

Mixture of Public–Private Partnership

Whether the public or private sector takes the dominant role in public services provision depends on the basic conditions associated with public services and infrastructure. The relative roles depend on the technology behind the cost function, including economies of scale and economies of network scope. They also depend on the demand, which is determined by consumer preferences and incomes. There is no simple theory identifying circumstances under which the private sector with profit-maximizing behavior has an advantage over the public sector. The latter involves rent-seeking activity and political log-rolling that can result in over- or under-supply of public funds. In addition, incentives for cost minimization are blunted in the 'partnership' mode. The optimal mixture of public–private partnership requires a deep understanding of the strengths and limitations of each organizing system.

Mechanism Design

For private initiatives to improve performance, it is essential to design a proper mechanism for private participation. It should satisfy a number of criteria, including incentive compatibility, governance, credibility, and transparency. The mechanism has to provide incentives for the private sector to bear risks, and the contract should clarify responsibilities and roles. To maximize value for money, the private sector can provide leadership, with intervention by the public sector not involving micro-management. Effectiveness depends on disclosure of information and transparency, particularly regarding the bidding system. Most developing countries and some developed countries, including Japan, have weak traditions in this area. In the UK, many procedures have been implemented in recent years; these include identifying necessary projects and signing the final contract so as to maintain transparency. However, this lengthy process increases costs for private firms to participate in the bidding process, and in some sectors, such as hospitals, getting the contracts right has proved difficult.

Credibility of the mechanism is also important for developing countries, since foreign investors and multinational enterprises are likely to be major participants in projects. They face various political as well as country risks, particularly in developing economies. Without credibility of the mechanism, nations will not be able to attract investment for infrastructure projects.

Supplementary Measures for the Introduction of Private Initiatives

Private initiatives are quite new to some countries, and it is often the case that economies do not have the economic institutions required for efficient private participation. Nations must establish those fundamentals on which performance of the private sector depends. Deregulation and the establishment of a legal mandate and adequate funding for oversight agencies are prerequisites for private initiatives: without institutional capacity, nations cannot be expected to promote improved performance. Thus private initiatives require a transformation in institutional systems.

Domestic reform in developing countries, however, is a sensitive issue, since their economic activities are often based on traditional systems, some of which are harmed by reform. Even though it is difficult to transform an economy, specific reforms should be selected carefully since poor policy can harm the economy. A good example of damages caused by rigidities is the East Asian economic crisis of 1997.

Because of deregulation and liberalization of the economy, substantial foreign direct investment entered East Asia, giving rise to the so-called East Asian miracle. The region was referred to as the growth center of the world. However, an economic crisis was triggered by speculation in East Asian currencies by foreign hedge funds. Such speculation was inevitable, since nations retained the traditional fixed exchange rate system. Financial liberalization, such as opening offshore markets, and the fixed exchange rate system contradicted each other. While it was hoped that the former would attract foreign funds, policy-makers also wished to maintain the latter to expand exports to the US.

Environmental, Congestion, and Security Issues

Global tensions affect perceived investment risks and real income growth. One of the most divisive issues among developed and developing countries is related to the environment. In terms of infrastructure building, the electric power industry, which utilizes fossil fuels, is typical. Certain types of pollution, like acid rain, affect local citizens and neighboring countries as well. As the US failure to adopt the principles of the Kyoto Protocol demonstrates, however, it is difficult to reach agreement on environmental protection. Developing countries give priority to economic growth while most developed countries wish to regulate uncontrolled emission of pollution-causing agents. Schemes that satisfy both developing and developed countries have to be sought, and continued negotiations are required. For some, global warming represents a policy challenge that warrants national and international intervention. Similar issues arise in the area of spectrum management, where scarcity requires cross-national coordination.

The greatest enemy of a 'good policy' is the pursuit of a 'perfect policy.' Policymakers should focus on the basics before attempting refinements! Those making decisions or coordinating policies across national boundaries will never have all the information they might like for optimal decisions. Nevertheless, efficiencies delayed are efficiencies denied. Delays by an agency can create expectations that deadlines need not be met by entities that are supposed to be complying with rules. The resulting pattern involves delay, noncompliance, and lack of sanctions. Such a situation damages the oversight agency's credibility. Ultimately, potential investors in and managers of infrastructure will adapt to such delays in ways that raise costs and waste resources. Infrastructure is far too important to let that happen.

The regulatory agency must also be a model of administrative fairness and effectiveness if it is to provide credibility to those who might supply capital and managerial techniques to infrastructure firms. No policy is perfect. The art of politics involves assembling coalitions around the positive aspects of an initiative, the better to address any potential problems that might arise from change.

With the recent terrorist attacks in the US, the global policy research community is turning its attention to security issues. The mix of public and private responses to external threats represents another example of how decision makers must prioritize objectives and select policy options that give citizens confidence in the institutional frameworks that affect income, health, and security. No one has a detailed map that can guide us in the decades ahead.

However, finding a firm path for the future surely requires that policymakers build on the principles and lessons outlined in this volume.

ACKNOWLEDGMENTS

Mitsuhiro Kagami assisted in the development of the themes outlined here. The editors gratefully acknowledge his leadership in organizing the workshop that led to this book. We also thank Patricia Mason for her editorial assistance. The volume could not have been completed without her careful review of the material and the energy she has given to this initiative.

Index